Arts *in* M

resource
directory

1998–99

BIBLE SOCIETY

BRITISH AND FOREIGN BIBLE SOCIETY
Stonehill Green, Westlea, SWINDON SN5 7DG

ARTS IN MISSION
193A Norwood Road, Herne Hill, London SE24 9AF

Published 1998 by British and Foreign Bible Society

We acknowledge with thanks permission of Bloodaxe Books and R S Thomas to use the
extract from his copyright material 'The Minister' from *Selected Poems 1948-68*
(Bloodaxe Books, 1986) on pp.13–14.

A catalogue record for this book is available from the British Library

ISBN 0564 040762

Printed and bound in Great Britain by Alden Press, Oxford
Cover printed by Swindon Press

Cover and text design and typesetting by
British and Foreign Bible Society Graphic Services Department

Arts in Mission aims to encourage, enable and equip Christians within the full spectrum
of the arts, to assist the whole Church in mission and to be a catalyst for dynamic
Christian communication through interaction between artists and the Church.

Bible Societies exist to provide resources for Bible distribution and use. The British and
Foreign Bible Society (BFBS) is a member of the United Bible Societies, an international
partnership working in over 180 countries. Their common aim is to reach all people with
the Bible, or some part of it, in a language they can understand and at price they can
afford. Parts of the Bible have now been translated into over 2,000 languages. Bible
Societies aim to help every church at every point where it uses the Bible. You are invited
to share in this work by your prayers and gifts. The Bible Society in your country will be
very happy to provide details of its activity.

contents

Preface   **7**
Using the directory   **8**
Stimuli

Vision brings life   10
Discovering God's heart for the arts   13
Paying the price   19
The art of God   27
Nurturing the creative gift   32
Life after rejection   34
On exhibiting paintings   40

The event

1 What are you aiming for?   44
2 Building your team   45
3 Looking at costs   48
4 Spreading the word   50
5 Arranging the event   53

Artists

Architecture / furnishings / interior design   58
Church organist / musical director   59
Classical music   60
Clowning / magic   65
Contemporary music   68
Dance   98
Drama   106
Fiction writing   117
Graphic design   120
Illustration   122
Journalism   124
Mime / physical theatre / circus   127
Other   130
Painting   134
Photography   141
Play writing   143
Poetry   145
Prose   149
Puppetry   151

Radio 152
Sculpting 154
Textile / fashion 156
TV / film / video / animation 159
Worship music 163

Services
Art galleries 178
Artist support groups 178
Audio / video recording 178
CD / audio / video / tape duplication 181
Conference centres 182
Counselling service for artists 184
Drama tutorial / workshops 185
Events venues 186
Graphic design studios 187
Management / agencies 188
Miscellaneous 190
Music publishing companies 193
Music tutorial / workshops 193
Production companies 195
Record companies 197
Recording studios 198
Scenery set production and hire 200
Sound and lighting hire 200
TV / film / video recording studios 202

Index **205**

Arts *in Mission*

Second national conference

GIANTS
GRASSHOPPERS

Visions of the Promised Land
Moving on in the arts

A conference for Christian artists of all disciplines, church leaders and church members actively interested in God's plan for the arts and artists in his Church and the postmodern world.

**The Hayes Conference Centre
Swanwick, Derbyshire
Wednesday 3 – Friday 5 February 1999**

For further details
and booking forms,
please contact:
Arts in Mission Office
193A Norwood Road
Herne Hill
London SE24 9AF
E-mail: HermioneT@aol.com

preface

Welcome to our second *Resource Directory*. If you are a church or organisation wishing to invite or commission artists and performers, I commend it to you. If you are an artist looking either to collaborate or build links with others or to find a service to help you perform or record your work, I believe you will find it just as useful. Around 750 individuals and groups are listed here and all of them are Christians committed to using their arts in God's service.

This time we have expanded the articles section to include, among others, a brief history of Arts in Mission and a guide to surviving rejection, an occupational hazard we all face in creating and promoting the arts! For our next edition we would like to include reports from Arts in Mission area groups and other articles which are burning on artists' minds and hearts. We invite artists to submit suitable material to the Arts in Mission office. We cannot promise to include all articles but we can promise to read each one carefully as we make our selection.

Arts in Mission is very grateful to Bible Society for underwriting and publishing this edition of the *Directory*. As before, we remind users that, while some artists and service organisations listed here are among the most skilled within their disciplines, we cannot vouch for the standard of each contributor. Please do interview, audition or visit as appropriate in the usual way. Happy reading!

Elizabeth Brazell (Chair)

April 1998

using the directory

The directory is split into two main sections:
- Artists' Entries and
- Service Entries.

The Artists' Entries are organised by category and, within each category, sorted alphabetically by artist (sur)name.

The Service Entries are also organised by category and alphabetically sorted within categories by company name.

A combined index can be found at the back of the book.

Entries for performing artists often show extra information with regards to performance arrangements. The symbols used have the following meanings:

❖   **Style** of music / art form

●   **Party** description: how many will be coming

■   **Venues** that the artist(s) will perform in regularly

£   **Fee** / Expenses

✸   **Technical** requirements

☼   **Demo** tape / CD or Portfolio available on request

Other abbreviations used are:

T   Telephone

F   Fax

Stimuli

vision brings life

A brief history of arts in Mission

Arts in Mission came to life out of a vision. A large red carpet was pictured, extending from the steps of an aircraft touching earth and spreading to the far horizon. Christian artists of every discipline paraded across the carpet, which was showered with music and light. Silks, banners and pictures arrested the eye, while tumblers, actors, potters and engineers were united in spontaneous celebration. And drawn by the vibrant sights and sounds, other people were walking on to the carpet, coming in from the 'blackness' outside. The artists greeted them, welcoming them into the Kingdom of God.

At close range, though, the artists themselves appeared tired and strained. There was a sense that God was wanting to communicate both his love for them and his longing for them to express the truth about Jesus through their work. He delights in their creativity and wants them to work that his Kingdom may come on earth as it already is in heaven. It was clear that he was also calling them to love and encourage one another. They were to make no distinction in this between professional and amateur, male or female, young or old: all are called to serve and follow and dedicate their gifts to his service.

In response to this vision, a 'think tank' was formed. This then evolved into a Council of Reference; a group of lay and ordained people willing to guide and give advice to an Executive who take a more active decision-making role in 'Artsim'. Arts in Mission also has various task forces who cover a variety of specialist areas and a central office run by the director, Hermione Thompson, who co-ordinates enquiries and planning of events.

Since the original vision was given and the 'think tank' of 1995, the following has happened:

November 1995	• Council of Reference and Steering Group formed
June 1996	• Regional launches in Birmingham, Cardiff, Edinburgh, London, Manchester and York
July 1996	• Publication of first *Resource Directory*
January 1997	• Formation of Area Groups
	• Appointment of Hermione Thompson as administrator
February 1997	• *Exodus*, first national conference held at Swanwick, Derbyshire;
	• Setting up of Friends of Arts in Mission

September 1997 • Administrative structure realigned: Task Forces introduced to replace Steering Group
October 1997 • Planning Task Force prayer day

At the last of these, the Planning Task Force of Arts in Mission met for a day of silent retreat and prayer to seek God's heart for the future. Various scriptures were given to us during the course of the day including Psalms 145 and 104. We sensed that the Lord was reminding us that he was present in both the secular and the sacred: nothing was set apart from Him. We also agreed that now was to be a rapid time of growth and a firm time of establishment for the organisation. The nation's response to the death and funeral of Diana Princess of Wales had revealed a spiritual movement in the heart of our land. The most abiding memories for many people were the song by Elton John, the address by Earl Spencer and the amazing gifts of flowers and poetry left at sites all over the world. We were reminded, however, that the love of God was revealed in the Cross and that saying 'it' with flowers or chocolates or poetry was insufficient. As Christian artists we have a wonderful opportunity to explain and portray the Cross of Jesus through art in all its various forms, and we needed to harness the energy to do this and to demonstrate the victory and joy we have in our relationship with our Lord Jesus.

The Lord seemed to be speaking to us through three visions given to different members of the Task Force. In the first he showed that Arts in Mission was like a plant, an English climbing rose. It was climbing rapidly and well supported on a frame of wood. The blooms were scented and beautiful, though each was only for a season. The wood was tough and strong but the thorns were sharp and dangerous. We prayed that God will continue to give sturdy growth, good blossom and defend us from evil. We also saw that the plant's roots needed water and sunshine to sustain life and prayed for our openness to God's life to flow through us. And reminded of the habitual growth or 'suckers' which needed recognition and pruning back, we also asked that God would direct and prune our future plans.

Secondly, one person 'saw' a large church building where an explosion blew the walls blew out. We understood that God was saying that the structure of the established churches can get in the way of the message of the good news of Jesus. God didn't want to destroy his Church but he desired to open it to the world and to communicate through the arts so that his power and love travel freely into the world.

Finally, God seemed to speak these words: 'I have given you the boldness and the resources to start this work. Be not afraid; I will provide all that you need to continue. You must train, teach, and encourage, and I will continue to guide and bless you if you heed my voice and spend time seeking my will.'

Here are our future plans for Arts in Mission. We welcome comments, ideas, and above all your prayers.

June 1998	• 15th–18th: Reaching the Unchurched Network (Run) Conference – Studio
November 1998	• 4th–6th: musicians' retreat at Acorn Christian Healing Trust
During 1998	• Quiet days (Retreats for Task Forces and Council of Refernce)
	• Retreats for drama groups and visual artists
	• Millennium Plans to be consolidated
	• Visits to all regional groups by Elizabeth Brazell and Hermione Thompson to pray with and encourage
	• Regional training days on invitation
February 1999	• 3rd–5th second national conference week, Swanwick.

We pray that God will bless us all as we continue to serve him, and that he may encourage and inspire the creativity of Christian artists and of the whole Church. News, comments and prayer needs from Christian artists are welcome at the Arts in Mission office.

Elizabeth Brazell

discovering God's heart for the arts

'Don't suppress it – let it out!' advises William Mather, a keen amateur painter and Vicar of St Peter's, Littleover, Derby. This article, which draws particularly on Exodus 31, is based on his talk given at the 1997 Arts in Mission 'Exodus' Conference.

For most of my adult life I have had a love–hate relationship with art and have tried unsuccessfully to suppress it. I have loved painting and I have painted sporadically ever since I can remember, but for years and years I could not handle the vivid emotions it evoked.

Although in the last six years I have had five solo exhibitions in the Derby area, this fresh creative stirring follows almost twenty years of denial of art and painting. Why such a conflict?

For me, the answer to this question came home sharply in the unlikely setting of a pub just beside Southwell Minster. In 1995 I had taken a sabbatical to study art and Christianity and, among many fascinating interviews I did, I met Canon Mike Austin, a keen painter. As I sipped a Guinness and he a fruit juice I found myself agreeing passionately when he said: 'There has been suppression of art and iconography since the Reformation. Art is about wholeness – *sozeo* – releasing your God-given gifts, being whole. The denial of art and iconography has for too long been a hallmark of too many Christians.'

I realised that this was the nub of it, and I found myself confessing to him my own part in such 'suppression'. Afterwards I sat for a long time in prayer in Southwell Minster and, in the stillness of that majestic Romanesque architecture, I did something that my Protestant roots had never encouraged: I lit a candle. I could hardly believe what I was doing. Yet for me it was an incredibly important act of prayer for the arts. I can see that little flame flickering still.

Perhaps such struggles are part of our western, scientific rationalism. The poet R S Thomas in his poem 'The Minister'[1] about a pastor called Morgan unable to connect with the culture of the Welsh valleys, writes:

Is there no passion in Wales? There is none
Except in the racked hearts of men like Morgan,
Condemned to wither and starve in the cramped cell

Of thought their fathers made them.
Protestantism – the adroit castrator
Of art; the bitter negation
Of song and dance and the heart's innocent joy –
You have botched our flesh and left us only the soul's
Terrible impotence in a warm world . . .

Powerful, prophetic, negative words.

Art and the impulse of the Spirit

It is salutary to contrast such thoughts with the ancient prayer uttered by painters of icons before they began their work: 'O Divine Master of all that exists, enlighten and direct the heart and the soul and the mind and the hand of your servant, for the glory, the joy and the beautification of your holy Church. Amen.'

While speaking at the Lee Abbey Conference Centre in North Devon in 1996, I found myself still struggling with suppressive thoughts. I woke at 5.00 a.m. one morning and found myself writing a poem about my subconscious battlings with the creative 'muse' of the Holy Spirit.

The poem is a plea for the Holy Spirit to be allowed access and creativity in our lives. Written in the form of a conversation between the muse and myself, it is called 'I long to let you open up'. The following are some excerpts:

O Muse that will not go away
You call me now to paint and play
You follow me, you urge me so
You move in ways I long to know

I am a Friend, just let me in
Don't banish Me, I'm not a sin,
I've been so long in exile too
I long for love and trust from you . . .

I will not force Myself on you
They call Me Love, compassion too
For intuition is My role
I come to free deep in your soul . . .

You never will exhaust My heart
To you I always will impart
The secrets that are always free
As you allow Me space to be.

Art in the studio of God

After a solo exhibition in Derby, favourably reviewed in the Church Times, I had a most encouraging conversation with the Rt Revd Keith Sutton, Bishop of Lichfield. While robing in a church vestry for a new vicar's licensing service, I was most surprised to discover that the bishop had read the review and, even more, that he recognised me. 'You must keep up with the painting,' were his words. 'It is vital. There must be the marriage of redemptive God and creator God, co-working and collaborating with Him.'

Bishop Sutton describes himself as a great lover of music and made particular mention of the way J S Bach used to write 'Glory be to God' at the end of his scores. Bach knew what many in the Protestant tradition forget, that our creativity is actually a mirror of the delightful acts of God.

The roots of human creativity and art are seen in the Bible's opening pages with the marvellous story of creation. It is clear from this that God delights to create and does so in and through us. His love for creativity is fundamental. It is right there in the beginning.

Later, in Exodus 31 verse 1, we see that implicit in all creativity is a relationship with God. It is clear that God is not a distant concept but a person who loves people and talks to them. He spoke to Moses then and he continues to speak to you and me today.

He goes on to say: 'I have chosen and called Bezalel.' There was something special about Bezalel's role, something that God had both called and equipped him to do. We are told that he was the son of Uri, grandson of Hur of the tribe of Judah. This is very personal information. God knows him and likewise Oholiab (verse 6) – both of them particular people set in place and time; just like you and me.

The name Bezalel means 'In the shadow or the protection of God'. The name Oholiab means 'The divine Father is my tent and tabernacle'. Both their names speak of a place of submission to God and relationship with him. Both are called to use their creative gifts in the framework of that special relationship.

Bezalel and Oholiab are given 'understanding'; and today the Holy Spirit gives us understanding through the Scriptures so we can understand God's purposes for our lives and our world. Both men are given skill and ability for every kind of artistic work.

Art in the college of God

Not only that, but we also read in Exodus 35 verse 34 that they were given ability to teach their crafts to others. When I first realised this, I recoiled: 'Oh no, I don't want that. I'm just interested in MY work, MY painting, MY creative development. I'm not interested in passing it on to others.'

People like the late John Wimber have been most helpful in this area. I remember at a conference in Harrogate in the mid-'80s hearing this colourful Californian pastor and teacher saying: 'We want to give away what God has given to us. We want to give it away so your ministry will increase and ours will decrease.' This was magnanimity with a capital 'M'. He meant what he said and he gave it away.

Here Bezalel and Oholiab were called to give away what they had been given. God's creativity is to be released in others also. For, as Exodus 31, verse 6 says: 'I have also given great ability to all the other skilled craftsmen so they can make everything I have commanded them to make.'

Like their teachers, Bezalel's and Oholiab's apprentices receive the same call to live in relationship and obedience to God.

Chapters 35 to 39 also supply an amazingly detailed list of the things God was commissioning: a tent, a covenant box with a lid, a table, a lampstand, a washbasin, an altar, furniture, robes, anointing oil, incense and so on. What we glean from this is God's love of detail and of the many different gifts that are needed for 'the glory, joy and beautification of His holy Church'.

Nor is artistic service a second-rung calling: significantly, the artist and teacher Bezalel is the first person recorded in the Bible to be filled with the Spirit (31.3). God has a heart for the artist and for all of us who have a concern for the arts. He wants all of us to be allowing the Holy Spirit to be coming upon us like Bezalel and filling us afresh.

Art and the community of God

There is also a very clear sense that this creativity was in the context of community. It was not the pattern of the lonely Van Gogh who, despite immense brilliance as a painter, was isolated, self-tortured and anguished.

It was tragic. From our Christian perspective today we can see how, Vincent, who drifted from his earlier deeply held Christian faith, greatly needed the healing and releasing work of Jesus in his life.

Through the many books written about him, we have become aware of his terrible loneliness, his acute depressions, his longing for company, his enjoy-ment of and influence by the Impressionists, and his dreams for an artists' colony founded by himself and his friend Gauguin. We are also aware of the singular support he had from his brother Theo and also his love for people expressed vicariously through his affairs with prostitutes. He also needed other people to be with him in some kind of supportive community. He was alone and vulnerable.

In Exodus 32 we see the reality of intense spiritual attack. Moses the Israelite leader was away having a wonderful time with the Lord on the top of the mountain. Meanwhile, his people with all their gifts suddenly started turning to other distractions and channelling their God-given creativity into making idols. Artists beware how quickly our energies can be distracted and diverted.

But we also see in chapter 35 verse 20 how the Holy Spirit came upon or 'stirred' people, making them want to make and give their creative giftings and offerings to the Lord for making the Tent of the Lord's presence.

In this way, they were bringing their artistic and creative gifts as offerings to the Lord. And this surely should be the way that we should view our art under the inspiration of the Holy Spirit. He is the one who inspires creativity for the glory, the joy and the beautification of God's Church.

Art as the messenger of God

Quite recently I was privileged to see one way in which my painting had been used as part of the Spirit's wider purposes. During my Sabbatical study leave in 1995, I had the wonderful opportunity to spend ten days alone painting in Venice.

One morning before breakfast I was profoundly struck by the sight of dozens of beautiful, delicate gondolas all chained to rough posts, bumping up against them and each other, shaking on the waves of the lagoon. I was mesmerised: it was such a contrast to the graceful craft I had seen being so skilfully manoeuvred over the lagoon and up narrow canals by the extrovert gondoliers.

All of a sudden, it was a scene begging to be painted. So, with a tremendous sense of excitement, I produced a large piece of paper, some charcoal and then a watercolour wash. It was tremendously quick but it said what I wanted: something to do with the great waste of potential there is in so many people who feel chained up when really they should be dancing free.

After breakfast I passed by the same way – not far from St Mark's Square – but this time all had changed. It was like an awakening. Where there had been dull, tired, tethered, immobile and uncreative boats, bumping against posts, now there was life. This was the gondoliers' rush-hour! They were all climbing into their wobbly gondolas and rowing off to work. Suddenly there was shouting and laughter, life, purpose and direction. Those delicately fashioned craft were dancing free over the bouncing waves, ready for the day's work, bringing joy to others. Again, another painting had to be done.

As I shared photographs of these paintings a year later at Lee Abbey, one person in particular identified with them very deeply as an illustration of her own sense of need. She felt chained up in her own life and was praying that somehow the gondolier – Jesus – would come and bring release to her. It was a tremendous joy, later, seeing this begin to happen.

We rarely realise how subconscious thoughts and feelings in our minds can be communicated powerfully and beneficially to others. This incident showed me afresh how much it is possible to convey as you respond to that Spirit-prompted sense of urgency to put something down, whether as poetry, writing, painting or music.

The key, it seems to me, is to plunge in fearlessly and wholeheartedly and using all the talent, skill and experience at one's disposal, thus attempt to co-operate with the dancing hand of God.

William Mather

The first of William Mather's paintings of gondolas appears with his entry in the Artists: Painters section; the second is found in the section of colour reproductions.

[1] 'The Minister' by R S Thomas, *Selected Poems 1948–1968* (Bloodaxe Books, 1986).

paying the price....

...for professional Christian help

The church's midweek meeting was distinctly sticky. No one seemed pleased to see each other. No one had much to say or pray about; there were long silences. Not sleepy, exactly; more as if something needed to happen, but no one knew what.

After a longer silence than ever, Tracy said in a small voice, 'I think God may be trying to say something to us.' She felt awful. This was only the second midweek meeting she'd been to. She hardly knew anyone. Who was she to make out she had a hotline to God?

'That's all right,' said the minister. 'What do you think God is saying?'

'Well, I think I must have got it wrong,' she said, 'But there are some words going round my head, "You are under a curse – the whole congregation of you because you are robbing me." '

Tuts and sighs of dismay all round! It was obvious she had indeed got it hor-ribly, almost blasphemously wrong. How could God put a lively church like them under a curse?

One or two wondered with a thrill if perhaps the church treasurer had been lifting the collection for himself. They stole quick glances at him, and he certainly looked stunned. But more with surprise than guilt.

Old Albert was thumbing through his Bible. 'Yes, I thought so,' he wheezed, 'It really could be God speaking. It's Malachi 3.9 – almost word for word.'

'So what can he mean?' asked the minister. 'How are we robbing God?'

Robbing God?

There is at least one way that many churches may be robbing God: in what they pay for professional services from fellow Christians.

Music

A prosperous suburban church with a strong musical tradition advertised for a new organist and choirmaster. The pay they offered was £1,500 p.a. Several qualified musicians sent for details but none applied, and the job went to a retired civil servant – a good amateur musician, but with no training. The church leaders thought they were offering adequate, even generous, payment; but in fact no musician could survive on such a low salary.

Think of it this way. The two Sunday services require the organist to be present for four hours. The choir practice and the organist's own practice take another three hours. The total is one fifth of a 35-hour working week. So how does the pay compare with a fifth of the salary of a similar full-time job – a school teacher, for instance? A salary of £20,000 would be below average; but even at that rate, the organist's fee should have been £4,000 p.a.

Guest speakers

Another church recently had a weekend away. Their guest speaker was the minister of another church nearby. He gave them a great time, and they wanted to express their heartfelt thanks. They gave him a book token for £25 and a bouquet of flowers for his wife.

These were of course meant and received as love gifts. And that, the church leaders assumed, was the end of their financial duty. They'd invited him – he'd said yes – he'd had no distance to travel – so what do you mean, 'financial duty'?

It never occurred to them that they were 'taking' (polite word for 'stealing') the speaker's time from his employer/paymaster, i.e. his own church. He was away from them for 48 hours and he spent a further two days in preparation. So his church lost four days of his time. When you work out the actual costs of paying a minister (including national insurance, pension and housing costs), the value that church lost was at least £300.

For a whole weekend, that is remarkably good value. I have researched the real cost of a speaker from a charity or missionary society visiting a church for a single day, and that too comes to £300 (bearing in mind proportion of salary, travel and other expenses, promotional literature and backup office costs). Churches might think themselves generous in sending a £100 donation in response; they would actually be draining (or 'robbing'?) the society of £200.

Training

A Christian writer on low income wanted to attend a training day over 100 miles from home. She asked her church to sponsor her by paying the £12.50 fee, while she would find the cost of the journey. They agreed with bad grace, by asking why the fee was so high.

The truth is, it is pitifully low – only achieved by the training agency paying less than it should for the hire of premises and the services of the trainer. Similar day courses run by secular agencies, advertised that month in writing magazines, ranged from £28 to £275, depending on the plushness of the venue and the number of trainers involved.

The stark fact, echoed by every Christian agency I've discussed it with, is that they keep charges to under half of their secular counterparts', but still get told they are too high. Churches seem to expect something for virtually nothing.

Published resources

You buy a Christian book or video, and you naturally assume you have paid for it in full. But that is not always so. One mission-minded, non-commercial publishing company put a 'subsidised' symbol by each of their products in the catalogue. 'It means we have subsidised the final cost from donations,' they explain. The true cost would be at least double, sometimes three times as high, because they do not include the editor's and project manager's time in the figure.

It is excellent to subsidise churches who really can't afford the full amount. But is it right for those who can?

Consultancy

A church decided recently not to renew their subscription to a Christian agency. Why? They had to pay for advice on the phone, whereas another organisation offered it to them free. But there's no such thing as a free phone call. The time spent giving the advice may come without charge to the calling charge, but somebody is paying for it – in this case, the organisation's general funds.

The question here – as with all the other examples – is should a reasonably wealthy church expect someone else to pay for them? Or are they really robbing God by taking it uninvited from another section of his people? And if we rob God, even without realising, don't we – according to what he told Malachi – lay ourselves open to his curse?

The question gathers force when we compare what we pay for services from those who are not Christians. Here – in marked contrast – we pay the proper amount. The gas bill contains no discount for church customers. The architect and builder are not subsidised by a missionary society. The local solicitors don't give 'free' advice on the phone (or if they appear to, it's because the cost is covered in overheads in your eventual bill). If we pay the going rate to the world, why should we defraud God's people?

Some churches get round some of this through friends in high places. As some firms with Christian partners are happy to give discounts to churches as part of their charitable giving. But that doesn't necessarily make it right for churches to get things on the cheap. It makes life harder for Christian agencies who have no non-church clients: they can't afford to offer the same discounts. They become the struggling victims of the curse.

Under a curse?

How did this bedevilled state of affairs arise? Largely, I suspect, through lack of clear thinking.

Blurred vision

Muddled thinking leaves us unclear about who should be paid and who shouldn't. Most church members are volunteers who freely give some of their time to Christian service. We don't pay John for handing out the news-sheets before the service, or Marion for pouring the coffee after it: they do it 'for love' as an expression of their church commitment. So it is easy to assume unconsciously that all Christian ministry comes unpaid.

It's possible to work that way. Paul had times when he worked in the week to finance his weekend pastoral work. An example was in Corinth where he met Aquila and Priscilla. He 'stayed and worked with them, because he earned his living by making tents, just as they did. He held discussions in the synagogue every Sabbath, trying to convince both Jews and Greeks' (Acts 18.34).

But it wasn't ideal; it was slow-going till the rest of his team rejoined him. 'When Silas and Timothy arrived from Macedonia, Paul gave his whole time to preaching the message' (Acts 18.5).

How was Paul now able to go full-time? It wasn't that Silas and Timothy took over the tent-making. It was because they brought money from the Macedonian church of Philippi as Paul later put on record: 'in the early days of your acquaintance with the gospel, when I set out from Macedonia, not one church shared with me in the matter of giving and receiving, except you only; you sent me aid again and again when I was in need' (Philippians 4.15–16). Paul and the others were able to get on with the work they had really come to do, because other Christians paid them to.

This approach wasn't an isolated one-off. It's God's will for the Church in every age: 'the Lord has commanded that those who preach the gospel should receive their living from the gospel' (1 Corinthians 9.14). So we are simply obeying God's orders when we pay people to do church work.

The obvious examples are church ministers and administrators. But in the same bracket come the staff of 'mission agencies' missionary societies and Christian organisations which exist to support churches in their activities. (For simplicity's sake, I shall from now on refer to all these Christian service-providers as mission agents or agencies.) We need to set them free to work full-time on their mission work; that means paying them enough to live on, free from worry or having to find extra work to pay the bills. They are professionals doing professional work; their employers should handle their pay at least as openly, generously and considerately as the best secular employers.

Tunnel vision

Here a second case of muddled thinking takes over. In some denominations ministers are paid at least reasonably (though obviously not as well as if they had gone for the best-paid job on offer). But sadly, disturbingly, many mission agencies pay their workers, especially the senior ones, only about half what they would be earning for similar work outside church circles. People have pointed out this blight for many years, but the inequality remains.

It is distasteful that the governing bodies of Christian mission agencies – many of them with well-paid jobs in business – set pay levels way below their own. It feels as if they are blind to the double standard. But, when challenged, they say with some justice that they are trapped by the small sums churches will pay for their products or give in donations. Perhaps that is where the tunnel vision begins.

It is a vicious circle, with vicious consequences. In the last few years most UK mission agencies have had serious financial problems. Some have had to let their reserves drain away; others have had to make staff redundant. Some may yet fold up altogether. Churches will then be starved of the help mission agencies could bring. Is this perhaps one form a divine curse takes?

This is of course not the whole picture. The crisis may be partly adjusting to the size of the market: perhaps there are too many mission agencies, and some of them may be too large. And the fault may partly be the agencies' own for giving the impression that their charges are realistic, rather than heavily subsidised. But the much more certain fact remains; the churches who make use of them do not pay them properly.

A way out?

What can one church do to reverse this widespread, long-standing abuse? LOTS.

Hold a policy discussion among those who control the church's spending. Are they happy that they get most Christian ministry on the cheap – subsidised by others' giving or by low levels of pay and investment? Or do they agree that churches who could afford to pay more are, in effect, robbing God?

Then the crunch question: are you a church who could afford to pay more than you do now? It is tempting to look at the financial pressures all churches face, and say, 'We don't pay more for anything.' So rephrase the question: 'In the light of our beliefs and priorities, should we pay more than we do now, assuming we could afford it?' Spend time in prayer before answering.

If you answer yes, adopt the twin policy of (a) paying the full cost whenever possible; and (b) working to raise the funds to make it possible. If you are a poor church, start with one or two of the more possible ideas here.

(a)   Paying the full cost

Repay hidden subsidies

- Develop an instinct for what is likely to be subsidised (this article has instanced musicians (include other artists), visiting speakers, trainers, books, videos and consultancy);
- ask the provider what is the real cost;
- give a donation on top of the asking price to make up the full cost;
- send SAEs with any correspondence wanting a reply.

This will save mission agencies from digging into their gift income to pay administrative costs.

Pay for people's time

When you book guest speakers, pay their employers for the time you take. Or if this is really impractical, thank whoever is really footing the bill for the gift they are giving you! As for the speakers, find out whether they are salaried or self-employed. Those already receiving a salary need only a token or honorarium for themselves; but those working freelance need full payment for their time.

Pay all expenses

Many churches think only of travelling expenses, when they offer to reimburse, say, a visiting speaker. But there are often other costs involved producing OHP slides, printing notes from computer, something towards the price of books read in preparation, etc. And those are only the direct expenses. If a mission agent comes from an office with a secretary, the overheads are almost as much again as the agent's own time-costs.

Review your attitude towards spending in general

Discourage meanness in your church accounts. God has lent you some money; be eager to pass it on to do good. This will mean:

- being generous not stingy in how you pay and look after your own staff;
- being 'good' spenders on things you need as a church, i.e. don't just go for the cheapest offer; buy quality goods which will work well and last, so costing less in the long run.

Get others involved

Where something is beyond your control as a single church (e.g. the way ministers are paid in some denominations), don't sit back and say there is nothing you can do. Go through the proper channels to those who have the power to do something.

(b) Working to raise funds

Keep educating the whole church membership about the need to give money, to pay your way properly.

How about a 'fair trade' campaign, for example? Many feel it is right to pay more for coffee and tea whose growers have received a fair price. Wouldn't it be good too to alert people to paying a realistic wage for mission agents? 'Next Sunday's preacher is fair-traded!'

More seriously, how many church members understand that God expects us to give generously, even sacrificially, to pay for his work? In Old Testament times, the 10% tithe was only part of what people gave. It paid the Levite tribe 'for the work they do while serving at the Tent of Meeting' (Numbers 18.21–24). But Israelites gave other offerings and sacrifices as well. And while the New Testament lays down no set proportions, we surely shouldn't give less than our ancestors in God's family. If every Christian gave an average of 12 to 15% of their income to churches and mission agencies, this article would not be needed.

But if church members are falling short in their contributions, whose fault is that? When did the people in charge of your church finances last spell all this out in a way that the rest of the church could understand and do something about?

From curse to blessing

God's word to his people through Malachi did not stop at the rebuke for robbing him. He told them how to lift the curse: 'Bring the whole tithe into the storehouse, that there may be food in my house. Test me in this,' says the Lord Almighty, 'and see if I will not throw open the floodgates of heaven and pour out so much blessing that you will not have room enough for it.'

We no longer gives tithes in food (except perhaps at harvest!) But the principle is clear; give God his due and blessing will replace the curse. Why not give it a try? He dares us to.

Lance Pierson

the art of God

Songwriter, musician and, now manager of Greenbelt Festivals, Andy Thornton argues that our art should reflect a balanced understanding of both God and ourselves as human beings. This article began life as a seminar at the 1997 Greenbelt Arts Festival.

Much of our endeavour is spent trying to understand the nature of God and conduct our lives in the light of it. But if we don't have an accurate understanding of the nature of human beings, then we are likely to completely miss the point of God. In short, we could fail to factor our biases into the equation. So half of the six million dollar question has to be 'what is a human'?

My friend has a 'Gin and Tonic' analogy which I've swallowed (but only metaphorically). It goes like this: if God is the true spirit and human nature is the tonic, then we only ever get to experience God as in the Gin and Tonic. You can't separate the two: they're mixed, irretrievably mixed this side of the grave.

This is the Gospel – God made flesh – and, although it's good news for our souls, it's sometimes bad news for the intellect that wishes to understand it all! The problem is that we have always to factor in the human aspect to any experience, theory, or revelation concerning God.

And the human aspect includes both individual and cultural ways of looking at God and at our experience. There's always a need for a hermeneutic, an understanding of the context and the effect of the context, when we come to think about God.

So the question remains, then: what are human beings really like and what do we learn when we attempt that difficult differential equation demanded by honest theological searching?

Here's my first point. That there's no single basic 'law' that can set the boundaries of our nature and God's – no reducible first principle. This is because most of our decisions about understanding and relating to God occupy points along a scale. At one end of the line is one viable position and at the other end of the continuum is another often equally viable position in a different situation. Take, for example, the flippant but sometimes tasking question 'How should I dress for church?' At one end of the line is the answer 'Dress up: you'd wear your best clothes for the Queen and, well, God's the

King, isn't he?' At the other end: 'Dress down: the Kingdom of God is for the poor and any display of conspicuous wealth would betray that'. So I must make the decision where I place myself on this continuum: dress up, dress down, dress middle… Different cultures will place themselves very differently on this scale. Many black-led churches, for example, place a high price on the dignity that comes from wearing smart clothes to a dignified event like church. This means our decisions are not clear-cut. We are left to find our place in society and culture as befits the occasion and where we put ourselves on the sliding scale of cultural decision-making.

I suggest that most of life's decisions involve these dialectics; seemingly opposing positions which are in tension with each other but whose extremes are seldom warranted in their entirety. Other examples include the freedom of the individual versus the obligation to the collective, 'I am normal' – 'I am special'.

Fundamentalist belief of any type usually thrives on adopting a position at one end of the continuum. There is security in adopting the black or white position. It's my belief, though, that behaving like this is against human- and God-nature. Life and spirituality is about finding the breadth of the options alive within yourself and choosing to participate in one of them with conviction and joy.

Here's my big assertion, then: that one of the most basic dialectics relating to human- and God-nature is a continuum which has at one end 'Logos' and at the other end 'Eros'. Now, having purloined these words from many famous thinkers, I need to explain what they mean.

'Logos', coming from the Greek for 'word', is the element of all things which can be measured, described, defined, trapped in time and communicated to others. So a fish, for example, would have a whole pile of aspects that could be measured which might help us define its 'fishness' scientifically. Similarly, there is much about God which Christians would describe as the knowableness of God. Jesus is described as God's Logos in the New Testament because he comes to make God known. Much of theology has to be about that which we can know about God.

'Eros', from which we get the word 'erotic', does not in my usage mean 'sexual', but means the unmeasurable, indescribable, undefinable, unable-to-be-frozen-in-time aspect of our experience and nature. It is the aspect which is often recognised as the role of the Spirit. Eros things need metaphors in order to be able to communicate something of their being. Because they cannot be measured or communicated makes them no less 'real'; they are real and enormously powerful. They are half of our humanity and half of God's 'Godness'. Eros is everywhere but most acutely in the mystery of God, the intuitive and gut-felt components of art and in our sexuality. A high Eros moment would be the point of orgasm where we can't control the moment, can't describe where we went to emotionally, can't describe it except in metaphor, but it definitely happened!

Good theology holds both of these qualities in tension. It understands the need for a 'knowing' and an 'unknowing'. This has biblical support and has been a universally and intuitively known aspect of being human until the Enlightenment elevated 'science' and 'progress' into their own idols.

This mystery of God in all things has been broadly lost in the post-Enlightenment West. It is floundering in the wings of evangelical Christianity but flying in the rafters of the High Church. Like most poles on any given dialectic, it is the source of division for those who can't contain and celebrate the breadth of our being. Those who want temporal security will run to one end and disparage the other.

This is why, I believe, evangelical Christianity is frequently death to the creative spirit. An artist will usually want to explore more of their internal world in order to externalise their experience in their craft. They are frequently more restless and, by temperament, often threaten those whose internal worlds are a source of discomfort or who are happy to accept emotional restrictions in order to be confident about their own Logos. The cultures that surround many types of Christianity have emotional parameters which feel like conformity to creative artists. What's missing is the Eros stuff.

The Eros stuff is threatening to church leaders because Western rationalism has infused our theological expectations and church leaders are expected to 'know' all the time. Moments of not knowing are not too welcome because they look like failure or upset people. So here are two examples of the destructiveness of a Logos-driven theology on the creative spirit:

A couple sit on the cliff top and stare out to sea. They are overwhelmed by the beauty of the Creator's design and simply sit within the moment, allowing it to speak to their spirits in humility. They are transformed by the experience. They have greater internal harmony and they leave praising the Creator for the stunning work of art that is that landscape.

On another day, the same couple stand before a work of art by another, human, creator. They look at it for a minute and ask each other 'What's it saying?' 'I don't know,' the other replies. 'Typical modern art, eh: says nothing.'

Funny that: they didn't ask the first creator what he was trying to say. They knew the moment was an Eros one.

The second example is a maxim: 'God has a plan for your life.' This phrase has been the source of so much serious psychological disturbance to many people I know. It's not really biblical as far as I can tell, and definitely not in the way it's taken up. This is how I think it's often heard: God is the great designer who sat making the blueprint for the big everything he was about to create. The blueprint is the way it should go, and there are lots of mini-blueprints he's pegged up for each individual who is to be born. Once redeemed, the believer has to get in to living out the blueprint…

The problem is that the metaphor is a Logos one. Here's an Eros option. In this scenario, God is an improvising musician. In God's mind there's this fantastic bit of music, a kind of half-finished symphony which will eventually come good when all the orchestra contribute their voicings and hear how it should be themselves. So God says to us, 'You start playing and I'll join in'. So you start playing and there's a bit of music which comes back to you that makes you sound a lot better than you've ever sounded. You gain in confidence. The music suggests to you where else you might go in your playing and enlivens your desire to contribute to the music. You play some more and God keeps the duet going and bringing new melodic possibilities to your hearing.

As time goes on, you're much more likely to be moving towards the far-off tune that God is hearing. You're inspired. You start playing with more people who can hear the tune and the harmony keeps growing. Slowly, over months, years, centuries, the tune becomes more and more like the one God can hear. The plan is happening. The plan was to make the most beautiful music ever, but to use all the players to make it. Each of us was needed to play and to listen, play and listen.

Now this I can work with! I'm drawn to love and want God more by this Eros metaphor than by the Logos one I started with. And I'll continually find myself needing to live to the Logos side of my personality and my Eros side, and find all stations in-between! To know that I can't know and I can know. I need to keep my breadth of being going. And if my art is drawing on my Eros at times when others can't see what the Eros is saying, then it doesn't mean it's saying any less. It might just be saying it to another part of my listener.

If Christian mission is about communicating God to others, we can't allow it to be all Logos when the totality, both of God and of humankind, is Logos and Eros together in creative tension.

I believe that Christian artists are part of God's mission to allow our full humanity to come alive in Christ. There is no obligation on artists to allow their imaginations to be limited by a Logos-defined mission context. However, we aren't to be lone rangers, but must live out our art in the context of a soul in submission to God, in service of the poor, and in harmony with our faith family. Sometimes we'll have to be militant to establish that the Eros dimension is as valuable as the Logos, but in so doing we will liberate our sisters and brothers in the Church and beyond.

Andy Thornton

nurturing the creative gift

An important facet of the Arts in Mission vision is to help more people within the Church recognise and grow their creative gifts. As a professional actress, Beth Ellis often performed in the West End and worked extensively in repertory and with touring companies. Here she describes the excitement of her present work, en-abling inexperienced drama volunteers to develop skills and realise their creativity.

I had been an actress in the world of secular theatre for over 40 years. In fact, that's where I was when the Lord eventually caught up with me at the age of 60. Like many who have late conversions, I threw myself headlong into learning everything I possibly could about Jesus and being his disciple.

A first stage was to fly off to the Pacific to join Crossroads, a 'Discipleship Training School' for the middle-aged, run – with some irony I think – by Youth With a Mission. 'How to become a disciple in twelve easy weeks,' I thought: if only I'd known! Following this, I went out for practical experience on the mission field in China, Korea and the Philippines, allowing God to fulfil the wonderful promise that this 'would be a life-changing experience'. It was!

I volunteered for another couple of years, and lost touch with my old world – my agent was baffled and so were my old friends – but the desire to perform was dying. It no longer fulfilled me. Perhaps it was never intended to . . .

A year ago, after a great deal of persuasion, I agreed to teach a complete week's drama workshops with a new performing arts team run by a young actor and his wife at YWAM's Midlands base. This was the first time I'd taught in a Christian environment, with young people who were aiming to use their skills working with neighbouring schools and churches. These were not pushy young 'wannabes' and I was very aware that I was dealing with inexperienced, vulnerable young people, who were looking to me to assure them that they had the necessary talent.

It was such a joy to see them growing in confidence every day, opening up with the realisation of their own creativity. I would go to my room exhausted, still needing to prepare the next day's sessions, but suddenly I realised I was in the right place, doing the right thing, using my 40 years' experience in the professional theatre and passing it on to be used in the Lord's Kingdom.

Since then, I've continued doing more workshops. For me, because it's such a blessing to see how people grow in confidence when they learn a bit more about the nuts and bolts of acting techniques – voice, movement, characterisation – I believe the Lord is telling us in Arts in Mission that one of our ministries should be as 'equippers' and 'enablers' in the fields we each know best. I shall let Dorothy M Sayers have the last word: 'I am perfectly certain that one has to encourage, encourage, encourage towards creativity, because people eventually become what they believe themselves to be.'

Beth Ellis

life after rejection

Reject *v. & n. v.tr.* **1** put aside or send back as not to be used, done or complied with etc. **2** refuse to accept or believe in. **3** rebuff or snub (a person)...

Concise Oxford Dictionary: Ninth Edition, 1995

There's a world of emotion lying behind these short phrases, 'sent back', 'refused to believe in', 'rebuffed or snubbed'. All of us have suffered rejection of one sort or another, and usually it hurts, sometimes deeply. This rejection can be inflicted by others, by ourselves, or we can even feel that God has rejected us.

How we deal with rejection in our personal lives as adult artists or art promoters is enormously affected by our past and present relationships with family, friends, colleagues, ourselves, and God. We can simply categorise these as relationships with:

- God
- ourselves
- others

So let's take them one by one.

Me and God: correcting the image

Our relationship with God is conditioned by our early life experiences of the adults who cared for us. Many of us tend to think of God and apply attributes to God's personality that we have derived from those who acted as our parents, carers and teachers in our early years. If they were distant, violent, ineffective, rigid or unpredictable, for example, from childhood on, we begin to think or feel that this is how God must be. We develop false images of him as an unfair, domineering, cruel, or distant figure which are far from the truth that he is continually concerned with our well-being and constantly offering us his unconditional love. Indeed, however loving and caring our early carers were, they cannot measure up to our Heavenly Father who knows all there is to know about us and still loves us with an everlasting and unchangeable love.

If we are to learn to deal with rejection in our adult lives, the first thing to do is to ensure our perspective of God our Father is centred on truth. He is not the same as our earthly parents, nor is he limited by any gender characteristics. The Bible tells us:

- He loves with an everlasting love;
- He is full of compassion and pity;
- He is immortal, invisible, unchanging;
- He is eternal and omnipotent;
- He wants us to trust and rest in him as a child would rest in its mother's arms or at her breast;
- He forgives all our sins;
- He has plans for our future;
- He has promised all who believe in him through Jesus Christ the amazing gift of everlasting life and a place (room/mansion!) reserved in Heaven.

My regular prayer is to say, 'Help me Lord to understand today your deep love and acceptance of me and to pass this acceptance on to others.'

Perhaps the hardest times to recognise God's love are when he is in the business of disciplining, refining or changing us. In Hosea 11 God talks of how, in the nation's early years, he loved Israel like a child, and later, through their rebellion and rejection, he lovingly disciplined them. A few years ago, I was having a Saturday with some of my children and grandchildren. One of the oldest, a delightful and wilful toddler, was having a busy and 'naughty' day – gas fires, coal buckets, fridge doors, window sills, doorknobs and sharp objects were all being pushed with investigative zeal and with no idea of the associated dangers. My daughter-in-law was patiently rescuing, mopping up and saying stern 'No's – cuddling and loving all day long – and my grandchild was alternately angered by the discipline and lapping up the love and comfort offered. Later, with a freshly bathed toddler safely in bed asleep, I recognised that the Lord had been giving us an illustration of Hosea 11. My little grandchild did not realise how strong and protective was the love of his parents. In fact, in his rebellion and frustration he sometimes felt they were thwarting him. So we as adults sometimes react to the love of God. Because he loves and protects us, he too has to rebuke, save or challenge us. If we are mystified, it is because his love is fathomless and his ways are so often not our ways.

So the first statement I suggest we put into our thinking is: 'God's love is unconditional and he accepts me just as I am.'

Me and myself: acceptance without strings attached

Now onto 'ourselves'. If we can begin to accept God's love for us, this will have deep consequences in our relationship with ourselves. We need to start to accept and indeed love ourselves unconditionally also. Many of us are not very good at doing this; self-critical phrases are frequently on our lips: 'What a fool I am'; 'I couldn't possibly do that'; 'I'm useless'.

Behind these thoughts lies an attitude of self-acceptance dependent on reaching certain conditions. Sometimes we are waiting to love ourselves until we are 'good enough' to be loved. Well, the good news is that God loved us when we were 'not good enough', and he goes on and on loving us even though we are still 'not good enough'. The key to a deep self-acceptance is in knowing ourselves, warts and all, and still accepting ourselves. As Christians, we have the treasures of God, Father, Son and Holy Spirit who have made their home in the ordinary clay and cracked pots of our lives (2 Corinthians 4.7). This treasure is everlasting and is there to comfort us and to shine out into the world.

God is not finished with us yet, of course. Indeed, he promises to change us from one degree of glory to another until we meet him face to face. But, if we offer acceptance to ourselves, we then rest in him and dwell more happily in him as his loving, and sometimes painful, refining continues.

My second thought, then, is: 'I must accept and love myself unconditionally, as God loves me.'

Me and others: passing the gift on

Therefore, we move to the third part, that is: 'I am called to love and accept others in the same way that God accepts me.' Perhaps the biggest test of this is the marriage relationship. Those of us who've experienced many years of married life will know the foolishness of having tried to change the other person into a person we could love. The biggest gift any person can give a spouse, or a friend, is to accept and love them as they are. I always remember the promises my youngest daughter and her husband chose to add to their wedding vows, one of which said, 'I promise to love God first and myself second so that I can love you properly'. They will spend a lifetime understanding and living out this promise, just as Denis and I are doing!

We can spend our lives criticising other people, noticing faults, seeking change and wasting valuable time when we could be accepting and loving. Paul in Philippians (2.1–5) wrote the following:

> Your life in Christ makes you strong, and his love comforts you. You have fellowship with the Spirit, and you have kindness and compassion for one another. I urge you, then, to make me completely happy by having the same thoughts, sharing the same love, and being one in soul and mind. Don't do anything from selfish ambition or from a cheap desire to boast, but be humble towards one another, always considering others better than yourselves. And look out for one another's interests, not just your own. The attitude you should have is the one that Christ Jesus had...

And Paul goes on to tell of the incarnation, crucifixion and resurrection of Jesus – all, as we know, inspired by God's love for the whole world.

Handling rejection: some practical steps

So what does it mean to *accept* God's love, ourselves and the people we rub shoulders with? Once again I turned to the Oxford Concise to discover:

> **Accept** *v.tr.* **1** to consent to receive (a thing offered). **2** give an affirmative answer to (an offer or proposal). **3** regard favourably; treat as welcome... **4a** believe or receive (an opinion, explanation, etc.) as adequate, valid or correct; receive as suitable...

As we move on to look at how we cope with rejection, we need to ask God to help us stand in a place of acceptance (knowing his acceptance, accepting ourselves and accepting others), even when others reject us.

Jesus has much to teach us about rejection, and it is challenging stuff. Firstly, there was his example: he was rejected, but endured it humbly and never said a word. And this was explained in his teaching: he told his disciples, 'You have heard that it was said, "An eye for an eye, and a tooth for a tooth." But now I tell you: do not take revenge on someone who wrongs you. If anyone slaps you on the right cheek, let him slap your left cheek too. And if someone takes you to court to sue you for your shirt, let him have your coat as well. And if one of the occupation troops forces you to carry his pack one kilometre, carry it two kilometres (Matthew 5.38–41).'

This is not the way of the world, is it? But remember Jesus called us to be 'in' but not 'of' the world. He also called us both to 'love our enemies' and 'pray for those who persecute us'

How do we work out this challenging example and teaching in our lives? We know the rejections we have experienced from people who have refused to give us jobs; disliked our offering of drama, art or music; judged us to have 'failed' auditions; returned unaccepted manuscripts and portfolios; criticised works that we have struggled with and prepared to our highest quality; told us that we weren't the 'right' person for the job. How do we cope with this?

I have experienced some of the above and I can only pass on the ways that I have received help, comfort and courage to continue. Initially, I find it helpful to know that I can 'hide', as it were, in the shelter of my Heavenly Father's love: I can go to him at times of rejection and receive his acceptance and comfort. Perhaps I simply sit in his presence, empty of words, and cry. At other times I pour my heart out to him, speaking aloud or silently or writing my feelings and thoughts to him in my prayer journal. Then I sit and wait and listen to his answers. There is nothing wrong about the feelings of anger and pain that we have. Our emotions and feelings are God-given. It is what we do with them and our reactions that are our responsibility and where we need God's help and direction.

After seeking God's love, I ask him to evaluate with me the rejection I have received. In the safety of his love, I find I can look more objectively at what has happened. Gradually, over many years, I have appreciated that when people reject or dislike my music, my drama, my teaching or preaching, they are rejecting what I do, and not who I am. This realisation enables me to stand firm in the centre of God's love while working at what I do and looking at the rejections or criticisms I receive. Probably the best thing to do at this stage is to forgive the person who has issued the rejection or criticism. Sometimes this is very difficult and we can't 'feel' forgiveness. Nevertheless, I always find, when I ask God to help me to make an act of will to forgive, that he immediately offers this help. I have to choose to forgive and he does the rest. I wasted years of my life as a young Christian, trying to forgive in my own strength, and only learned that it was impossible! It is also foolish to wait until we feel like forgiving.

Then I have needed to move on to forgive myself – again to choose to do this, to stop blaming myself for 'not getting it right' or 'not being good enough'. Again, when I ask God for help to do this, he turns up trumps and helps me to walk in peace with myself. Sometimes I have needed to 'forgive' God – I know that God is perfect and without sin but in my sinfulness I have blamed him for rejections I have received. When I have confessed this to him, I also have received a sense of peace and freedom to move on. Of course the whole process of choosing and walking through forgiveness takes a long while. I have found that it requires patience with myself and with God.

I also have found it helpful, perhaps at a later stage, to share this experience of rejection with a trusted Christian friend. This can of course make one vulnerable to more hurt and misunderstanding (because my friends aren't perfect either!) but it can also be very constructive and helpful.

Above all, at the moments of rejection or criticism I hold fast to God's prom-ise that whoever else rejects me, even those who are closest to me, he will never reject nor forsake me. That is one of the gospel truths that sets us free.

I am by training a musician and I realise now that one of the reasons I decided to study music and to work as a pianist, conductor, teacher and examiner was that as a musician I could never get the music 'right' but I could always get it 'better'. Most of us as artists will recognise in ourselves this striving after perfection. The good news is that the perfect is there, it is within our reach, but it is not in ourselves: it is in God!

God's love is ours. If we receive it and accept ourselves, we shall have the security to accept and help each other. In the strength of the Lord, we can face 'failure' and 'rejection' squarely, learn from it and dismiss the irrelevant. There is great encouragement in the writings of Paul: 'the one thing I do . . . is to forget what is behind me and do my best to reach what is ahead. So I run straight towards the goal in order to win the prize, which is God's call through Christ Jesus to the life above.'

Further reading: Russ Parker, *Free to Fail* (Triangle); Mary Pytches, *A Child No More* (Hodder and Stoughton); Steve Hepden, *Rejection* (Explaining Series, Sovereign World); Floyd McClung, *The Father Heart of God* (Kingsway)

Elizabeth Brazell

on exhibiting paintings

The pain of exposure;
Paintings on view;
  not many
But oh so terribly
  vulnerable.

 Naked before the eyes
  of others:
Every nerve taut, fearing
Rejection –
 A callous word
  A quick dismissal
  A supercilious
   raised eyebrow
    A walking by . . .

So much at stake;
Heart poured out
  on canvas and paper;
   precious moments
   of powerful emotion
   encapsulated in Time.

Will they be swept away
  Or passed by?
Will there be recognition,
  the quickening pulse,
  the sense of 'Yes',
   the excitement of
   identifying?

Will eyes be opened
  to a new truth,
   or even an old one?

Will they appreciate
    the agonies
        the tensions
        the heart aches
        the exhaustion
        the study
            the prayer
            the love?

Or will they walk by
    On the other side
        with barely
        a glance?

There has been
    Encounter;
        Experience
        of numinous
Moments in time
    transcended
        and transfigured;
Fearful ecstasies
    of powerful
        emotion.

Time to think,
    reflect
        and pray
And meditate
    a while . . .

William Mather

on wings
LIKE EAGLES

a retreat for musicians

led by Elizabeth Brazell and Hermione Thompson

at Acorn Christian Healing Trust
Bordon, Hampshire

4–6 November 1998
(beginning evening of 4th,
ending teatime on 6th)

Cost: £90.00 per head (inclusive)

Please send application form to: Hermione Thompson, Arts in Mission Office, 193A Norwood Road, Herne Hill, London. SE24 9AF

Arts *in Mission*

I wish to book _____ places at On Wings like Eagles

Name_____

Address _____

_____ Postcode_____

Telephone_____

I enclose a deposit of _____ (£30.00 per head),
the remainder payable by 24 October 1998.
On receipt of your deposit, you will receive
travelling instructions and further details.

The event

1 what are you aiming for?

Before anything else is decided you should be sure of your aims for the event. Unless your objectives are clearly defined before you proceed with any bookings or make any plan of action, you might discover that your event is not the success that you hoped for. Ask yourself the following questions:

What is my target audience?

Be sure of the group of people that your event is aimed at, whether you want to attract mainly teenagers or children, the middle-aged or elderly, church-goers or non-churchgoers.

What kind of evening's 'entertainment' do I wish to provide?

An inspiring wholesome evening's entertainment for the church community, an evangelistic opportunity or the chance to present people who would not normally set foot inside a church with good 'alternative' entertainment? Once these aims are clearly defined, it makes it much easier to be de-cisive about matching your venue and artist to your target audience.

What programme will suit my purpose best?

There is a wonderful and diverse bunch of musicians, comedians, singers, theatre companies and so on, all of whom have different ministries, abilities and objectives. Do some market research! Just because long-haired hippy Harry brought you to Christ in the 1960s or Larry Lurex greatly entertained your Church youth group in the 1970s, does not mean to say that they will have the same appeal for a group of 15- to 18-year-olds at the end of the 1990s. Equally so, hippy Harry might not be a great crowd-puller as far as a group of cheese- and wine-consuming 40- to 50-year-olds are concerned! Find out what young people are 'into'. Go and see your potential artist 'live' and be aware of the kind of audience they have attracted.

Once you have decided on a suitable programme, then familiarise yourself with the concept. Immerse yourself in the artist's latest CD, read any biographies or relevant literature. Do whatever it takes to ensure that you and your team are 100% committed and 100% enthusiastic about your 'product'.

2 building your team

Good teamwork is an essential part of organising a successful event. No matter how gifted or multi-talented one person may be, it is simply not possible to achieve a level of success unless other people's talents, time and energy are recruited.

How do I chose my team?

How you answered the questions in chapter one will partly determine how you answer this one. If your target audience is 18s to 25s and you are 52, it will be a great asset to have people who are within that age group as part of your team, to be sure that your objectives are met.

It might also be helpful to involve people who have connections with the venue. For example, a concert in a school hall will be made smoother if a committed and enthusiastic school representative is invited onto your committee. All in all, your team should consist of those who are as committed as you are to the success of your event and the suggestion is that they should fulfil the following roles:

Chairperson

Overseer of all meetings and activities prior to the event and the person who liaises with the artist or agency. Someone who initiates and co-ordinates and, most importantly, delegates, as this is the key to good leadership.

Secretary

A person responsible for taking minutes, writing circulars, dealing with post and generally assisting anyone on the team with administrative matters.

Treasurer and ticket sales co-ordinator

A person to set up and manage the bank account and to take responsibility for the finances. This person would also be responsible for distributing tickets. This doesn't mean that one person alone would be the ticket seller. The job would entail allocating and delegating batches of tickets to others. This is explained in more depth in chapter 4 under the heading 'Active Selling'.

Publicity co-ordinator

A person to communicate with the media, targeting local television and radio and any local newspapers, as well as liaising with the local community and churches. This person would also be responsible for co-ordinating the distribution of posters and handbills.

Co-ordinator for the work involved on the day

This person would be responsible for the venue, co-ordinating the different groups of volunteers and overseeing hospitality. He or she would also be responsible for putting together the schedule for the day of the concert and making sure that people and equipment are in the right place at the right time.

It is advisable to keep to a maximum of ten committee members although this shouldn't exclude the involvement of others. Each committee member should be responsible for various sub-groups which should involve your additional volunteers as well as other committee members.

The co-ordinator for the day can organise a team to run hospitality, a technical support group and stewards to run the venue.

The person responsible for promotion can organise a team of leaflet droppers or a team of people committed to making contact with the target audience, visiting schools, colleges, churches, youth groups and so on.

If your event is on a much smaller scale, it will obviously not be necessary or even possible to involve so many people. If this is the case, then each team member can be responsible for more than one job, providing you limit your prep-arations accordingly so that objectives and targets can be more easily met.

Your meetings

The size and complexity of your event will determine the number of meetings needed to organise it properly. Too many meetings will put people off, but too few will mean that you're likely to lose the momentum. Most people need the deadline of the next meeting to motivate them to meet their objectives. Good minutes and action lists serve to keep everyone informed and active, the secretary playing a vital role in this respect. Try to keep your meetings as efficient as possible. It is better to have a short business part of the meeting and enjoy one another's company afterwards, having given those who are very busy the chance to depart, than to have long, cozy meetings every time. This will make your meetings both efficient and pleasurable.

The spiritual motivation

Make sure that you have a good prayer support network so that you do not lose sight of your spiritual motivation and objectives. Remember you are treading on territory that the enemy considers to be his and he is not going to accept lightly what you are planning to do. However, art was created by God for his pleasure as well as ours. All we are doing is reclaiming the territory! Remember the authority we have and tread boldly.

Make sure that your team members are supportive of one another. If your aims and objectives are well grounded in prayer, then it will be much easier to inspire and encourage each other.

Make specific prayer requests and expect specific answers! Keep your prayer support network informed at all stages even of the smallest endeavour or step forward Finally, very importantly, though sadly often forgotten, give praise once the event is over!

3 looking at costs

It is absolutely vital that a realistic budget is determined right from the start. Although you will find that there are those willing to contribute their skills, labour and goods for free, it is most likely that there will be a bill to be paid at the end. You will need to decide whether you want the event to be free to those attending, whether tickets should be sold or whether a love offering should cover the costs. Whatever you decide, adequate provision needs to be made. Here are examples of three different budgets:

Fig 1: **Examples of budgets for three different-scale events**

	A	B	C
Publicity costs – printing, photocopying, postage	£50	£50	£250
Hire of venue and additional costs, e.g. extra staging, hiring of caretaker or venue staff	–	£150	£500
PRS (Performing Rights Society) fees	–	£40	£75
Artists' fees and travel costs	£150	£250	£400
Sound and lighting hire	£75	£150	£400
Additional costs, e.g. overnight accommodation and meals	–	–	£200
TOTAL AMOUNT	**£275**	**£640**	**£1825**

Tickets

If this is your chosen method of recouping all your expenditure, then it is important to be clear when setting your ticket price. In most cases this is the best way to meet your budget objectives. Once a ticket price has been determined and your budget is established it is easy to calculate how many tickets you need to sell in order to cover all your outgoings. For example, with Budget B, if you set a ticket price of £4.50, you will need to sell 143 tickets to reach your break-even point. It is usually better to set a slightly higher ticket price rather than the absolute minimum so that you can afford to allow for group discounts and other ticket-buying incentives and any complimentary tickets.

Ticket sales are not only a more reliable means of covering your expenditure, but they are also a quantifiable way of measuring your pre-event success. The general public are also very used to paying for their entertainment and might even come with a lower sense of expectation if the event is free. Free entry might make them suspicious of your motivations or might make them think that you are not convinced of the entertainment value of your performers. Young people in particular are used to paying for their entertainment. Bear in mind that a cinema ticket these days costs anywhere between £4.00 and £8.00. Obviously, if a severe lack of money is a consistent factor in your target audience, then a lower ticket price needs to be set. This might mean that your budget requirements will not be met through ticket sales alone and will benefit from being boosted by pre-concert donations.

Underwriting

This is an important way of easing the financial burden. If you can spread your budget so that there is more than one person prepared to absorb the financial risk, then it will certainly make it easier for you to commit yourself to the venture in the first place. It may be something that your committee is prepared to take on, or if no one is in the financial position to do so, then it is certainly a good idea to approach those who are. These might be wealthier members of the church or local business people who are not able to get involved on a practical level but would happily underwrite part or all of your budget and would feel that in this way they can contribute to the success of your venture.

Boosting income

This can be done by selling refreshments. Another possibility is to sell programme booklets with the costs of pro-duction met through selling advertising space. This means that the booklet sales will generate extra income for you. Most people like to have a programme, lyrics, images or photographs to guide them through the evening and also something to take home with them afterwards. Selling advertising space is also another way of making sure that your community is aware that an event is taking place.

4 *spreading the word*

However convinced you are of the crowd-pulling potential of your event, you should never hold back from actively promoting it. People will not only need to know about the event, they will also need to be convinced that it is an attractive alternative to an evening in front of the television. It is becoming increasingly difficult to persuade people to tear themselves away from a form of entertainment which is generally unthreatening and unchallenging, and even more difficult if you want them to invite other people!

Motivate the motivators

Churches are often key places to attract an audience and you will need their support even if your event is aimed primarily at non-Christians. Be aware of those around you who might be able to sell tickets for you. Issue challenges! If your event is something that you are proud of, then be brave about asking people to invite their neighbours, people at work or school, family and friends. One of the worst comments you could hear after an event is 'If only I'd known it was going to be that good I would have invited Audrey and her six children!'

Make use of the network of people that make up the Christian church and if you feel that you don't have access to a network, then this is your chance to develop one. You are really making it easier for yourself as far as future events are concerned. If your evening proves to be the success that you hope for, then people will want to come again to anything else that you organise. You will establish for yourself a good reputation for organising enjoyable and successful events.

All of this might sound easy in theory but in practice it requires a great deal of persistence and determination. If someone asks you for two tickets, see if you can persuade them to take four.! If your event is aimed at young people, challenge your youth group to sell a substantial batch.

There is a general tendency for 80% of tickets to be sold in the last two weeks leading up to the event. By getting more tickets moving earlier, you will find that you will actually sell more tickets in total. Set yourself the task of changing this percentage. Create a general excitement by making your event the topic of conversation! You might be living, breathing and sleeping your event but that doesn't mean to say that others are even aware that anything is going on! Commit yourself to meeting your break-even point through your pre-concert ticket sales and, above all, don't convince yourself that most people will buy their tickets on the night. Statistically only 10 to 25% of tickets are sold at the door.

Active selling

This is by far the best way to sell a substantial number of tickets prior to the event. Your ticket co-ordinator needs to divide the tickets into blocks of five or ten and then give them two months prior to the event to those you have identified as motivated to sell them for you. This could involve your family, friends, youth groups, choirs and other church groups and could even be intensified with a little bit of healthy competition between groups or group members! Incentives can be introduced to motivate them further, with free or discounted tickets being given with every batch sold. Any unsold tickets and money collected should be returned the week before the event. It is wise to check sales on a regular basis so as not to be surprised by some less successful sales.

The publicity campaign

The distribution of handbills and posters, direct mailing and even cover-age on radio and television should never be perceived as a way to sell tickets. They should be viewed as a way of generating interest, sustaining momentum or reminding people of something they have heard about already. People are saturated with advertisements and publicity, so it is never enough in itself to expect a poster or radio interview to persuade the average person to come and see someone they have possibly never heard of.

Having said all of this, your publicity campaign is still important for all the reasons mentioned and when deciding your strategy you should take the following things into consideration:

- Be sure that the publicity materials that you use are visually impactive with a corporate image and strong and clear design.

- Be sure about the timing of your publicity, especially as money and time will be limited. Don't put posters up too early. Most posters put up in public places are defaced or removed fairly quickly.

- Be sure to follow things up correctly. It is simply not enough to mail out a standard letter to church leaders in your area. It is very often a waste of time and resources, as your letter is probably one of many received that week and most likely not considered to be of enough importance as to be dealt with immediately. Don't rely too heavily on direct mailing when junk mail is becoming an increasing source of irritation to most people. Pre-empt it with a phone call and then, once they have received the information, make a follow-up call and ask if they would be interested in selling some tickets for you! Again persistence is required!

- As far as radio and television is concerned, your event will probably not be considered for anything more than a 'What's On?' type of slot. A way to give it more status would be to present stations with an 'angle' to make your event really newsworthy thereby giving it more coverage.

- Random leaflet distribution is very often unconstructive and a waste of resources. Be specific about who you are giving leaflets to and try and follow it up wherever possible.

- Church services are very often a good way actively to promote your event. Try and enlist the enthusiastic support of one person in each church who would be prepared to actively promote and sell tickets for you! This will also make it easier for you to place adverts in church magazines and make announcements, hand out leaflets or even play a 'trailer' before, during or after church services.

5 arranging the event

Your choice of venue

This is something that needs to be considered right at the beginning and relates to all the questions asked in chapter one. Your choice of venue should be determined by:

(a) your target audience

If you are aiming mainly at attracting a non-Christian audience then you would be wise not to choose a church as your venue, as this can dissuade people from attending.

(b) The type of event

It is important that your venue is suited to the type of event you have chosen. If it is not possible to find one that is ideal, then it certainly needs to be adaptable. If your programme requires an intimate wine-bar-type setting then make sure that an appropriate atmosphere can be created.

It is also very important that your venue meets the practical and technical requirements of your event. Find out if there is a sufficient power supply, adequate dressing room facilities, the right kind of staging or if more specific requirements can be met: for example, an effective blackout or facilities for the use of AV equipment.

A team of helpers

You will definitely need different teams to assist in the smooth and efficient running of all the different aspects of your event. They will probably consist of the following:

- Those responsible for refreshments;
- A team to help with the loading, unloading, setting up and taking down of all the PA and lighting equipment, scenery, sets, etc;
- Stewards to be responsible for admission, selling of tickets and programmes, and looking after the venue and the audience;
- A team to set up, look after and take down the CD, tape and book stall.

Hospitality and accommodation

It is important that your performers and crew are well looked after, so it is advisable to have a person who is responsible for hospitality. This would involve being aware prior to the day whether there are any specific requirements regarding times of meals, any dietary specifications and also to make sure that the dressing rooms have mirrors, hand towels, are adequately heated and that there is a good supply of refreshments for everyone involved. It is also important to be clear about the accommodation arrangements. Some artists prefer to be in guest house accommodation and some are happy to stay in people's homes. If home hospitality is the case, be sure that this doesn't involve lots of people cramming into one room, people sleeping on the floor, having to share a double bed or being wakened at four in the morning by a screaming baby! After the event most artists and crew long for a good and undisturbed night's sleep!

The day of the event

As you are only too aware, there will be a great deal to think about on the day! Be sure to schedule the day's events so that all involved are aware of what time they are to arrive, at what time various things will start and how long they are likely to take. This involves careful liaison with the various groups involved and a clear and comprehensive timetable. See Fig. 2 as an example.

Be aware of those involved by putting yourself in their shoes

Imagine yourself as the audience

What are your first impressions? If the venue is a school hall, have any attempts been made to create a warm, welcoming and exciting environment with a careful use of subtle lighting and screens? Is the refreshment area well laid out? Are there enough toilets and are they clean and well signposted?

Imagine yourself as the artist or artists

As the organiser be sure to welcome the artist so that a relationship is established right from the start. Combine this with the option of a hot drink and a snack. This is almost certain to be very welcome, particularly as the artist will most probably have travelled a fair distance. Make sure that the dressing rooms are welcoming and that the general atmosphere is not one of panic and chaos.

Fig 2: **Sample timetable for an evening event**

14:00 Arrive at venue with hospitality team and stewards to prepare hall and dressing rooms and refreshments for artists

14:30 PA, lights, props and scenery/staging arrive, as well as a team to assist with unloading and setting-up

15:00 Artists arrive

15:30 Sound check

16:00 Team arrives to set up book, tape and CD stall. Team arrives to prepare and set up refreshments for the audience

17:00 Sound check finishes

17:30 Meal for those who wish to eat before the concert

18:30 Prayer time

19:00 Doors open

19:30 Event starts

21:00 Interval

22:30 Event ends

22:45 Team to assist with taking down and reloading

23:30 Meal for those who wish to eat after the concert

24:00 Take artists and crew to their accommodation

Imagine yourself as the crew

Make sure that there is a good supply of hot drinks and snacks. Be sure that you have a good team of helpers, preferably the same ones to set up and take down so that they only have to be instructed once. Make sure that there is easy access to the stage and that you have made sure that the crew are able to have a good and direct relationship with the venue staff.

Imagine yourself as a local helper

Give clear instructions on when helpers should arrive and what each designated task entails. Be sure that your volunteers feel included, respected and valued.

It is important to try and keep everyone happy, as dissension and misunderstanding is not conducive to an enjoyable day, no matter how successful your event might be. Give clear instructions and be encouraging. In this way you will avoid irritation and stress and will also ensure that you have a team of volunteers who will be happy to work with you next time. Creating the right environment and providing adequate helpers, facilities and hospitality will mean that you have enabled the artists and crew to work and perform to their best ability. This will also mean that your audience will have had a very enjoyable evening's entertainment.

Being an event organiser can often be a thankless task so make sure that you have a reliable, supportive and encouraging team. Be sure that you are organised well in advance and pace yourself so that you avoid unnecessary stress and difficulty. Above all enjoy yourself and you will find that the evening you have been responsible for will have moved, entertained, inspired and challenged many people.

Aad Vermeyden

Artists

A C Design
Alex Clennett
BA (hons) BArch

8 Springwell Gardens, Churchdown, Glos, GL3 2AL
T (01452) 531 112 or 712 054
Dwellings designed to clients' requirements, extensions, barn conversions, listed building work and small scale industrial projects. Also experienced in theatres, church extensions, shops and offices, etc.

Peter J Berry – Stained Glass Artist

The Old Apple Store, Pinkney Park, Malmesbury, Wilts, SN16 0NX
T (01666) 840 739
I provide a complete service from design to installation carrying out private, commercial and ecclesiastical commissions, repair and restoration work.

Jane Campbell

34 Alexandra Road, Kings Langley, Herts, WD4 8DT
T (01923) 260 903 F (01737) 242 374
Has created and installed countrywide figurative, symbolic and abstract stained glass windows, sandblasted and moulded features and enamelled toughened glass doors/internal screens for churches and public buildings.

Kevin Colbear

8 Keable Road, Riverdale, Wrecclesham, Surrey, GU10 4PW
T (01252) 733 478
My work manifests my desire to see humanity standing free of worldly facades, through the use of two- and three-dimensional expression, (metal, interior and exterior).

John Eynon

33 Fairlands Avenue, Thornton Heath, Surrey, CR7 6HD
T (0181) 684 9866 F (0181) 665 9871
Practising architect and ordained minister, with special interest in the relationships between faith, mission and architecture. Able to advise on and enable all aspects of building projects.

Graham Laird Fine Furniture
Graham Laird

4 The Hilders, Ashtead, Surrey, KT2 1LS
T (01372) 275 683 F (01372) 271 719
Designs and makes furniture of the highest quality. Graham believes that church furniture should be simple and elegant and be a real aid to worship.

Timothy Rawe

74 Leswin Road, Stoke Newington, London, N16 7NQ
T (0171) 254 7294 F (0171) 923 0741
E-mail TIM.RAWE@TRA.NDIRECT.CO.UK
A professional interior designer and guitarist/worship leader in Lifeline Community Church.

Alan Reed

See main entry under Painting section.

58

Christine Brand   *See main entry under Classical Music section.*

Peter Holland   *See main entry under Worship Music section.*

David Mitchell   *See main entry under Contemporary Music section.*

Tony Newnham   *See main entry under Classical Music section.*

The Other Phil & Jon   *See main entry under Contemporary Music section.*

Jan Payne   *See main entry under Worship Music section.*

Paul Poulton   *See main entry under Contemporary Music section.*

Mark Pullinger   St Stephen's Church Office, St Stephen's Terrace, London, SW8 1DH
T (0171) 735 8461 or 735 1619
Involved in the use of music in liturgy and worship, particularly the integration of music of all traditional and contemporary styles, for the congregation's encouragement.

Raymond Smith & The Hillside Singers   White Coppice Farm, Anglelarke, Chorley, Lancs, PR6 9OF
T (01257) 277 633
Director of Music at Hillside Methodist Church, Brinscall, Chorley. Choir sing during worship, concerts and religious musicals. Recently performed 'Samuel' with 400 children.
❖ Contemporary ● 55 ■ Churches around North West England
£ Minimal ❀ Electric Socket ✿ No

David Snowdon   *See main entry under Worship Music section.*

Angela Tilley   45 Bell Lane, Broxbourne, Herts, EN10 7HD
T (01992) 443 520
Trained as a classical singer, I am now organist and musical director at United Reformed Church Broxbourne, and for 'Churches Together in Hoddesdon' musical ventures.

David W J Williams   Harmony House, 12 Marnham Road, Torquay, Devon, TQ1 3QW
T (01803) 324 850
I direct an ecumenical choir and vocal group who are available for advice/information on music in worship and to share in worship events/services.
■ South-West England £ Travelling expenses + donation to trust
❀ Organ piano keyboard if possible

church organist / musical director

Nicola Ellis Andrews
9 Kite Hill, Eaglestone, Milton Keynes, MK6 5BL
T (01908) 242 485
Composer/performer (flutes and piano). Perform at evangelistic events and in worship. Some compositions devised collaboratively with poet Phil Andrews McGovern expressing our faith and have been performed in concerts and experimental services.
❖ Contemporary classical music ■ Concert and church venues
£ Variable ✿ n/a ♻ Yes

David Ashmore-Turner
75a Palmerston Road, Buckhurst Hill, Essex, IG9 5NS
T (0181) 505 9698 F (0181) 281 0318
E-mail turner75a@delphi.com
Freelance operatic tenor. General Director of Dominion International Opera (see separate entry), and lay evangelist.
❖ Operatic ● Minimum myself and accompanist ■ Freelance opportunities both secular and Christian based £ Negotiable
✿ Piano ♻ Yes

Christine Brand
19 Bennett Park, Blackheath, London, SE3 9RA
T (0181) 318 3181
Pianist/accompanist – Christine is a fine and experienced performer. She offers a tasteful approach to worship, classical and lighter musical styles. Confident in classical, worship and lighter music styles. Her skilled improvisations provide an anointed dimension – useful in ministry outreach situations.
❖ Classical, worship-free, light music ● Solo performer
■ Conferences, services, weddings, concerts, outreach venues
£ Negotiable ✿ Keyboard, piano ♻ Yes

Peter Bye
14 Avenue Elmers, Surbiton, Surrey, KT6 4SF
T (0181) 390 5896
Arranger, composer, musical director, pianist.

Philip Carter
18 Marlowe Road, Broadwater, Worthing,
W Sussex, BN14 8EP
T (01903) 230 984
Classically trained singer experienced in opera, operetta, musicals, oratorio, and sacred song, hymns etc. Available for concerts, church events with programmes tailored to your needs.
❖ Opera singer (baritone) ● Solo ■ Concert halls, churches, theatres etc. £ Negotiable ✿ Tuned piano ♻ Yes

Sophy Cartledge
1 Sinclairs Cottages, 47 Palace Road, Bromley, Kent, BR1 3JY
T (0181) 290 5223 or (0973) 697 786
Sophy Cartledge is a freelance harpist who has worked in England and abroad playing both orchestral and solo work. She plays regularly at her church and also for the New English Orchestra (a Christian orchestra).
❖ Classical, some traditional Irish/Welsh ■ London, Kent, Birmingham – anywhere! £ solo for background/functions/weddings: approx. £150–£200 ♻ No

Christine Cottingham
LGSM LTCL

The Lodge, Bletchingley Road, Godstone, Surrey, RH9 8LL
T (01883) 742 925

Singing teacher, soprano soloist. Also with 'Living Proof', a concert group of singers, using Christian and secular music of many styles, to reach people not used to church attendance.
❖ Classical/country and western etc. ● 6 ■ Churches, church halls, any venue considered £ Expenses ❀ Piano in good order ○ No

Dominion International Opera
David Ashmore-Turner

PO Box 62, Woodford Green, Essex, IG9 5NY
T (0181) 504 6228 F (0181) 504 6228
E-mail dio@dlsoft.com Website
http:www.dlsoft.com/dio/
A charitable trust using opera in mission. A professional quality operatic resource offered to churches and Christian organisations to reach out with the gospel at home and abroad.
❖ Operatic concerts/events ● 36043
■ Churches, festivals, TV mission events, radio £ Negotiable ❀ Piano and PA ○ Yes

Stuart A Ellsmore

Mount Pleasant, Whiteshill, Stroud, Glos, GL6 6AU
T (01453) 758 538
I am a freelance orchestral trumpeter and soloist. I also conduct youth orchestras. Play in worship bands and am a deacon in a Baptist church.

Garden Music Duet
David Burden

10 Mayfield, Welwyn Garden City, Herts, AL8 7EL
T (01707) 333 409
Professional musicians using the language of music (ranging from Bach to the Beatles) with contemporary Christian songs and testimony to communicate the message of Christ.
❖ Basically classical but arrangement of contemporary music and Christian songs ● Duet: guitar and violin/oboe/voice ■ Churches and other Christian organisations £ A gift to cover expenses ❀ Chairs (x2) and mics (x2) ○ Yes

Sandra Graham
LRAM, GRSM, Dip RAM

6 Black Eagle Close, Westerham, Kent, TN16 1TF
T (01959) 865 038
Trained Royal Academy of Music. Sing mostly on the operatic stage and oratorio. Have been soloist for Langham Arts 'Prom Praise' and All Souls Church.
❖ Classical singer (light classical also) ● Myself and accompanist (if required) ■ Opera, church, oratorio £ £75–£100 + travel (accompanist extra) ❀ Piano, PA system if available ○ No

Robin Hagues
MA (Oxon)

36 Westbrooke Road, Sidcup, Kent, DA15 7PH
T (0181) 309 9308
Pianist, music transcriber, arranger, copyist/engraver, proof reader, editor, harpsichordist, composer, songwriter.
❖ Various ■ Theatres, churches £ By negotiation ○ Yes

Graham Hepburn

332 Rectory Road, Bensham, Gateshead, Tyne Wear, NE8 4SR
T (0191) 420 1913
Clasical/jazz/piano for evangelistic events and charity events. Good for Alpha courses or 'bring your friends' evangelistic events. I tailor my programme to the type of church.

Alison Holmes

c/o 6 Gresham Road, Hillingdon, Middx, UB10 0HT
T (01895) 234 261 E-mail andywilson@dial.pipex.com
Classically trained grade 8 pianist and flautist. My repertoire includes Rag. I also have several years' experience of playing in a variety of worship situations.
❖ All styles catered for ● Solo and group experience ■ Church and social situations £ Negotiable ❀ Used to playing acoustically and have own digital equipment ✿ Yes

London Magnificat Orchestra

Gerard le Feuvre

19 Crossway, Harpenden, Herts, AL5 4RA
T (01582) 462 668 F (01582) 462 668
High quality professional orchestra whose members are committed Christians.
❖ Classical with much humour ● 10–50 players ■ Harpenden (at YWAM base) and London £ Rarely available for expenses, fee £1000 plus ❀ Good lighting and seats ✿ Yes

David McArthur

Milestone, St Nicholas Avenue, Great Bookham, Surrey, KT23 4AY
T (01372) 457 755 or (0468) 404 557 F (01372) 450 525
E-mail maestosc@cix.compulink.co.uk
Have performed as solo pianist and accompanist in over twenty countries worldwide.
❖ Classical music £ Negotiable ✿ Yes

Phil Andrews McGovern

See main entry under Poetry section.

Stephen Morris

29 Legard Road, Highbury, London, N5 1DE
T (0171) 354 3281
Freelance violinist – worked with Nigel Kennedy, Oasis, most London orchestras, Jason Carter, Carnelian Quartet, Kammerspiel trio, film and commercial work, previously leader of All Souls orchestra.
❖ Classical violinist/crossover/rock/folk/ commercial ■ Worldwide £ Variable according to venue/programme ✿ Yes

Mosaic Theatre

See main entry under Drama section.

Tony Newnham 9 North End, Southminster, Essex, CMO 7DN
T (01621) 773 548
Music for all – a blend of classical and easy listening, played on organ, piano and electronic keyboards with a low key evangelistic slant. I also record and produce radio programmes etc.
❖ Classical easy listening ● 1 and sound engineer ■ Anywhere
£ £70 + travel (negotiable for evangelistic events) ✿ Mains supply
☼ Yes

Jan Payne *See main entry under Worship Music section.*

Heidi Pegler 16 Glazbury Road, Barons Court,
London, W14 9AS
T (0171) 602 1257 F (0171) 602 1257
Trained at Trinity College of Music; soloist for Langham Arts "Prom Praise", All Souls Church, Bloomsbury Baptist Church; Songs of Praise and special presentations with Springs Dance Co.
❖ Classical soprano ● Myself and accompanist if required
■ Churches, concert halls, recital venues, theatres £ Equity rates
✿ Accompanist and PA if possible ☼ Yes

Elizabeth Rodger 25 Nutbrook Street, London, SE15 4JU
T (0171) 732 3734
Professional concert and opera singer (soprano). Training: Choral Exhibitioner (St Catharine's College, Cambridge); Opera Course, Guildhall, London. CV: UK, France, Italy, Spain and Greece (Glyndebourne, English Touring Opera, Opera North, BBC, ITV etc.).
❖ Classical – oratorio/operatic (but not heavy – I don't have a big vibrato!) ■ Theatres, concert halls, recital venues, churches
£ Negotiable ✿ Amplification if performing with acoustic instruments ☼ Yes

Roquefort Duo
Gerard le Feuvre

19 Crossway, Harpenden, Herts, AL5 4RA
T (01582) 462 668 F (01582) 462 668
Entertaining recitals given (light or substantial) presented with much humour.
❖ Classical and light classical ● 2 men ■ Throughout the UK and abroad £ £250 plus ✿ A good piano ☼ Yes

Ruth Scott 457b Kingsbury Road, London, NW9 9DY
T (0181) 206 2564 or 533 1372 (diary service)
As a freelance orchestral musician I have worked with many orchestras, including the Academy of St Martin in the Fields, the Chamber Orchestra of Europe, the City of Birmingham Symphony Orchestra and English National Opera, also do solo work, and am member of a trio available for functions.
■ Concert halls or more informal venues £ Musicians' Union Rates

Audrey Thomas
147 Stafford Road, Caterham, Surrey, CR3 6JH
T (01883) 346 196
Professional accompanist and piano teacher. Worship leader (on the piano) in church. Works often with husband – Edgar Thomas.
❖ Classical piano (and charismatic worship), generally accompanying singers and instrumentalists ■ Churches, old people's groups, etc.
£ Negotiable ❀ Piano! ☼ Yes

Edgar Thomas
147 Stafford Road, Caterham, Surrey, CR3 6JH
T (01883) 346 196
Professional classical tenor – now retired from the professional performing scene, but able to sing for churches, old folk, etc. Also teaches singing.
❖ Classical tenor ■ Churches, old people's groups, etc. £ Negotiable
☼ Yes

Ellie Ulmer
Music Promotion Ltd, 12 Hinde Street, Flat 18, London, W1M 5AQ
T (0171) 835 9608
Song cycle (piano and mezzo-soprano) with illustrations of Ernst Bahan (sculptor), multi-media approach. German lyrics with translation.
❖ Modern classical; song cycle on sculptures ● Ensemble, mezzo-soprano ■ Galleries £ Depends on number of musicians, negotiable ❀ Piano ☼ Yes

Carlyon Viles
19 Debdale Road, Barrowby, Grantham, Lincs, NG32 1BD
T (01476) 67 281
I am a classical composer writing in a contemporary modal idiom. Currently working on a psalm book. I hope to write opera on biblical themes.

Wedding Songs – Catherine Francoise
71 Leachcroft, Chalfont St Peter,
Bucks, SL9 9LD
T (01753) 882 646 Mobile (0850) 617 775
F (01753) 408 089
Professional singer with career spanning West End and repertory theatre, opera, oratorio and concerts. Available for both Christian and secular performances including personal events such as weddings.
❖ Classical and contemporary singing ● 1
and accompanist or backing tapes
■ Churches, art centres, theatres, schools
£ Negotiable ❀ Piano if possible ☼ Yes

Mark Brooke: The Mill

See entry on p.134

Barbara Dawe: Crucifixion
Mixed media
See entry on p.135

Alan Reed: High Bridge, Newcastle upon Tyne
Available as a limited edition print
See entry on p.139

Charlotte Wright: Fire by Night No.2
Oil and wood dye on canvas on wooden panels - 31 x 83 cm
See entry on p.140

William B G Mather: Gondolas - off to work! Venice 1995
Courtesy of Mr Lothar Wesemann, Vienna
See entry on p.138

Susan M Cook: Daily Bread
Stained glass
See entry on p.131

Laurence Pusey: Rachel
Pastel - 58 x 43 cm
See entry on p.138

Colin T Hale: Gas Street Basin, Birmingham
See entry on p.136

Bijou Theatre   *See main entry under Drama section.*

Clownin'g   2 Deacons Road, Kilsyth, Nr Glasgow, G65 0BN
Glory   T (01236) 825 379
Ann Gallagher   *We do circus skills workshops with a Christian theme. Unicycling, juggling, plate spinning, rhythm sticks, diabolo, face painting and balloon animals.*

Brian Colling   88 High Street, Carisbrooke, IOW, PO30 1NU
T (01983) 522 460 or 282 500
Brian is an entertainer who uses the art of illusion and sleight of hand to show Christian truths and make Bible stories fun to learn.
❖ Humorous or serious as occasion demands ● Usually work alone ■ Churches, halls and schools £ £20 + expenses ❀ Self-contained, raised platform preferable ✪ No

Gof The   The Rectory, The Green, Stanford-le-Hope,
Clown   Essex, SS17 0EP
Revd John Guest   T (01375) 672 271 F (01375) 672 271
Prophetic Balloon modelling Chaos/magic (it goes wrong!). Parastuntology. Storytelling/Dramatic reading/Clownselling/Awful Jokes – GOF ("God's Own Fool") can't wait to be at your service [Semper Ninquam Annis Tuis!].
❖ Clown ● 1 (occasionally 2, very occasionally 20) ■ Anywhere £ Negotiable (£35 per 1/2 hr for children's parties) + expenses ❀ Adult supervision! ✪ No

John   47 Whitestone Road, Halesowen,
Hardwick   W Midlands, B63 3PU
[Creative   T (0121) 550 5794
Communication]   *I use unicycling, juggling, clowning, storytelling, puppets and music to present the Christian message in an exciting way. I work in association with Saltmine Trust.*
❖ Children's family evangelist ■ Schools and churches £ Donation + 25p per mile ✪ Yes

Steve Legg   104 Kingsham Road, Chichester,
W Sussex, PO19 2AL
T (01243) 778 892 F (01243) 781 279
E-mail 106644.1462@compuserve.com
Steve Legg uses his skills as a professional escapologist to entertain, and challenge young and old to understand how Christ can set them free.
❖ Comical ● 2 ■ Streets, schools, colleges, churches, events £ POA ❀ PA and mic ✪ Yes

Ludo the Clown (These Foolish Things)
Stephen Ashcroft

81 Gladstone Road, Wimbledon, London, SW19 1QR
T (0181) 715 3938
Clown ministry – shows, walk around, workshops, etc. Christianity presented afresh using clown skills and idiom. "Release the Clown in You", also story- telling.
❖ Clown ● Individual clowns or troupe of 2, 3, 4 or more as needed ■ Churches (services), charity events, fêtes, etc. £ Negotiable, depending on requirements ✹ None ○ No

Lulubelle the Clown
Valerie Ashcroft

81 Gladstone Road, Wimbledon, London, SW19 1QR
T (0181) 715 3938
General clowning, church services, fêtes, workshops, charity events. Story- telling.
❖ Clown ● One, two, three or more clowns as required ■ Churches, fêtes, charity events, etc. £ Negotiable, depending on requirements ✹ None ○ No

Peter D McCahon

Oasis Trust, 87 Blackfriars Road,
London, SE1 8HA
T (0171) 928 9422 F (0171) 928 6770
E-mail PETER-MCCAHON@compuserve.com
Presenting the gospel to all in a relevant, creative way using illusion, comedy and escapology. Also involved in workshops, seminars etc.
❖ Comedy magician illusionist ● Solo act ■ Churches, educational, festivals, clubs £ Negotiable ✹ Mic on stand ○ No

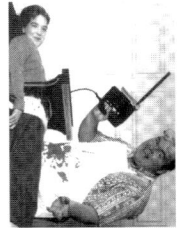

Newby Entertainments
Ricky Newby

100 Fotheringham Road, Enfield,
Middx, EN1 1QE
T (0181) 366 6051
Close-up magician for corporate events or private children's party. Entertainment with magic, clowning, balloon modelling etc. Gospel magic and entertainment organiser for adults and children.
❖ Varies with age range ● 1 ■ Greater London and around £ Negotiable ✹ Self-contained, need plug socket ○ No

'Rokey' the Clown
Richard James

93 Horns Road, Barkingside, Ilford, Essex, IG6 1DQ
T (0181) 554 7986
A joyful clown with a full range of clowning and circus skills. Can provide training and day workshops. Contact for 'Holy Fools UK' Christian clown organisation.
❖ Joyful clowning ● Individual and group clowning ■ Churches £ £30+ (negotiable) ✹ Somewhere to change and a space to perform ○ No

Roly

Revd Roly Bain

285 North Street, Bristol, BS3 1JP
T (0117) 963 6490 F (0117) 963 6490
Performing clown using slapstick, story and circus to preach the gospel in my own foolish ways. Workshops too.
❖ Auguste Clown ● Me ■ Anywhere £ £100 + travel ❀ Radio neck mike and lots of space ✿ Yes

Captain David Woodall, CA

1 The Esplanade, Frenchwood, Preston, Lancs, PR1 4PJ
T (01772) 828 706
Church Army evangelist who uses clowning and conjuring to present the gospel and other aspects of the Christian faith to Christians and non-Christians.

clowning / magic

Acacia
Anna Littler

PO Box 200, Bromley, Kent, BR1 1QF
T (0181) 464 3101 F (01942) 820 671
*Original songs and monologues for Christians and non-Christians alike.
(Various styles and themes.) Also involved in UK and overseas missions
as a soloist and worship leader.*
❖ Modern ballads and jazz ● Soloist with guitar ■ Churches £ No
fee, expenses appreciated ❀ Facility for using backing track tape on
occasion – not essential ✿ Yes

Agape
Graham Daw

54 Girnhill Lane, Featherstone, Pontefract, W Yorkshire, WF7 5NN
T (01977) 796 281
*Agape is a two-piece unit vocal/inst/midi technical support. Outreach/
worship. They perform well-known Christian music as well as their own
material. Member British Equity.*
❖ Contemporary, traditional, various ● Male two-piece ■ Arranged
concerts £ Negotiable ❀ Prefer stage with lighting ✿ Yes

As If...
Philip Goss

Glebe Farm, Ludgershall, Nr Aylesbury,
Bucks, HP18 9PL
T (01844) 237 916 or (01869) 340 643
E-mail AS IF@vision.org.uk
*We play concerts, festivals and outreach events
all over the country. We are signed to Spirit
Records, and have our own PA, lighting, and
laser systems.*
❖ Dance, techno, rock ● 3 plus 3 stage crew ■ Anywhere £ Price
negotiable but usually £350 ❀ Please ring ✿ Yes

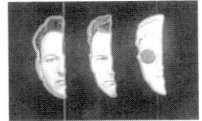

Rob Ash

13 Bristol Street, Aberkenfig, M Glam, CF32 9BW
T (01656) 722 589
*Full-time singer/songwriter musician travels anywhere. Venues include
schools, concert halls, pubs, churches, colleges, etc.*
❖ Contemporary, rock, blues ● Solo artist ■ Schools, church
organisations £ £100 per night, according to distance ❀ Good
lighting rig (have own PA) ✿ Yes

Asylum
Vivienne Neville

12 Gullwer Road, Rift House Estate, Hartlepool,
Cleveland, TS25 4AL
T (01429) 232 904
*We are a five-piece evangelistic band who work to promote the gospel
and moral structure to young people.*
❖ Contemporary Christian rock music ● Stuart (keys/vocals); Paul
(guitar); JP (bass); Jason (drums); Viv (keys/voc) ■ Music festivals,
churches, youth clubs, etc. £ Depends on location + distance ✿ Yes

Keith Ayling

PO Box 61, Lytham St Annes, Lancs, FY8 1SS
T (0585) 472 607
*Singer/songwriter with band Kato and available for acoustic
performance; youth co-ordinator for Lifelink – North West.*
❖ Guitar-based pop ● 35886 ■ Clubs, festivals, youth events
£ Price on application ❀ Dependent on gig ✿ Yes

Jim Bailey, Kingdom Creative
See main entry under Worship Music section.

Baly's Cream Jazz
Paul Baly
13 Travers Walk, Stoke Gifford, Bristol, Avon, BS12 6XW
T (0117) 979 9018
A Christian jazz band, performing contemporary Christian music with a jazz flavour, original compositions and jazz standards.
❖ Jazz ● Line-up of 6 men (voc/sax/guitar and harmonica and double bass + keyboards and drums and rhythm guitar) ■ Churches, halls, pubs, clubs, weddings £ £25 per person (max. 6 people) ✾ 2x mains outlets ✧ No

Beehive
Hadyn Wood
Beehive, The Sound Foundation,
PO Box 3001, Wokingham, Berks, RG41 3YQ
T (0118) 962 9100 F (0118) 962 9100
E-mail beehive@soundfoundation.co.uk
1997 MOBO award winners, best gospel act. Beehive have a vision to take the gospel into pubs, clubs, colleges and universities by delivering an exciting innovative blend of popular music relevant for today's culture.
❖ Jazz, funk, nu soul, and R&B (not blues) ● 5 ■ Pubs, clubs, universities, colleges, festivals £ £500 + travel ✾ We have a small PA but no lights ✧ Yes

Theo Bessem
5 Banbury Road, Walthamstow, London, E17 5SY
T (0181) 531 4977
CCM and praise and worship.
❖ CCM ● Soloist ■ Concerts, conventions, seminars, church services £ Love offering ✾ Good mic and fold back ✧ Yes

Kate Beswick
25 Crossman Street, Sherwood, Notts, NG5 2HR
T (0115) 962 5809
Singer/songwriter, guitarist and keyboardist. Solo or with band. Also into writing drama, art/design and video. Seeking to communicate the gospel and encourage Christians.
❖ Contemporary folk ● Lots of jelly and ice cream? ■ Pub, prison, theatre, church £ Variable ✾ Variable ✧ Yes

Beyond Jordan
See main entry under Worship Music section.

Big Boss
Mark Hilditch
Big Boss Management, 204 Harvie Avenue, Glasgow, G77 6ZZ
T (0141) 616 0591 F (0141) 616 0591 E-mail
gibbleol@globalnet.co.uk
Christian techno – dance music act. Energy, dancing, amazing light and video show. Played throughout UK including Brixton Academy and recently returned from gig in Belgium.
❖ Club/dance music ● 5 ■ Churches, youth clubs, events, schools £ £200 + travel ✾ Call to discuss each booking ✧ Yes

'Big Jack' Kelly
John Kelly

31a Grove End Road, Farnham, Surrey, GU9 8RD
T (01252) 710 517 F (01252) 718 104
My work is a combination of live music, DJ-ing and various mixed media attempting to speak of my faith in culturally relevant voice.
● Musicians and graphic designers and DJs and interior dec.
■ Clubs/similar £ from £50–£2000 ❀ Sound system lights ☿ Yes

The Big Picture
Alvin Allison

41 Chatsworth Avenue, Haslemere, Surrey, GU27 1ED
T (01428) 641 665
Intelligent rock played by experienced musicians, featuring outstanding Christian musicians.Concert show now incorporates video and multimedia. CD recording available.
❖ AOR, intelligent, hi-energy rock ● 5-piece rock band ■ Concert halls, churches, stadiums! £ Details available on application
❀ Sound, lights and video provided by band ☿ Yes

Rob Blackman

53 Storr Gardens, Hutton, Brentwood, Essex, CM13 1HT
T (01277) 231 961
Contemporary/worship (distinctly both) from professional guitarist/ vocalist. Teaches popular guitar and is also in secular country rock and jazz funk bands.
❖ Rock, jazz, country, funk? ■ Wherever asked, churches, pubs, clubs £ Negotiable ❀ Electric power ☿ Yes

Bluestone
Pete Rawlings

207 Moorside Road, Bromley, Kent, BR1 5ES
T (0181) 461 4452
Quality, non-preachy pop music, complete with a live string section.
❖ Electric pop ● 8 ■ Churches anywhere £ Negotiable ❀ We have our own PA ☿ Yes

The Bogle Band
Albert Bogle

St Andrew's Manse, Bo'ness, W Lothian, EH5 19DP
T (01506) 822 195 F (01506) 511 492
Do you like melodic/Celtic country rock? Want to be entertained, enjoy strong harmonies and vocals, a good sense of humour, love stories and challenge to think about faith in today's world – that's Bogle Band!
❖ Celtic/country rock ■ Colleges, universities, hotels... £ Variable
☿ Yes

Caroline Bonnett
Derek and Su Elliott

The Music Works, PO Box 1193, Cheddar, BS27 3BF
T (01934) 741 281 F (01934 743 222
E-mail 106620 2522@compuserve.com
A unique and experienced singer/songwriter with three solo albums to date, numerous TV and radio appearances. Caroline also works with and produces other artistes.
❖ Contemporary keyboard-based ● Solo or with other musicians
■ Halls, theatres, churches £ Please call The Music Works ❀ PA and lights ☿ Yes

The Boot Brothers
Ben Boot (administrator)

Christian Centre, 104 Talbot Street, Nottingham, Notts, NG1 5GL
T (0115) 950 4506 F (0115) 950 4506
A full-time contemporary Christian band specialising in all forms of evangelistic outreach. Also available for conferences and full ministry programmes.
❖ Funk rock ■ Youth clubs, churches, conferences, festivals
£ Negotiable ❀ Supply our own full PA system ☼ Yes

John T Bowman
GLCM (Hons) LLCM (TD)

96 Talbot Road, Abington, Northampton, NN1 4JB
T (01604) 460 614
I specialise in composition, from wedding music to full-scale musicals. I write, record and produce my own work, with a particular interest in jazz.
❖ Various ■ Anywhere (pubs – churches) £ Various ❀ Power ☼ Yes

Dr James Bragg

20 Brent Road, Horfield, Bristol, BS7 9QZ
T (0117) 951 3619
Part of Christian band 'Strange Blue World' – rock/dance music. Play guitar and keyboards. Have computer recording set up. Also interested in painting and computer art.
❖ Rock/dance music ● Guitar and keyboards ■ Clubs, pubs, youth clubs and Christian events £ Negotiable ❀ Reasonable PA and technician ☼ Yes

Henry Bran

El Salvador Music, Frampton Park Baptist Church, Frampton Park Road, Hackney, London, E9 7PQ
T (0181) 533 2477
Poet, writer, songwriter and singer. Composer of praise and worship. Promoter of Salvadorean culture and the only artist from El Salvador living in Great Britain. Working in Spanish and English.
❖ Latin American folk music ● One person ■ From church services, school assemblies to international concerts £ Negotiable ❀ Two microphones (guitar and voice) ☼ Yes

Paul Brittain

21 Kingswood Road, Wimbledon, London, SW19 3ND
T (0181) 543 3191
Singer/songwriter. Accompany myself on acoustic guitar. Variety of styles, mainly ballad-type songs. Also some poetry. Ministry and evangelistic material. Married, 43 years old.
❖ Folk bias, but various styles ● Solo ■ Informal gatherings, church services £ None fixed ❀ Electric socket, amplification ☼ Yes

Capitaan
Ron Fernihough

Promotential, Kingbury House, Leasowe Road, Wirral, L46 3RE
T (0151) 604 0070 F (0151) 677 1977
Formed in London in February 1995 by two university graduates, this new and exciting set-up blended together various styles including commercial Acid Jazz, Pop and Rock to form 'Corrosive Funk', the driving rhythm of Capitaan.
❖ Acid Jazz ● 5 band members ■ Pubs, clubs, festivals, churches
£ By negotiation ❀ Full PA and lights required ☼ Yes

Jason Carter
Alison Ciantar

80 Denecroft Crescent, Hillingdon, Middx, UB10 9HY
T 01895 256 410 F 01895 812 910
E-mail 100335.751@compuserve.com
Solo concert artist; classical/jazz/flamenco guitar. Composer of guitar and chamber music.
❖ Spanish Guitar ● 1 ■ Concert halls – USA, India, Mexico, Europe £ Min. £150 + expenses and travel ❀ PA system and mic ✿ Yes

Marc Catley

5 Olive Bank, Woolfold, Bury, Lancs, BL8 1TQ
T (0161) 797 5066
Manchester-based singer/songwriter/recording artist. Satire or progressive rock. Ten albums including 'Make the Tea' as heard on Radio Four. London Bible College graduate.
❖ Humour and satire ■ Church, clubs, festivals £ Negotiable ❀ Audience ✿ Yes

Andy Chance
Kathy Humphries

7 Portlock Drive, Luton, Beds, LU2 9LL
T (01582) 615 049
Using video and music Andy performs thought-provoking entertainment, preaching the Good News with a fresh approach.
❖ Light-hearted family stuff ● Varies from full band to solo ■ Churches, prisons, schools, etc. £ 25 ❀ PA system and large TV? ✿ Yes

Michael Clements

66 Connaught Road, Fleet, Hants, GU13 9QY
T (01252) 628 451
Experienced guitarist and arranger with rock and blues roots, mainly involved in musical shows, both Christian and secular, and in worship events.
❖ Rock/blues/musical shows ● Just me as session musician or arranger ■ Churches, theatres, school halls £ Expenses only for Christian events ❀ 240V–2A power source, I provide equipment ✿ No

Gerry Cohen-Stone

See main entry under Drama section.

Alexander Cook

3 Wilton Place, Estcourt Road, Watford, Herts, WD1 2PY
T (01923) 219 090
Vocals/drummer; live work, TVB, Jonny Markin, Derek Bond, Sue Rinaldi, Judy Bailey, Flamme, Sister Brothers. Studio; Praise Mix '96, Mick Gibsey, Jonny Markin, TVB (at ICC).
❖ Rock, pop, etc. Jazz, fusion, etc. ■ Throughout UK and Europe, clubs, festivals, churches, etc. £ Approx £50 per gig, £100 per day studio, + expenses ❀ Drum kit ✿ Yes

Dave Cooke

26 Lebanon Park, Twickenham, Middx, TW1 3DG
T (0181) 892 3393 F (0181) 744 2787
Film and TV music composer; advertising for TV and radio. Record producer. Owner of fully equipped digital recording facility. Song writer and arranger.

Shiloh Crew
W F C
(Warrior 4 Christ)

37 Bamford Road, Pennfields, Wolverhampton, WV3 0AT
T (01902) 340 015
I have been in the music scene singing rap, soul, gospel for 4 years. I perform in concerts, open airs and church services.
❖ Rap, soul, gospel and ballad ● Young and cool ■ Liverpool and London areas £ None ❀ PA system and lighting (1000 watt) ♢ Yes

Maggie Croft/Alison Holmes
Maggie or Alison

93 Dartmouth Road, Ruislip Manor, Ruislip, Middx, HA4 0DG
T (01895) 676 202 or (0181) 841 3897
Maggie, vocalist performed professionally with bands for seventeen years. Alison is a classically trained Grade 8 pianist and flautist; repertoire includes rag, secular and Christian music.
❖ Easy listening ● 2 ■ weddings, functions, cabaret style events, worship £ negotiable ❀ standard PA ♢ No

Crossfire
Andy Sayner

34 Fountayns Street, York, YO3 7HL
T (01904) 642 363 or 761 593 (Dave)
Four-piece rock band playing in pubs and clubs etc. Influenced by Phil Keaggy, Dire Straits etc. Grew out of church worship band.
❖ Rock ● 4 people ■ Pubs, festivals, anywhere really £ Depends on distance we have to travel ❀ Mains electricity ♢ Yes

Andy Cullen

3 Mersey Drive, Partington, Manchester, M31 4LD
T (0161) 776 2076
Having been out of circulation for three years, I've recently begun work on a new collection of songs which I believe have led to Now.
❖ Easy listening, experimental ● Me! ■ Churches, halls, etc. £ In agreement with organiser ❀ PA/DI ♢ No

Anita Cuttill

33 Stonehill Avenue, Birstall, Leicester, Leics, LE4 4JE
T (0116) 267 7973
Recently formed a jazz/blues duo with James Williams to perform my songs about life and faith for local church-based evangelism. Can produce publicity material, 1st Dip. Photography, Nat. Dip. Media Studies.
❖ Jazz/blues ● 2 ■ Churches but willing to go anywhere £ Travel costs for Christian gigs only ❀ A piano preferred (we have a keyboard) ♢ Yes

Jeff and Susanne Cutts

Evangelism Through the Arts, Green Pastures, Buxhall, Stowmarket, Suffolk, IP14 3DX
T (01449) 736 628 or (0374) 272 381 F (01449) 737 677
Full-time musical missionaries reclaiming and using the arts for the Kingdom of God. Training and leading one-year evangelistic teams for young adults.
❖ Contemporary music/multi-media ● Creative! ■ Youth groups, churches, streets, schools £ Travel expenses and gift or offering ✹ PA and lights for larger venues ✿ Yes

December Blue
Raymond McFeeters (manager)

3 The Brackens, Newtownabbey, County Antrim, N Ireland, BT36 6SH
T (01232) 839 310 F (01960) 352 375
Based in Belfast, December Blue's reputation for dynamic live performances and relevant personal lyrics continues to gain respect and recognition from the wider Christian music industry.
❖ Highly original female vocals ● Female vox; guitar; keyboards; bass; drums ■ Christian music events, concerts, festivals £ Contact manager ✹ Professional PA and lighting rig ✿ Yes

Dave Deeks

13 Pentland Grove, West Moor, Newcastle Upon Tyne, Tyne & Wear, NE12 0NY
T (0191) 268 4749
Singer/songwriter. Albums 'Let Go Let God' (1985) and 'Solid Ground' (1990). Mostly local ministry, powerful testimony, including healing from paralysis.
❖ Contemporary Christian music and testimony ● Myself, wife, son (keyboards) and 1 helper ■ Local churches/prison £ None ✹ None – own PA etc. ✿ Yes

Deliverance Ablaze
Ian Henley

1 Water Road, Gornal Wood, Dudley, W Midlands, DY3 2NH
T (01384) 821 161 F (01384) 455 974
E-mail ian_henley@pandp.co.uk
Deliverance Ablaze are a four-piece Christian rock band from the West Midlands who believe in ministry through music.
❖ Rock music ● 3 guys, 1 girl in band, manager and sound engineer ■ Wherever possible, Christian or secular £ Negotiated due to venues circumstances ✹ Basic PA system (which we can arrange) ✿ Yes

Discovery
Allison Berry

37 Perne Road, Cambridge, CB1 3RX
T (01223) 245 021
Five-piece pop/rock covers band, playing live hits from 1960s to present day. Much experience in clubs and functions. Adaptable, reliable, professional!
❖ Pop/disco/soul/rock from 1960s to present day charts ● Function covers band – 5-piece (all live music) ■ Clubs, dinner dances, hotels, parties, etc. £ (Depends on distance) £250 minimum ✹ Power supply (we have own PA and light show) ✿ Yes

Distant Light
Andy Strong

100 Edgeworth, Yate, Bristol, BS17 4YP
T (01454) 319 503
Melodic rock, early Seventies style, guitar-based, and songs about contemporary issues from a Christian perspective.
❖ Rock ● 5-piece band ■ Schools, pubs, clubs, churches, prisons, festivals £ Negotiable ❀ Power supply ☼ Yes

Paul Douglas Band

PDMM, PO Box 15, Nottingham, Notts, NG6 9JZ
T (0115) 976 0935 or (0585) 222 127 F (0115) 976 0935
E-mail pauldouglas@innotts.co.uk
Sounds of the '90s merged with classic pop style of the '60s and '70s. Amidst reggae guitar, jazz trombone, syntus and a cool groove comes the versatile voice of Paul Douglas.
❖ Classic pop songs with a cool groove ● 35950 ■ Churches, halls, theatres, pubs, clubs, festivals £ £300–£350 in the UK ❀ We provide ☼ Yes

John East

15 Burgess Green Close, St Annes, Bristol, BS4 4DG
T (0117) 971 1996
1. Bass player and backing vocalist available for session work (all styles). 2. Singer/guitarist available for live performance in contemporary or worship setting.
❖ Performance; contemporary folk/rock ■ Churches, studios, most venues £ Session work: £15–£20 per hour, performance negotiable ❀ PA with foldback preferred ☼ Yes

Colin Elliott

8 Drumnacanvy Lodge, Drumnacanvy Road, Portadown, Armagh, N Ireland, BT63 5XY
T (01762) 362 432
I perform both as a solo artist and with my band 'Inside Out', spreading the gospel through song to the young people throughout Ireland.
❖ Folk, blues ● 35886 ■ Youth gatherings throughout Ireland £ Love gift ❀ Small vocal PA ☼ Yes

Emmaus Road
Andy Sheldon

34 Darrell Close, Chelmsford, Essex, CM1 4EL
T (01245) 284 820
We are a rock/pop band who play university college bars, Christian Unions, youth groups etc. Our aim is to try and challenge people about Jesus Christ.
❖ Pop/rock ● Five ■ Student venues, church youth events £ Travelling expenses ☼ Yes

Endgame
Sarah Hay

17 York Avenue, Jarrow, Tyne & Wear, NE32 5LP
T (0191) 489 7455 F (0191) 378 2885
E-mail simeon.hope@gexpress.gn.apc.org
Quality rock/pop/danceable music, Christian band, but playing mainly secular venues for over 18s.
❖ Rock/pop/danceable ● 6 ■ Arts centres, pubs, not for children £ 150 ❀ PA needed for larger venues only ☼ Yes

Envoy
Paul Worthington

14 Willow Green, Caerleon, Gwent, NP6 1EA
T (01633) 420 886
Envoy combine their own hard-edged rock and strong Christian lyrics to put over the gospel message in a way that is both exciting and original.
❖ Christian rock band ● 4 musicians: vocals, guitar, bass, drums ■ Festivals, church halls, concerts, youth clubs £ Travelling expenses only ❀ 2/3 accessible electrical supply points ✿ Yes

Euphoria
Ricky Wright

27 Carwood Avenue, Newtownabbey, County Antrim, N Ireland, BT36 5LW
T (01232) 835 502
Website http://www.niweb.com/dnet/dnetorfo/
We are a band who spread the gospel through music in a relevant way to today's culture using a mixture of secular hits and Christian songs. We mostly play youth events, missions and concerts.
❖ Rock ● 4-piece band ■ Youth events, missions £ 50 ❀ We provide sound – light can be hired at extra cost ✿ Yes

Malcolm Evans

28 Greenridge Road, Handsworth Wood, Birmingham, B20 1JP
T (0121) 358 3788
A singer, songwriter and church elder who now performs solo, following 10 years with the group 'Dunamis'. Experienced, versatile performance for Christian gatherings or evangelistic events.
❖ Varied to suit venue, folk/rock ● Solo ■ Churches/Christian gatherings £ Negotiable ❀ None apart from power source and OHP ✿ Yes

Eve and the Garden
Paul Cudby

Flat 2, 46 Chalk Hill, Watford, Herts, WD1 4BX
T (01923) 250 758
Soaring melodies, elaborate harmonies and rhythms, and a mature attitude. The debut album 'Quiet Earth and Shining Stars' released April '96 on FFG Records.
❖ Celtic folk/world-influenced contemporary rock ● 5-piece (vocals, violin, lead/acoustic guitar/synth, bass and drums) ■ Church organisations, festivals, secular clubs (anything considered) £ No set fee, expenses only (gift appreciated, if able) ❀ Lights needed, can supply PA

Excursion

See main entry under Worship Music section.

Face to Face
Stephen Pitkethly

c/o Lime Tree Studios, Welgate, Mattishall, Dereham, Norfolk, NR20 3PJ
T (01362) 858 015 F (01362) 858 016
E-mail limetree@paston.co.uk
Acoustic guitar-based songs, some with backing tracks. Available for concert/performance events or increasingly as leaders of worship. Call for details and demos.
❖ Contemporary folky pop/rock ● 35950 ■ Churches, church halls and outside £ Negotiable ❀ Mains sockets ✿ Yes

FGOT (Fine Gentlemen of Trout)
Richard Lee

1 Bramble Drive, Maidenhead, Berks, SL6 3NX
T (01628) 823 438 F (01628) 823 438
We provide lively contemporary style music of high quality, coming from a strongly Christian direction, often for youth events and celebrations.
❖ Energetic, sensitive, guitar-based, strong rhythm ● 3 young males: guitar/vocals, bass, drums and guest musicians ■ Church youth centres £ Expenses as relevant ❀ Mains power ✪ Yes

Andrew Flannagan & Peter Ryan

3 Sandhill Court, Bleary, N Ireland, BT63 5XP
T (01762) 343 671 or (01426) 643 806 (pager) or:
39 Casaeldona Avenue, Belfast, N Ireland
T (01762) 793 828 Mobile (0410) 362 006
Our performing is really about one thing – COMMUNICATION – not in it to do anything else! It's been fantastic to see the songs work at many levels, getting a response from real people.
❖ Acoustic-based thought-provoking songs ● 2 ■ Festivals, youth events, nightspots, anywhere £ None ❀ Decent PA 2 vox, 3 guitars, keyboard, percussion ✪ Yes

Steve Flashman
Soapbox Music

14 Cranbrook Terrace, Cranleigh, Surrey, GU6 7ES
T (01483) 271 015 F (01483) 273 872
Contemporary rock with a prophetic cutting edge to schools; prisons; colleges; clubs. Seven albums released to date, demo available.
❖ Contemporary acoustic/electric rock ● One plus a technician ■ Schools, colleges, clubs, churches £ Donation basis only ❀ Own PA and lighting rig ✪ Yes

Flow
Andy Hooge

124 Broad Hinton, Twyford, Reading, Berks, RG10 0XH
T (01734) 344 190
Flow are a five-piece indie/pop band playing guitar-driven, original music in venues in the Thames Valley/London area. Recent shows: Garage, Mean Fiddler, etc.
❖ Indie/pop ● 5-piece band ■ Pubs, clubs, live venues £ £100 fee (negotiable) plus expenses ❀ Vocal/instrument PA ✪ Yes

4th Dimension
Dave Flowers

10 Sycamore Road, Hythe, Southampton, Hants, SO45 5EJ
T (01703) 848 245
Experienced Christian rock band, many gigs, many top bands supported, we bring a powerful gospel message with testimonies mixed with heavy rock and powerful ballads.
❖ Rock ● Drums, bass, 2 guitars ■ Churches, pubs, youth events, festivals £ Expenses ❀ None – we have PA and lights ✪ Yes

Catherine Francis

Elined Music, 46 Crown Lane, Southgate, London, N14 5ER
T (0181) 361 1092 E-mail catherine_francis@ipc.co.uk
Catherine's powerful, thought-provoking songs have led to bookings at festivals, churches and youth groups around Britain, radio airplay and a deal with Nu Life Records. Currently working as a senior sub-editor of Woman's Own magazine. Has also contributed to Christian titles CrossRhythms and Aware, plus various women's magazines.
❖ Ambient folk pop ● Solo singer, songwriter, pianist ■ Churches, youth groups, festivals, CUs £ No set fee (offering, expenses, nothing) ❀ PA for larger venues; lights if required ☼ Yes

Fresh Claim
Simon Law

236 Sebert Road, Forest Gate, London, E7 0NP
T (0181) 534 8500
Christian rock band committed to evangelism in any situation. Sponsored by the Wavelength Trust.
❖ Rock and blues ● 4 ■ Schools, youth clubs, pubs, festivals, prisons £ £50 in London, then distance ❀ Power supply ☼ Yes

Funktion Junktion
Mark Green

3 Wharf Cottages, Stonebridge Wharf, Shalford, Surrey, GU4 8EH
T (01483) 452 486 Mobile (0966) 455 036
Funktion Junktion is a quality Christian function band. We provide entertainment for any kind of function (weddings, corporate events, etc.) We are highly professional, polite and very funky!

Gethsemane Rose
Derek and Su Elliott

The Music Works, PO Box 1193, Cheddar, BS27 3BF
T (01934) 741 281 F (01934) 743 222
E-mail 106620,2522@compuserve.com
A modern rock band singing mostly original material to a variety of venues. A well established act, with an ambition to take the gospel to rockers.

Phil Glover

70 Okebourne Road, Brentry, Bristol, BS10 6QP
T (0117) 950 3370
My aim is to present the gospel in an entertaining way through music using a variety of styles, via electric and acoustic guitars/backing tracks.
❖ Blues, pop, rock, jazz, funk ■ Church, youth group, youth rallies £ Travel expenses only ❀ PA if possible, but can provide if necessary ☼ Yes

grace

See main entry under Worship Music section.

Colin Green

72 Avondale Road, Wavertree, Liverpool, L15 3HF
T (0151) 733 6781
Contemporary singer/songwriter with humorous presentation. Also promoter and compère of Christian Songwriters' Showcase since 1993.
❖ Thoughtful acoustic songs ■ Songwriters' Showcases on Merseyside £ Expenses only, but would not turn down fee! ❀ Mic and stand and PA ☼ No

Mark Andrew Green
3 Wharf Cottages, Stonebridge Wharf, Shalford, Surrey, GU4 8EH
T (01483) 452 486 Mobile (0966) 455 036
Experienced drummer/percussionist. Spent last 5 years in church-based missions to secondary schools with Soapbox Communications Trust and the Powerhouse Christian funk band.
❖ Western rock/fusion to jazz, latin and Afro C.ban styles ● I work with various musicians, including Sue Rinaldi ■ Schools, clubs, pubs, private concerts £ Negotiable ✿ Can supply all equipment required ✺ Yes

Steve Gregory
47 Balham Park Road, London, SW12 8DX
T (0181) 673 5642 F (0181) 333 9446
Saxophones, flutes, arranger, composer. Many praise and worship sessions. Recently with Van Morrison, Chris Rea, Graham Kendrick, Bryn Haworth, Matt Redman. Best known solo George Michael's 'Careless Whisper'.
❖ Pop, jazz, R&B, latin ● Playing in band and worship groups
■ Studios, clubs, theatres, churches, conferences, etc. £ Negotiable
✺ Yes

Iver Grimstad
See main entry under Worship Music section.

Robin Hagues
See main entry under Classical Music section.

Bryn Haworth
48 Chatsworth Avenue, London, SW20 8JZ
E-mail brynuk@aol.com
International session guitarist, songwriter, recording artist and worship leader. Currently touring with solo production titled 'Water from the Rock'. Available also with his band for rock and rhythm and roll gospel nights.
❖ Electric and acoustic/rock blues/worship ● solo or 4 with a band
■ Churches, concert halls, colleges etc. £ On application
✿ Professional PA required and lights ✺ Yes

David Heming
Beryl Heming
2 Henley Avenue, Ipswich, Suffolk, IP1 6RN
T (01473) 259 399
A professional saxophonist with contemporary orientation. Two solo albums under Word label, performed at Spring Harvest, Greenbelt, Expo in Spain, Salzburg Festival. Available for concerts, outreach functions.
❖ Contemporary, classical, jazz, alternative ● Solo but sometimes with keyboard player ■ Wide variety of venues – UK and continent £ Negotiable, according to event and venue ✿ Own PA available✺ Yes

Graham Hepburn
See main entry under Classical Music section.

Garth Hewitt
Beth Todd/
Beki Bateson
The Amos Trust

St Saviour's Church & Centre, Woodridge Road, Guildford, Surrey, GU1 4QD
T (01483) 453 592 F (01483) 453 593
Singer/songwriter – re: worldwide mission, storytelling, world issues and how to get involved. With forgotten peoples – justice and peace organisation = Amos trust – also lots of projects/speakers for young people.
❖ Contemporary ■ Churches, halls, events, etc. £ £500 plus travel @ 38 pence ✾ Bring own PA/lighting/engineer (inc. in fee) ✿ Yes

Nick Hodges

Woodcroft, 19 Kingsweston Road, Henbury, Bristol, BS10 7QT
T (0117) 950 €960
Songwriter/musician, currently working in home studio, with others, producing contemporary Christian music.

HOG
Lee Jackson

PO Box HP122, Leeds, W Yorkshire, LS6 4XX
T (0113) 275 €152 or (0973) 146 407
Coming from Leeds HOG (Lee Jackson and Justin Thomas) have been together since 1989 and are still one of the only Christian rap groups in the UK. Their performances are lively and humorous and tailored to suit the event.
❖ Hip Hop (Rap Music) ■ Anywhere £ £200 + mileage ✾ Please contact ✿ Yes

Phil Holburt

35 Patterdale Avenue, Richmond, Whitehaven, Cumbria, CA28 8RX
T (01946) 691 023
Music ministry including: worship, evangelism and encouragement via song and the spoken word. Formal preaching also undertaken.
❖ Contemporary acoustic ● 1 plus driver ■ Churches or anywhere that will have me £ Expenses + gift (no set fees) ✾ A larger PA needed for big events ✿ Yes

Chris Hymus

7 Conwy Street, Rhyl, Clwyd, LL18 3ET
T (01745) 344 429
I am a student in Prestatyn High School completing my A-level course.
✿ No

Inreverse
Ian Milen

55 Avignon Road, Brockley, London, SE4 2JT
T (0171) 635 8355
Inreverse lead worship and perform using their own material, which is a unique blend of dance/indie music. Inreverse are based at 'The Bear' youth church, part of the Ichthus fellowship.
❖ Dance/indie worship music ● Six-piece band ■ Youth events/clubs £ £400 + expenses ✾ Good PA rig ✿ Yes

Inside Out
Colin Elliott

172 Old Kilmore Road, Lurgan, County Armagh, N Ireland, BT67 9LR
T (01762) 329 207
Inside Out is a four-piece Christian folk/blues band, involved in youth work throughout Ireland. We are also interested in bookings further afield.
❖ Folk, blues ● 4-piece band: drums, bass, keyboard, guitar and vocals ■ Youth gatherings throughout Ireland £ Left to discretion of organiser ✿ Two 13amp plugs, I have own equipment ✿ No

IONA
Simon Hicks

PO Box 2950, London, W11 3ZX
T (0171) 727 2275
Contemporary Christian music – Celtic rock.

William J Jack

28 Elmtree Avenue, Allenton, Derbys, DE24 8EU
T (01332) 761 680
Ian Evans – guitar/bass, Pete Merry – drums and Jack – singer/songwriter/bass/vocals. We play NE where we can 2 spread God's word.
❖ Gospel – jazz/funk – soul/R&B ● 3 of us ■ Festivals, pubs, clubs, church, carnivals, etc. £ travelling expenses (whatever you can afford) ✿ PA for guitars, bass, drums and vocal ✿ Yes

Ira Jackson

See main entry under Worship Music section.

Steve James

The Rectory, Church Road, Bebington, Wirral, L63 3EX
T (0151) 643 9526 F (0151) 643 9664
An evangelist musician – ordained in the Anglican Church. I like to do a concert with band (6 others) and give a short evangelistic message at the end as appropriate.
❖ Light rock ● 7 in the band and sound engineer ■ Any venue 100–500 people £ £200 + expenses ✿ We bring our PA ✿ Yes

Helen Jayne
Doug McKellar

Safe Music Ltd, c/o 10 The Broadway, Woking, Surrey, GU21 5AT
T (01276) 31881 F (01276) 35241 E-mail mckellar@pncl.co.uk
Helen Jayne is a gifted singer/songwriter originally from Wales, whose debut album 'Safe' (on Word Records) is receiving international acclaim.
❖ Contemporary Christian rock/pop ■ Nationwide £ Varies ✿ Yes

JNR MACK

Mission Promotions, Studio 1, 54 Weatherby Road, Luton, Beds, LU4 8QS T (0973) 403 968
DJ specialising in Gospel music available for parties, weddings, concerts and any other form of celebration.
❖ Gospel DJ ■ Indoor or outdoor £ Negotiable ✿ PA ✿ No

Jo and Matt
Joanna Davies

15 Church View Close, Arnold, Nottingham, Notts, NG5 9QP
T (0115) 967 0901
We are a Christian music duo, who write and perform our own songs. Our aim is to present Christianity in a simple and effective way.
❖ Popular ● Female singer/lyricist and male musician/composer ■ Churches, church venues £ Gift but ask that expenses at least are covered ✿ Tested 13 amp sockets ✿ Yes

John de Jong

c/o VCF Manchester, PO Box 490, Manchester, M60 1ET
T (0161) 834 9565 F (0161) 839 7667
E-mail 101357.244@compuserve.com
A singer/songwriter playing contemporary music either solo or with band, involved in pub/club/outreach/church events. Director of the Vineyard School of Worship providing foundational and practical teaching.
❖ Contemporary acoustic (solo), rock/pop (with band) ■ Vineyard events, churches, pubs/clubs, schools £ Negotiable ✿ Depends on size of gig ✿ Yes

Jubilee
William and Evelyn Hamilton

27 Park Avenue, Bishopbriggs, Glasgow, G64 2SN
T (0141) 772 0219
We write our own material which we use for evangelism. We are working on a worship tape. Our programme is flexible, except for the message.
❖ Contemporary and worship ● 4 members, keyboards, bass, elec. and ac. guitar, 2 vocals ■ Various church groups from YF to rallies £ Expenses gift ✿ We provide our own ✿ Yes

Kato
Keith Ayling

PO Box 61, Lytham St Annes, Lancs, FY8 1SS
T (0585) 472 607 or (01253) 730 944
Britpop from Blackpool. Regular festival appearances including Greenbelt main stage. Large fanbase and own gigline. Travel anywhere.
❖ Britpop ● 4 ■ Clubs, festivals, youth events £ POA ✿ Dependent on gig ✿ Yes

Joe King

58 Nowell Terrace, Leeds, W Yorkshire, LS9 6HX
T (0113) 249 5381 F (01977) 682 088
At present, my songs and presentation are a very varied mixture of material but mainly focused on people who are hurting, going thru the 'valley'. Songs about intimacy or lack of it with people and God. There's also a 'worship' aspect to the performance when necessary and appropriate. I perform in all sorts of contexts both Christian and totally unchurched.
❖ Music influences: Beatles, Celtic ● I perform solo. Have a sound engineer and bring my own PA ■ Anywhere! TV, church, prison, night clubs, youth clubs £ £150 plus 25p per mile petrol ✿ A good attendance ✿ Yes

KiS
John and Sue Ritter

Rockingdown House, 16 High Street, Weedon, NN7 4PX
T (01327) 341 535 F (01327) 341 535
KiS perform concerts and roadshows to an audience age range 12-20 years. Lots of audience participation!
❖ Pop/dance music ● Hi-tec duo, includes roadshow ■ High schools and one-nighters £ negotiable ✿ Stage 10'x12' and 2x13amp sockets ✿ Yes

**David
Knowles**

Flat 1, 66 Upton Park, Slough, Berks, SL1 8DG
T (01753) 821 921
*I write and perform songs inspired by the Holy Spirit. I am also a
worship leader.*
❖ Folk, blues, rock – singer/guitarist ● Solo artist ■ Church
meetings, Christian gatherings £ Travel expenses ❀ PA ✿ Yes

Label of Love

Carolyn Salt

20 Hilton Avenue, Scunthorpe, S Humberside, DN15 8BD
T (01724) 846 228
*A full-time ministry available to churches of any denomination for work
in comprehensive schools and a multi-media concert. Excellent
references available on request.*
❖ Rap, rock, dance music, drama, multi-media concert ● Full-time
schools team: 2/3 people ■ All day in schools. Weekend/evening
concerts in schools, halls, churches £ £500 approx for a full week in
school and a multi-media concert ❀ For the concert a stage area
approx. 20'x20' ✿ Yes

Steve Lawson

c/o Elined Music, 46 Crown Lane, Southgate, London, N14 5ER
T (0181) 361 1092
*Experienced freelance bass guitarist, studio and live and bass tuition.
Also loads of experience in youth work, schools work and evangelism.*
£ Negotiable ✿ Yes

**Phil
Lewthwaite**

See main entry under Worship Music section.

**Lighthouse
Christian
Rock Band**

John Smithy

15 Cardigan Close, St Johns, Woking, Surrey, GU21 1YP
T (01483) 480 576
*Our aim for each event is that the audience will go away knowing that
we are Christians, and have some idea of what that means.*
❖ Contemporary rock band ● 5-piece band, guitar, synth guitar,
bass, sax, drums ■ Youth clubs, outreach events, pubs £ We play
for expenses ❀ Only power required, PA and lights included free
✿ Yes

Living Horns

Chris Mitchell

3 Delamere Road, Earley, Reading, Berks, RG6 1AP
T (01734) 267 754 F (01734) 267 754 E-mail
cmitchell@worldscope.net
*Professional horn section with years of experience working with a
mixture of contemporary bands and worship leaders. Also work as
freelance arranger/musical director and trombonist.*
❖ Rock, pop, black gospel, R&B, jazz ● Solo or brass section from
2 players up ■ Full range of venues at home and abroad
£ Negotiable ✿ Yes

Loose Goose
Carolyn Stilwell

56 Holland Road, London, W14 8BB
T (0171) 371 1891
Loose Goose was formed in 1995. The album is distributed by Nelson Word. The band came out of a worship ministry at St Barnabas Church, Kensington and has a Celtic feel.
❖ Celtic and ministry ● 2 or full band – 7 ■ Festivals, churches, outreach events £ Negotiated fee + expenses ✿ Depends on venue and size of band ✿ Yes

Julie Lord
Julie Silversides

15 Glenhurst Drive, Whickham, Newcastle-Upon-Tyne, NE16 5SH
T (0191) 488 1937 F (0191) 488 2307
E-mail 101370,1612 @ compuserve.com
Experienced singer, mostly in hotels but always available for private functions and church socials. Fully self-contained with quality backing tracks and 600 watt system.
❖ Various – 60s to 90s, including some original material ● Solo vocalist ■ Pubs, clubs, restaurants, hotels, weddings, church events £ Negotiable, church events at a much lower rate ✿ An electric mains socket ✿ Yes

Malaika Ministries
Malaika

35 Crossland Road, Chorlton-Cum-Hardy, Manchester, M21 9DU
T (0161) 861 0859
Recently returned from 12 years' full-time ministry in America/Canada in 27 different denominational churches; prisons; nursing homes; conferences; concerts; women's aglows; FGBMI's; TV; rallies; etc.
❖ Gospel singer, speaker, evangelist £ Free will offering, expenses + hospitality ✿ Yes

Iain May

9 Nursery Avenue, Hale, Cheshire, WA15 0JP
T (0161) 941 6368
Singer/songwriter – lead singer of band 'In The Clear'. Currently working on the rock opera 'Francesio of Assisi' to be produced as a professional show.
❖ Dramatic song performance ● Rock band/performance artist ■ Prisons, churches, clubs £ £250 for band ✿ PA system ✿ Yes

Felix McCabe

54 Wolseley Road, Bishopton, Bristol, BS7 8EN
T (0117) 975 4017 F (0117) 975 4017
I am a singer/songwriter indie/dance music. Also in band Strange Blue World. We have had TV, radio and journal exposure. Into secular and Christian work.
❖ Indie/dance ● 4-piece band ■ Clubs, secular, Christian, pubs, etc. £ £120 minimum ✿ PA, lights possibly ✿ Yes

Howard McCalla

See main entry under Radio section.

Chris Menist

Gronbear Farm, Withleigh, Nr Tiverton, Devon, EX16 8LA
T (01884) 257 848 or (0421) 354 139
Freelance musician specialising in percussion. Ideal for films, videos, theatres and dance. Created in 16-track digital and acoustic studio.
✿ Yes

Mission through Music
Colin Woodcock

PO Box 6, Prudhoe, Northumberland, NE42 6YY
T (01661) 831 030 F (01661) 831 030
Mission through Music is a registered charity. It arranges conferences, concerts and seminars aiming to build the body of Christ through music, training and witness; is committed to supporting music and teaching ministries in this country and abroad.

David Mitchell Morning Star Music

91 Relugas Road, Edinburgh, EH9 2PX
T (0131) 668 2744
Musician and biblical scholar.
❖ Folk/rock ● Varies ■ Wherever £ Negotiable ❀ Negotiable
☼ Yes

Marion Montgomery
c/o Ann Zahl

51 Great Cumberland Place, London, W1
T (0171) 402 8868
Vocalist – radio – TV – stage – concert – cabaret – actress – writer. One-woman show 'My Southern Heart', trustee of Montgomery Holloway Musical Trust. Critic with Crescendo Magazine.
❖ Popular, MoR, jazz music ■ Concert halls, art festivals
£ Negotiable ❀ Grand or b/grand piano, sound, lights and operator
☼ Yes

David Lyle Morris

PO Box 46, Beckenham, Kent, BR3 4YR
T (0181) 658 2153 F (0181) 658 0427
Singer, acoustic guitarist and songwriter: a) performing concerts; b) leading worship; c) backing other artists live and d) recording sessions (tenor lead and harmony group vocals, acoustic guitar).
❖ Acoustic ● Solo, or with band (percussion and acoustic bass)
■ Churches, schools, university, pubs, clubs, TV, radio £ £100 + petrol money, add £150 for band of 2 ❀ Standard PA ☼ Yes

Giles D Morrison

39 Renshaw Road, Greystones, Sheffield, S Yorkshire, S11 7PD
T (0114) 266 6409 (evenings)
Freelance bassist with wide gigging experience (contemporary and worship). Available for groups/bands playing all kinds of music, rockers.
❖ Most contemporary styles ■ Variety of venues £ Mileage
❀ Provide all own bass equipment ☼ No

Mosaic Theatre

See main entry under Drama section.

Mudheads Monkey
Matt Sims

Belmont, Tarnwell, Stanton Drew, Near Bristol, BS18 4EE
T (01275) 332 558 E-mail trevor.sims@bris.ac.uk
A rock band flavoured with roots, indie, brit pop, punk and grunge. They tire you out just watching them. Recently been supporting Eden Burning, Iona and Why?
❖ Indie, brit pop, rock ● 4 piece band ■ churches, pubs, clubs, schools, prisons and festivals £ £150 + travel ❀ PA can sometimes be provided if necessary ☼ Yes

Steve Nelson
49 Fort Street, Ayr, KA7 1DH
T (01292) 28C 265
Professional gu:tarist/saxophonist currently studying at the National Jazz Institute, Strathclyde University. Play all styles. Involved in praise/worship, rock evangelism.
❖ Jazz, rock – all styles ● Single musician ■ Professional session gigs £ None for Christian work ❀ Guitar/bass – 240V, sax – none ✿ No

Network Music
See main entry under Worship Music section.

Never on a Monday
Andy Atherton
4 Compton Close, Carleton, Poulton, Blackpool, Lancs, FY6 7TJ
T (01253) 892 994 F (01253) 892 994
We proclaim our faith in our words and the way we act. Not by out and out preaching.
❖ Indie rock ● Rock band that combines folk and rock and Christianity ■ Nationwide Christian and secular venues and festivals £ Expenses + £150 ❀ 2kW PA rig and lighting ✿ Yes

Nia
Kevin D Hoy
Nia Management, PO Box HK 70, Leeds, W Yorkshire, LS11 6YR
T (0113) 279 8636 F (0113) 279 4808
Since entering full-time ministry at age 17, Nia has spent 9 years sharing the Good News all around the world, through professional, challenging and inspiring concerts.
❖ Melodic rock/pop with ballads and worship included ● Soloist performance travels with full sound rig and lights, special effects and engineer ■ Church, theatre, school, conference £ By negotiation individual to event ❀ None – all provided ✿ Yes

No Limits
Mike Ikwuemesi
66 Surrey Grove, Sutton, Surrey, SM1 3PN
No Limits are a 7-piece band that play a fusion of soul, rock, and gospel with a tinge of jazz!
❖ Soul/funk/rock/gospel and jazz ● 7 ■ Most places ❀ PA system depending on size ✿ Yes

Nuffsed
Kati Rigby
120 Pooles Lane, Short Heath, Willenhall, W Midlands
T (01922) 497 128 or (01922) 495 401
We are a Christian roots (acoustic based) music/ministry band. We have played universities, churches, cathedrals, festivals, prisons, Christian centres and local radio.
❖ Roots ● Band ■ Nationally (see write-up) £ £150 + expenses (but we are negotiable) ❀ None – we have our own PA and lights ✿ Yes

The Ocracy
See main entry under Worship Music section.

Richard O'Conor
See main entry under Worship Music section.

Organised Chaos
Steve Mimmack

170 Great Clowes Street, Salford, Gt Manchester, M7 9XU
T (0161) 792 6820 F (0161) 835 3000 (work)
I write, record and perform my own songs, which I hope will glorify God, touch hearts and save lost souls by planting the good seed.
❖ Ambient industrial contemporary music ■ Local church, sometimes streets and prisons £ Free ✽ PA system (if possible)
✪ Yes

The Other Phil & Jon
Pat Harrison

16 Sefton Drive, Worsley, Manchester, M28 2NQ
T (0161) 794 2580
A teacher and a kitchen salesman (brothers) who enjoy using music and singing as a way to get the gospel message across to (especially young) people.
❖ Easy listening ● Two young men (brothers) ■ Churches and youth groups £ Negotiable ✽ Plug sockets ✪ Yes

Graham Owen

519 Abbey Road, Popley, Basingstoke, Hants, RG24 9EP
T (01256) 410 715 E-mail 100334.2150@compuserve.com
Guitarist/songwriter

Steve Parsons
Ruth Shirlow
(administrator)

Living Praise Ministries, 1 Old School Grange, Hengoed,
M Glam, CF82 7NY
T (01443) 862 603 F (01443) 862 603
Steve is a full-time Christian singer/songwriter whose ministry includes gospel concerts, outreach events and evangelism. His ministry challenges, encourages and reaches the lost. Amen!!!
❖ Pop MoR ■ Churches, outreach events £ Lives by faith ✽ None
✪ Yes

Stuart Penny

c/o Tomorrow Trust, Christ Church, Glebe Road, Bayston Hill,
Shrewsbury, Salop, SY2 6PJ
T (01743) 368 581
A Christian communicator, singer-songwriter and evangelist. Stuart uses music, humour, chat, verse and worse to entertain and explain the gospel.
❖ Contemporary singer-songwriter ■ UK and abroad. Churches, colleges, etc. £ Negotiable ✽ Good PA system ✪ Yes

John Perry

PO Box 93, Walton-on-Thames, Surrey, KT12 2RS
T (01932) 252 815 F (01932) 252 815
Outreach type concerts (evangelistic or just looking type). Musical and chatty in style... informal. Also worship leading at events and conferences etc. Seminars on worship.
❖ Pop, rock, worship (evangelistic in nature) ■ Church £ Negotiable
✪ Yes

Persuasion
Simeon Hope

1S Fir Avenue, Brandon, Durham, DH7 8AT
T (0191) 378 2885 F (0191) 378 2885
E-mail simeon.hope@gexpress.gn.apc.org
A contemporary music trio, we specialise in danceable rock/pop with a cutting edge and thought-provoking lyrics. We aim to entertain, evangelise and stimulate.
❖ Contemporary rock/pop/dance music ■ Youth events, pubs, clubs, Christian or secular £ £50 + travel ❀ Have own small (600W) PA. Need lights if possible ✿ Yes

Pilgrim
Paul Symonds

175 Quarmby Road, Quarmby, Huddersfield,
W Yorkshire, HD3 4FE
T (01484) 460 321
Pilgrim fuses high quality rock music with a strong desire to glorify Jesus, to create an effective channel through which the gospel can be proclaimed.
❖ Melodic rock ● 4-piece band (ages 21–29) ■ Churches, youth groups, prison £ No set fee, but would appreciate at least expenses ❀ PA (for over 100 people) and preferably lights ✿ Yes

Poetic Justice
David Casswell

HMP Wolds, Everthorpe, Brough, N Humberside, HU15 2JZ
T (01430) 421 588 F (01430) 421 589 E-mail
mark@fredblog.demon.co.uk
'Remember those in prison...' Heb 13.3. Fronted by prison chaplain, David Casswell, Poetic Justice carries this theme and a challenge about the penal system today.
❖ Folk/rock and various ● 6-piece band ■ Prisons, churches, colleges, festivals £ Petrol @ 15p/mile min ❀ PA for 5 vox, bass, keyboard, guitar, but we can provide ✿ Yes

Paul Poulton
Lorraine
(Christians in Music)

35 Stanhurst Way, Bustleholme Mill, West Bromwich,
W Midlands, B71 3QT
T (0121) 588 7959
Paul Poulton is a singer/songwriter both solo and with a band. Humour, fun and communicating spiritual truth are the hallmarks of his concerts.
❖ Rhythm and blues ● 1 ■ Churches, theatres, halls, etc.
£ Negotiable ❀ PA system ✿ Yes

Pray Naked
Mark Houston

38 Queens Avenue, Barnsley, S Yorkshire, S75 2AZ
T (01226) 207 749
Four good-looking lads who play alternative styles of rock from punk to metal. Original material plus covers by Neil Young, The Undertones, Steve Taylor.
❖ Rock band ■ Pubs, universities, colleges £ £50–£100 ❀ PA
✿ Yes

Pure Silk
Anthony Brightly

231 Lower Clapton Road, Hackney, London, E5 8EG
T (0181) 533 7994 F (0181) 986 4035
Pure Silk is a contemporary gospel group, singing lovers rock, reggae style gospel – young and enthusiastic, they have lots of talent and spirit.
❖ Gospel lovers (reggae) ● 6-strong team ■ Church and clubs
£ Depending on event ❀ Full PA ✿ Yes

The Radiators
Lawrence Langton

9 Woodend Lane, Speke, Liverpool, Merseyside, L24 3TQ
T (0151) 448 1754
The Radiators are a four-piece rock band playing mostly original songs in an indie rock and blues style of performance occasionally unplugged and acoustic.
❖ Contemporary rock ● 4-piece band, 3 guitars and drums ■ Church halls, Christian outreach £ Expenses or gift ❀ Fully equipped (except lighting) ۞ Yes

Julie Rayne

33 Barnsbury Street, Islington, London, N1 1PW
T (0171) 359 1497
My work includes theatre, pantomime, revues, television, records and radio. I have been a Christian since 1966 and have been included in outreach and worship projects.
❖ Middle of the road cabaret ● Solo artiste ■ Theatre, clubs, churches, small and large venues £ £100 (plus fee for pianist) + expenses ❀ Microphone/lights/PA, etc and both piano or keyboard for an accompanist ۞ Yes

RDA
Adie Mitchell

7 Falkland, Birch Green, Skelmersdale, Lancs, WN8 6RA
T (01695) 725 068 E-mail frankb@ehche.ac.uk
RDA play a blend of electric and acoustic style rock music with a wide-ranging appeal to both teens and twenties.
❖ Acoustic rock music ● 3: drums, bass, lead/rhythms and vocals ■ Church youth groups, schools, festivals, SUs £ Costs/gift (up to organisers) ❀ PA (but will provide own if nec.) ۞ Yes

Paul & Sharon Reid

28 Collinbridge Road, Glengormley, Newtownabbey, N Ireland, BT36 7SN
T (01232) 849 092
1. Working with youth at camps weekends. 2. Leading worship ministry. 3. Recording artists.
❖ Contemporary pop ● 2 ■ Events, weekend conferences £ Negotiable ❀ Have own PA and equipment ۞ Yes

Return to Eden
Leslie Haynes

'Pagasa', 4 Inney View, Laneast, Nr Launceston, Cornwall, P45 8PN
T (01566) 86943 F (01566) 86943
We are dedicated to spreading the full gospel through the music and our sharing of Christ, wherever God calls us to preach or play!
❖ Indy, folk rock ● Drums, bass, rhythm guitar, vocals ■ Anywhere we're asked £ Expenses only ❀ Full PA (we have a small PA ourselves) ۞ Yes

Revelation
Andrew Bunting

PO Box 5264, Birmingham, B14 7EA
T (0121) 441 3575
We are a Catholic Christian pop/rock band using music to help spread the gospel message in schools, universities, pubs, churches, etc.
❖ Pop, rock music ■ Schools, churches, universities, pubs, anywhere! £ Negotiable ❀ We have our own small PA system ۞ Yes

Noel Richards
PO Box 79c, Esher, Surrey, KT10 9LP
T (01932) 862 129 F (01932) 862 129
Available for concerts with full band, leading worship and teaching at seminars.
❖ Rock ● Full six-piece band ■ Concert halls, theatres £ For concerts £1,500 to £2,000 plus VAT ❀ Full PA and lighting provided by Noel Richards ✿ No

Sue Rinaldi
124 Portsmouth Road, Cobham, Surrey, KT11 1HX
T (01932) 867 652 F (01932) 867 652
Singer/songwriter/communicator, Sue travels as a solo artist or with band. Regularly giving concerts, Sue is also involved in worship events, and popular as a speaker and writer.
❖ Singer/songwriter or band (dance!) ● Solo or with 6-piece band ■ Larger venues, churches, schools £ Solo: £250 + expenses; Band: £600 + expenses ❀ Solo: full rig and foldback; Band: full rig and SM58 mics. ✿ Yes

River
Ali Loaker
9a Broad Street, Ely, Cambs, CB7 4AJ
T (01353) 663 583 (after 6:00pm) E-mail Riv@LHouse.Win_UK.net
River are a rock band made up of devoted and passionate, churchgoing Christians. We play punk/metal songs with strong melodies.
❖ Rock ● Four young Christian men ■ Festival, most venues £ Usually just travel and eating expenses ❀ PA, lights, good publicity ✿ Yes

Ian Roberts Photography
See main entry under Photography section.

Rodd & Marco
Elaine Palmer
28 Moray Park, Dalgety Bay, Fife, KY11 5UN
T (01383) 824 533 E-mail 101761,143@compuserve.com
Rodd and Marco are a comedy/musical/dramatic duo. They are Kingsway artists. Produced two critically acclaimed CDs Jurassic Church/The Acts Files. Full-time, cover all UK. Put on a fun concert.
❖ Outrageous, satirical music/comedy/drama mutation ● 2 ■ The whole spectrum of churches, prisons, festivals, youth events, high schools
£ £150 a day plus travel ❀ We have own PA. Lights needed ✿ Yes

Shane Rootes
Downtown Productions, 49 Kingsland Road, Worthing, W Sussex, BN14 9ED
T (01903) 207 197 F (01903) 207 197
Shane Rootes is a gifted musician/songwriter. He has served at Spring Harvest, Stoneleigh, and Elim Bible Weeks. He travels the UK extensively doing concerts, family roadshows, and training seminars.
❖ All music styles ● Available with or without band ■ Churches, missions, conferences, concerts, Bible weeks £ £200–£300 + 35 pence a mile ❀ None ✿ Yes
❖ Heavy rock metal/pop ● 5 ■ Festivals/pubs/halls etc. £ £150 + travel ❀ PA with monitors, stage and lights ✿ Yes

Peter James D Round
15 Bryntirion Drive, Prestatyn, Clwyd, LL19 9NT
T (01745) 853 977 F (01745) 853 977
Experienced contemporary vocalist and songwriter, with 23 years as solo artist and with groups. I play acoustic guitar, bass and drums.
❖ Various ● Solo performer ■ Anywhere £ Expenses only ❀ PA equipment ✿ Yes

The Rumours are True
Richard Coates
(Band co-ordinator)
141 Fossway, Huntingdon Road, York, YO3 7SQ
T (01904) 422 501
Available for concerts or worship. 'Spiritual stuff, serious, fluid, enchanting, the delivery is subtle, the sound is bang on. The audience was mesmerised.' (Yorkshire Evening Press).
❖ Jazzy Celtic rock ● 5 band members plus 1 sound engineer ■ Public venues, pubs, arts centres, churches, etc. £ Negotiable, please ring to discuss details ❀ Can provide own PA, etc. ✿ Yes

S'dANCE
See main entry under Worship Music section.

Nancy Sawyer
Brian Taylor (New Dawn Management)
1 Beech Close, Towcester, Northants, NN12 6BL
T (01327) 351 799 F (01327) 351 146
I am 24 years old, a Christian singer songwriter who is simply using the gifts God has given me. I work alongside 'As If' Phillip Goss to keep originality there.
❖ Pop ● 1 ■ Churches £ POA ❀ PA system ✿ Yes

Secret Archives of the Vatican
Vince Millett
70 Birdhurst Road, South Croydon, Surrey, CR2 7EB
T (0181) 680 0331
Musician creating postambient fourthworld electronica distributed worldwide through the cassette underground and independently of mainstream music industry.
❖ Postambient fourthworld electronic music ● Vince Millett and invited guest musicians ■ Festivals, clubs £ Negotiable, but must cover expenses ❀ Stereo PA, DAT or CD player, good foldback ✿ Yes

Signature
Tom Langlands
81 Hecklegirth, Annan, Dumfriesshire, DG12 6HL
T (01461) 205 719
Contemporary music group that also writes and performs own music and drama.
❖ Pop (contemporary Christian) ● 6 adults: drums, keyboards, guitars, brass, vocals) ■ Churches and charity events £ Nominal expenses ❀ Electricity supply ✿ Yes

**Simeon &
John**
John Gerighty

PO Box 1193, Cheddar, BS27 3BF
T (01934) 741 281 F (01934) 743 222
E-mail 10662C.2522@compuserve.com
_Simeon & John give concerts and make recordings of their unique style of
instrumental music, using panpipes, flutes, classical and acoustic
guitars._
❖ 'Contemporary/ambient' ● Informal, yet thought-provoking
concert of instrumental music ■ Small theatres, festivals, churches,
etc. £ £380 inclusive (but can be lower depending on circumstances)
❀ No sound equipment required up to 400-seater; above that, sound
equipment and engineer required ✿ Yes

**The Fiona
Simpson Band**
Brenda Adams

15 Foxhall Road, Timperley,
Altrincham, Cheshire, WA15 6RW
T (0161) 928 6672
_We play contemporary songs presenting the
Christian message to believers and non-
believers of all ages in an entertaining, non-
threatening way. We have performed in
various venues including churches, folk clubs, prisons and hotels._
❖ Acoustic/electric/various styles of music from folk to rock
● 5 ■ Church premises £ Expenses ❀ Power supply ✿ Yes

Claire Smith

55 Whitton Dene, Hounslow, Middx, TW3 2JN
T (0181) 894 1087
_I spent a year singing in a youth missionary band and since then have
travelled widely. I aim to communicate in an evangelistic and
contemporary way._
❖ Popular music ● Solo artist ■ Outreach events, churches and
conferences £ 100 ❀ PA system with tape recorder ✿ Yes

David Smith

242b London Road, Mitcham, Surrey, CR4 3HD
T (0181) 648 9113 or
Jet Star (0181) 961 5818
_Second album 'Coming' scheduled for release
summer of '97. 14 essential tracks – whatever your
taste in music you will love this!_
❖ Gospel reggae ● Solo ■ Concert halls, churches
£ £100–£150 ❀ PA system and microphone
✿ Yes

**Gordon
'Honky Tonk'
Smith**
Gordon Smith

70 Legsby Avenue, Grimsby, N Humberside, DN32 ONE
T (01472) 361 725
_Singing and talking about Jesus using contemporary Christian country
music – playing guitar, piano or pedal steel guitar to prepared backings.
Format to suit._
❖ Christian country music ■ Churches in Britain, EEC, Romania,
pubs, dances £ £50 + travel (negotiable) ❀ None – self-contained
✿ Yes

Jean Smith 4 Woodcroft Hollow, Ballymena, County Antrim,
N Ireland, BT42 1GB
T (01266) 652 742 F (01266) 652 742
Presently I sing solos, mainly in church services although I have taken part in fund-raising concert and I have produced one gospel tape.
❖ I sing mainly gospel, worship and MoR music ● I sing with backing tracks ■ Churches around the country, church halls ❀ PA, including tape deck

**Raymond Smith
& The Hillside
Singers** *See main entry under Church Organist Music Director section.*

Adrian Snell 1 Combeside, Lyncombe Vale Road, Bath, BA2 4LU
T (01225) 423 113 F (01225) 423 113
E-mail adriansnell@compuserve.com
Composer, performing and recording artist. International concert touring schedule (particularly Europe, East and West). Seventeen albums recorded over twenty years.
❖ Contemporary music rooting in classical rock ● Solo or with other musicians ■ Concert halls, churches, festivals, etc. £ Negotiable ❀ PA/lights, depending on production ✿ Yes

**David
Snowdon** *See main entry under Worship Music section.*

Brenda Sokell 7 Welbury Way, Southfield Lea, Cramlington,
Northumberland, NE23 6PD
T (01670) 734 754 F (01670) 731 233
I like to work in a cabaret-style evening, creating a non-threatening atmosphere for non-Christians. For example: a pre-Alpha evening?
❖ Jazz and contemporary (various) ■ Pubs, clubs, but prefer private functions £ When I worked through an agent it was £50–£100 but now I work on my own I haven't set a fee ❀ I have my own PA if needed ✿ Yes

Julie Steventon *See main entry under Worship Music section.*

Stonehouse
Andy Hutchinson 27a Adelaide Street, Plymouth, Devon, T (01752) 220 804
Powerful songs, sensitively hard.
❖ Powerful ■ Churches £ Petrol, as Lord leads ❀ PA if possible, though can be arranged ✿ Yes

**Graham
Stovold** 27a Devonport Road, Stoke Village, Plymouth, Devon, PL3 4DJ
T (01752) 509 935
Since conversion 8 years ago I've appeared at Kensington Temple, Cross Rhythms, Greenbelt etc. Also events by Shaftesbury Society, Walk of 1000 Men and others. Good thoughtful songs.
❖ Acoustic or band available ● 35916 ■ Churches, events £ Negotiable ✿ Yes

Swarm
Suzi Clark

28 Kestrel Avenue, Herne Hill, London, SE24 OEB
T (0171) 738 4061
Swarm offer a compact yet uncompromising set brimming with ideas, narratives and emotions. They also provide computer-generated visuals which are synchronised to their songs.
❖ Laid back pop with an alternative edge ● Two piece singer/songwriter band ■ Cafes, restaurants, wine bars, pubs £ £100 plus expenses ❀ PA plus video projector (if desired) ♻ Yes

Target
Andy Dickinson
(manager)

Hardley Pentecostal Church, Hardley Green, Hardley, Southampton, Hants, SO45 3NN
T (01703) 326 704
Target are a 'wacky' rock band who love to preach while playing.
❖ Indie-rock ● 1 guitarist/singer, 1 bass player, 1 drummer ■ Anywhere £ Depending on venue ❀ None ♻ No

Elaine Taylor

132a Agar Grove, Camden Town, London, NW1 9TY
T (0171) 813 7572
I feel called to reach the world through contemporary prophetic worship and to provide quality backing vocals/encouragement for artists producing music of all types.
❖ Mainly contemporary ■ Church/recording studio £ Travel expenses ♻ No

TEN
John Powell

14 Waverley Road, Steeple View, Laindon, Basildon, Essex, SS15 4HU
T (01268) 542 741
Modern, lively 6-piece band playing up-tempo dance/rock music. Live performances include Greenbelt, Brixton Academy, Mean Fiddler. Received Radio 1 airplay with debut single.
❖ Lively dance, rock, pop, contemporary music ● Six-piece group: vocals, drums, guitar, keyboards, bass, sax ■ Clubs, festivals, London rock venues £ £200–£250 + expenses ❀ 500–1000W PA and fairly large stage ♻ Yes

Tina Thomas
Tina Reibl

2 Lock Mead, Maidenhead, Berks, SL6 8HF
T (01628) 33509 F (01628) 770 808
Singer and lecturer for Performing Arts. Solo work as singer – guitarist. Appearing as 'Tequila Sunrise' with keyboard player. Also dinner-jazz. Tina works a a session singer on a regular basis.
❖ Folk, jazz, rock, pop, cabaret ● Available as duo or in a band ■ Restaurants, hotels, functions £ £200 for the duo ❀ A powerpoint ♻ Yes

Jason A Thompson

13 Argyle Terrace, Newbiggin by the Sea, Northumberland, NE64 6PR
T (01670) 810 370 or (0589) 044 869 F (01670) 854 652
Composer, recording engineer and producer for independent projects. Recently released 'Crunchy Maggotts' album, now working on high energy dance worship for 'The Deep End', Arlington.
❖ Composer/producer

Neil Thompson   *See main entry under Worship Music section.*

Charles   24a The Square, Titchfield, Hants, PO14 4AF
Timberlake   T (01329) 845 265
Pianist/composer of quiet, reflective and thought-provoking piano music.
Co-writer of carols and worship songs.
❖ As above, plus own arrangements of well-known ballads and
popular songs ■ Churches, plus private parties/functions
£ Negotiable ❀ At present, not fully mobile with own equipment
✿ No

Rob Turner   62 Peristone Street, Ibstock, Leicester, LE67 6NU
T (01530) 263 740
Singer/songwriter. Born again 1984. Songs often experience-based,
always Holy Spirit-driven. Melody, harmony and lyrics of equal
importance.
❖ Folkish ● Solo ■ Churches and folk clubs £ Travel ❀ PA system
if available. If not, no problem ✿ Yes

Sarah Tyler   c/o Northumbria Community Trust, Heyton Hall, Chatton, Alnwick,
Dave Hay (Nice &   Northumberland, NE66 5SD
Safe Management)   T (0191) 373 7481
A singer/songwriter who tackles issues from a hard-edged, Christian
perspective, but with a subtlety that is accepted anywhere from pubs to
churches!
❖ Indie, roots, acoustic ● Up to 4 people ■ Anywhere – pubs,
church events, SUs, youth events £ Sometimes nothing, talk to us!!
❀ Normal electrical supply ✿ Yes

Unity   8 Montcliffe Crescent, Whalley Range, Manchester, M16 8GR
Mike Vell   T (0161) 226 6946
Using various styles of music we communicate the word of God to
Christians and non-Christians, working in churches, public concert halls
and outdoor venues.
❖ Varied – to reach a broad cross-section ● Young, respectful and
gospel dedicated ■ Around the North-West of England £ Negotiable
❀ Church or concert setting ✿ Yes

Steve Urwin   142 Newport Road, New Bradwell, Milton Keynes,
Bucks, MK13 0AA
T (01908) 319 771
Active drums/percussion. Singer/songwriter. Midi studio etc. Songs for
the lost and found and relationship with God evangelism/worship. Very
interested in involvement with media projects.
❖ Mellow to rock/jazz ● Alone at the moment. Craves pro-Christian
musician ■ On a Christian level in church/secular level in pubs etc.
£ Negotiable ❀ PA ✿ Yes

contemporary music

Marianne Velvárt
70 Oakley Road, South Norwood, London, SE25 4XQ
T (0181) 656 3080
I have worked extensively on the festival arts circuit, recorded several albums, no stranger to radio or outreach work. A member of PRS, I describe myself as a street-wise singer/ songwriter and poet.
❖ Jazz-rock-funk-blues-folk-gospel ● Solo or with band if required ■ Anywhere £ Yes depending on gig ✹ Basic PA system ✪ Yes

Visual Ministries Concert Choir
Junior Spence
82 Nevill Road, Stoke Newington, London, N16 0SX
T (0171) 241 1901 or (0956) 599 729
Not just another gospel choir, but a choir that possesses experience and professional quality. The choir is made up of some of the best lead singers drawn from other well-known gospel groups and choirs.
❖ Traditional/contemporary ● 21 professional singers ■ Nationally £ £500–£1500 ✪ Yes

Wedding Songs – Catherine Francoise
See main entry under Classical Music section.

Where's Harry?
Keith Thom
125 Brediland Road, Linwood, Paisley, PA3 3RX
T (01505) 320 765 Mobile (0585) 726 626
A 5-piece Christian rock band able to perform solo or as support playing original material with a clear Christian message. Also able to play praise and worship, to lead celebration or youth services.
❖ Guitar-driven rock gospel ● 5 musicians and sound and lights ■ Prisons, schools, colleges, church £ By arrangement ✹ None, own PA and lights available ✪ Yes

Ali & Karen Wilson
15 Robert Street, Newport on Tay, Fife, DD6 8BJ
T (01382) 541 178
We are husband and wife singers/songwriters who write and play material from jazz/funk to light rock. We also do session work.
❖ Light rock to jazz, funk music ● Husband and wife team ■ Churches (but anywhere considered) £ Travel expenses plus donation ✹ PA (at least 4 channels) ✪ Yes

Sharon Winfield
c/o St Paul's Church, Holgate Road, York, YO2 4BB
T (01904) 658 820 F (01904) 780 152
A female vocalist able to adapt to all audiences; pubs, prisons, churches, mission tents, open air. Whole self-contained set or warm-up for speaker.
❖ Folk/vocal and acoustic guitar ■ Anywhere, prisons, churches, pubs, etc. £ Negotiable ✹ A socket ✪ Yes

Nigel Worner-Phillips
6 Magill Close, Spencers Wood, Reading, Berks, RG7 1BW
T (01734) 882 036
Vocal guitarist performing ballad-type music with a personal and evangelistic message.
❖ Vocal guitarist ● Myself ■ Anywhere £ Expenses ❀ PA ✿ Yes

Tessa Wrightson
39 Calbourne Drive, Calcot, Reading, Berks, RG31 7DB
T (01734) 455 413
Songwriter, music and lyrics. Christian and melodic rock material. Vocalist.

contemporary music

Andy Au
Megan Tasdeller

City Gate Centre, 84–86 London Road, Brighton,
E Sussex, BN1 4JF
T (01273) 693 807 F (01273) 682 248
E-mail CITYGATE.TRUST@ukonline.co.uk
*Andy dances in worship using props such as flags
and ribbons. Much of his work involves encouraging
and teaching others to worship through movement.*
❖ Celebratory ■ Christian conferences
£ £150–£180 per day ❀ Minimum 8x8 space
♢ No

Liz Babbs

29 Cropton Crescent, Beechdale Mews,
Aspley, Notts, NG8 3FG
T (0115) 929 4008
*Dancer, teacher, retreat leader specifically
working with ME (Myalgic Encephalomyelitis)
sufferers and currently writing a book. Uses
dance to increase public awareness of this
illness.*
❖ Contemporary ● Solo ■ Churches,
cathedrals, retreat centres, theatres £ Negotiable ❀ Sound
equipment. Clear space preferably raised ♢ Yes

Ella Barker
Fenella Jane Barker

'Courtside', 13 Darlington Close, Amersham,
Bucks, HP6 5AD
T (01494) 727 739
*Has danced choreographed live theatre, TV, and
film including Springs Dance Co, MAS Dance,
Cooperative Dance Theatre and Nomad Dance
Company. Teaches all ages and abilities.*
❖ Dance (contemporary; contemporary/jazz;
Spanish) ● Solo, but also work as duet with
Frances Clarke ■ Theatres; churches; cathedrals;
arts/community centres; schools £ Min. £15/hour teaching;
performance is negotiable ❀ Sound equipment (cassette recorder);
clear space min. 10'x10' ♢ No

Erica Bebb

21 Bramble Drive, Stoke Bishop, Bristol, BS9 1RE
T (0117) 968 2153 E-mail 101741.1546@compuserve.com
*Described as a prophetic dancer; my platform is the International
Christian Dance Fellowship. Also lead group 'Daughter of Zion'. Vision a)
teach Jewish roots of faith b) minister reconciliation (2 Cor 5:18) c)
prepare the Bride.*
❖ Varied, workshop presentation ● Max 8 ■ Church, theatre, hall
£ Acc. to requirements ❀ Clear space ♢ Yes

Beyond Jordan

See main entry under Worship Music section.

Beyond the Barricades
Anne and Derek Marr

26 The Chesters, Newcastle-upon-Tyne, NE5 1AF
T (0191) 267 4808
Beyond the Barricades seeks to encourage exploration of faith beyond the security of the familiar, finding simple movement expressions across the boundaries of mime, dance, drama and sign.
❖ Teaching, workshops, presentation ● All ages, various skills, adaptable, ecumenical ■ Schools, churches, outside venues £ Voluntary contributions as possible ❀ Power source only ✪ No

Fru Bird

Flat 2, 19 Bromley Common, Bromley, Kent, BR2 9LS
T (0181) 460 0637
Teaching and performing within the Church and education, Fru's work ranges from fun to profound; she has danced and taught extensively and is currently Artistic Director of Springs Dance Co. Fru is experienced with people with special needs.
❖ contemporary dance ● 1 ■ Churches,schools, festivals, outreach events £ variable fee + expenses. £100–150 per day ❀ Space, sound and lights ✪ No

Philip Bollen

3 Edith Road, West Kensington, London, W14 0SU
T (0171) 603 4166
I have trained in ballet, contemporary, jazz, composition, bharatha natyam and have performed with several small companies, with roles in productions such as Nutcracker, Coppelia, etc.
❖ Classical and contemporary ■ Small venues ✪ No

Heidi Bomber

16 Bellwell Drive, Four Oak, Sutton Coldfield, Birmingham, B74 4AH
T Year 1998: (01992) 448 144,
Year 1999: (0121) 308 5998
A CDFB member. I am a professionally trained contemporary dancer specialising in encouraging men and women to worship through movement via workshops discussion. Available weekends.
❖ Contemporary, worship, creative ● Solo ■ Churches and Christian celebrations £ Gift which includes travel expenses ❀ Plug, sockets, smooth flooring, heat/air conditioning ✪ No

Elizabeth Anne Bristow

See main entry under Worship Music section.

Jane Burton

7 Collingbourne Road, Shepherd's Bush, London, W12 0JG
T (0181) 740 0951
Performance: ballet, jazz, contemporary, period dance on stage, TV, film, founder of Christian dance groups: 'Springs' London, 'Prepare' Sydney. Teaching: London, Australia, Europe, USA. Choreography: all styles.

Cedar Dance in Worship & Theatre Company
Janet Randell

42 Gunton Road, London, E5 9JS
T (0181) 806 4609 F (01691) 791 486
Cedar offer a unique opportunity to Christians, whatever their standard of dance, to develop a creative expression of their faith and to bring worship and liturgy alive. Cedar uses the medium of dance to communicate Christian spiritual truths to both Christian and non-Christian audiences. Selecting performances, residencies, master classes and lecture demonstrations for Christian conferences/ outreaches/churches.

Andrea Clarke

15 The Priors, Lowdham, Notts, NG14 7BA
T (0115) 966 3161 F (01636) 816 602
I was a professional dancer and now I teach. I am particularly interested in the Christian arts and in teaching and encouraging the oppressed and abused.
❖ Contemporary dance ● Myself, my ghettoblaster, my literature
■ Anywhere £ As a teacher £60 per day, all inclusive ✿ Yes

CRE 8
Karen Dalziel

20 Grosvenor Road, St Albans,
Herts, AL1 3BY
T (01727) 839347 or (0973) 662 707
CRE 8 is a young lively dance company. Our aim is to celebrate our faith through dance and share our faith with the wider church through performances and workshops.
❖ Jazz, modern pieces ● 8 ■ Churches, theatres, concert halls
£ £200 approx ❀ Tape CD player

Carol Cruickshank

30 Park Avenue, Chelmsford, Essex, CM1 2AB
T (01245) 287 112
Organises and choreographs dance for Christian events, conferences, church meetings, outdoor evangelism. Also runs workshops on worship and creativity in all its aspects.

Alison Eve Cudby

Flat 2, 46 Chalk Hill, Oxhey, Watford, Herts, WD1 4BX
T (01923) 250 758
Dance, expressive mime, song (mezzo) combined. Contemporary and various styles. Solo, live accompaniment possible. Also workshops in expressive mime and liturgical/contemplative dance: 'Prayerdance'.
❖ Expressive mimetic dance in contemporary style ● Solo (live accompaniment possible) ■ Festivals, churches – anything considered £ Negotiable ❀ Tape/CD player. Mains power ✿ No

Carol Dale

15 The Nursery, Burgess Hill, W Sussex, RH15 0LR
T (01444) 235 642
I do solo, creative dance/drama to contemporary Christian and non-Christian music, expressing all aspects of Christianity.
❖ Creative dance ● Solo ■ In local church services ❀ Tape amplification – good lighting ✿ No

Dance for Christ (DFC)
Mark and Mary Fleeson

1 Mulberry Close, Tring, Herts, HP23 5DZ
T (01442) 827 838 F (01442) 891 838 (ring first)
E-mail dfc@dfcuk.demon.co.uk
DFC presents the arts by providing support and teaching to others who are using the arts in their churches and by working as a challenging and inspiring presence in the Christian community.
❖ Dance, mime and movement – not classical ● Between 2–6, depending on event ■ Where invited – but not as 'entertainment' £ No charge, love offering accepted ❀ Power point ✿ No

Kathryn Sarah Davies

Old Vicarage Ministries, The Old Vicarage, 77 Addington Village Road, Addington Village, Croydon, CRO 5AS
T (01689) 842 952 F (01689) 800 205
'Just the way you are', 'Time', 'The Mask', bridge-building through dance. The message portrayed with secular and Christian music. Thought- provoking, inspirational! and entertaining!!
❖ All kinds, incl. modern, jazz, ballet, tap ● Soloist ■ Cabarets, church services, celebrations £ Expenses (e.g. travel). Fee from £25 ❀ Audio equipment ✿ No

Diakonos Physical Theatre

See main entry under Drama section.

Dunamis Dance Company
Dot Soltay

28 Chatburn Park Drive, Brierfield, Nelson, Lancs, BB9 5BU
T (01282) 698 327
Heavenly contemporary, jazz, contact/release, street, tap, tackling issues with its feet firmly on the ground! Performances, workshops.
❖ Contemporary dance ● min. 3 ■ Church, street, theatres, festivals £ Expenses plus negotiable fee ❀ PA with tape/CD playback, raised area to perform ✿ No

Essential Theatre Company

See main entry under Drama section.

Gof The Clown

See main entry under Clowning / Magic section.

Mal Grosch

32 Temple Dwellings, Old Bethnal Green Road, London, E2 6QG
T (0171) 739 0589
Barn dance/ceilidh caller. Can provide band or work with client's band or with tapes. Mixture of accessible British and overseas dances. Good fun for church social.
❖ British/overseas dances ● With band or tapes ■ Social functions £ Negotiable but c. £400 with band or £100 with tapes ❀ Large wooden floor, church hall, gym, etc. ✿ No

Candida Hadler-Mayor

26 Cavendish Road, Chesham, Bucks, HP5 1RW
T (01494) 791 876 F (01494) 791 876
I am joint national co-ordinator of the Christian Dance Fellowship of Great Britain. I offer Christian dance workshops covering both worship and evangelism, and performances.
❖ Contemporary, character, worship dance ● 'Connections' dance company, my husband Roger Mayor, solo ■ Churches, schools, theatres, conferences £ Negotiable ❀ Smooth flooring, preferably raised, access to plugs ○ Yes

Susanna Harrington

4 East Mill, Halstead, Essex, CO9 2EJ
T (01787) 474 561
The grace of bharatha natyam, the classical dance of Tamil Nadu in South India lends itself to the worshipful sharing of the gospel of Christ.
❖ Bharatha natyam – classical Indian dance
● Freelance individual ■ Churches of all denominations and schools £ Fee £20 per hour + travel at 15p per mile ❀ 11x12ft space and a power point, sprung wooden floor is preferable ○ Yes

Ken Hodgson

10 Highland Croft, Beckenham, Kent, BR3 1TB
T (0181) 658 0972
Using coloured flags in worship, expressing love to God, extolling Jesus, interpreting Scripture, prophetic ministry, international highplace praise/prayer. Workshops and training seminars.

Sylvia Mary Hughes

22 Millbrook, Leybourne, West Malling, Kent, ME19 5QJ
T (01732) 871 405
SE Regional Co-ordinator for Christian Dance Fellowship of Britain. I specialise in workshops which encourage, motivate and enable people and groups to move forward. Also Israeli dance and flags.

JNR MACK

See main entry under Contemporary Music section.

Livingstones Dance
Freda Leask

'Fjael', Quarff, Shetland, ZE2 9EY
T (01950) 477 285
A young group who use music, song, dance, drama and mime to convey the gospel. Age dance 7+ late teens. Between 20–30 members.
❖ Lively, contemporary ● Young, enthusiastic, full of life!
■ Concerts, church, street £ Donations to charity ❀ PA for tape recorder and 2–3 mics ○ Yes

Audrey Marriott

2 Bridgefield Close, Banstead, Surrey, SM7 1LR
T (01737) 216 894
I dance with a small group and specialise with banners and ribbons taking adult and children's workshops. I often work with Capt'n Alan Price, Tecknon Trust, Derby.

Bill Miller

39 Eastcote Lane, South Harrow, Middx, HA2 8DE
T (0181) 426 8236
Currently, I dance freelance amongst a team of three churches and teach once a week. I am looking to start a dance company in the East Anglia region.
❖ Contemporary dance ● Work alone, but willing to work with others ■ Churches £ Negotiable ❀ Sound system, cassette/CD capabilities ☼ No

Gill Moore
Artistic Director –
Phoenix Performing
Arts Trust

PO Box 11073, London, SE15 4ZE
T (0181) 299 2021 F (0181) 299 2021
A performer teacher with skills and 16 years' experience in dance, improvisation and physical theatre. Workshops offered include contemporary dance, technique, improvisation, creative movement with children/youth and groups with disabilities.
❖ Physical theatre, contemporary, improvisation ● Solo to three ■ Theatres, studios etc. £ Professional rates, equity, negotiable ❀ 20x20 stage and sound system ☼ Yes

New Jerusalem Dancers
Vera Chierico

128 Hollydale Road, London, SE15 2TQ
T (0171) 277 7073 F (0181) 692 8431
I teach, lecture and present Davidic dance (2 Sam 6:14) including the biblical, historical and modern revival of this ancient form of dance worship from the Israelites.
❖ Davidic dance (Jewish) ● 14 dancers ■ UK and Europe £ Various ❀ Phone for details ☼ Yes

The Ocracy

See main entry under Worship Music section.

Joanna Pegler

16 Glazbury Road, London, W14 9AS
T (0171) 602 3194
Joanna Pegler – graduate of the Royal Ballet School and former member of Springs Dance Company, is able to offer creative dance within a Christian context.
❖ Contemporary ● 1 dancer ■ Churches, missions, festivals £ Gift + travel expenses ❀ Decent size space, sound system, lights ☼ Yes

Sandy Phillips

62 Ash Lane, Hale, Cheshire, WA15 8PD
T (0161) 980 6138
I am a professional dancer/choreographer. I've mainly worked in theatre, West End and tours. I have also worked alongside Adrian Snell on 'Song of an Exile' and 'Alpha & Omega' tours.
❖ Modern, jazz ● Solo or within dance team ■ Theatres, concerts, tours £ £50–£100, depends on venue ❀ Floor space, lighting ☼ No

Phoenix Performing Arts Trust

See main entry under Drama section.

Andy Raine

'Settled', 3 Lilburn Terrace, Holy Island,
Northumberland, TD15 2SA
T (01289) 389 351
*Involved in Christian dance since 1975 – teaching, choreographing,
leading teams – emphasis on streetwork, dance in evangelism. I work
primarily with untrained dancers, and men's dancework.*
❖ Varied ● Various ■ Streets, schools, parish missions, festivals,
etc. £ Love-gifts ❀ Tape and amplification for large events ○ Yes

Janet Randell

42 Gunton Road, London, E5 9JS
T (0181) 806 4609 F (01691) 791 486
*International choreographer, teacher, writer and artistic director of the
Cedar Dance Theatre Company. Worked in China and USA.*

S'dANCE

See main entry under Worship Music section.

**Kate
Snowden**
Mrs Heather
Snowden

'Peterbridge', Pyrford Woods Close, Woking, Surrey, GU22 8QN
T (01932) 348 672
*I graduated from the Royal Ballet School in '95 and on leaving, secured a
contract with a large classical ballet company in Berlin.*
❖ Ballet ■ Deutsche Oper Berlin ❀ Suitable stage for pointe work
○ Yes

**Christiane
Spivey**
Director Phoenix
Performing Trust

PO Box 11073, London, SE15 4ZE
T (0181) 299 2021 F (0181) 299 2021
*My training has been in contemporary dance,
improvisation and subjective mime techniques.
Performance and teaching draw from these
disciplines with the addition of vocal work
including poetry and text.*
❖ Contemporary, improvisation, physical theatre
● Solo – three ■ Theatre venues/studios etc.
£ Professional rates/negotiable ❀ 20x20 space,
sound equipment ○ Yes

**Springs
Dance
Company**

Fru Bird – Flat 2, 19 Bromley Common, Bromley, Kent, BR2 9LS
T (0181) 460 0637
Frances Clarke – 49 Ellesmere Road, London, E3 5QU
T (0181) 981 5428
*Springs' repertoire is diverse and thought-provoking, demonstrating
biblical themes and truths through performance and teaching. Its
members are professionally trained dancers, teachers and
choreographers.*
❖ Contemporary ● 3 dancers ■ Schools, colleges, universities,
churches, outreach missions, festivals, theatres £ £300 a day –
negotiable. Plus special packages ❀ Space (20ft by 20ft), sound
system ○ Yes

Vivienne Tsouris

'Tregudda', West Hill, Wadebridge,
Cornwall, PL27 7EW
T (01208) 816 421
Powerful dramatic dance in contemporary style often addressing issues of social concern. Also to encourage other dancers in teaching seminars/ workshops. Writer of poetry short stories.
❖ Classical, contemporary ■ Theatre, festivals, schools, etc.
£ Travel + gift ❀ Powerpoints. Tape/CD player ☼ Yes

Linda Wells

5a Longmeadow Close, Sutton Coldfield, W Midlands, B75 7SQ
T (0121) 311 1073
I marry the languages of dance and British sign language after discovering the two create a powerful tool to communicate the Christian life and message. It also bridges the gap of misunderstanding between the deaf and hearing.
■ Churches, deaf clubs, colleges £ £70 per day or £10 per hour
☼ Yes

Virginia White

Ginny White

'Two Hoots', 38 Wentworth Road, Thorpe Hesley, Rotherham,
W Yorkshire, S61 2RL
T (0114) 245 1599 F (0144) 245 1599
'Davidic dance' – worship dance using Hebraic music and steps. Workshops are done throughout UK teaching Davidic dance. Member of 'Messianic dance North'.

Paul Alexander
Triple 'C' Terry
Anne Preston

PC Box 199, Horley, Surrey, RH6 9YF
T (01293) 824 840 Mobile (0850) 878 814 F (01293) 824 840
Professional actor, 30 years. One-man shows: St John's Gospel, The Psalms, Shakespeare, Dreams of Power and Passion, Miracles & Parables, Francis of Assisi, The Old Testament. All one and half hours.
❖ Solo, dramatic story telling ● One ■ Churches, art centres, festivals, schools, theatres ✸ Clear space, basic lighting ✿ Yes

Gill Ashton

117b Grove Avenue, Hanwell, London, W7 3EX
T (0181) 566 5603 Mobile (0956) 313 660 F as phone on request
I am a professional actress/singer, having worked in theatre, stage, TV and film. I write short plays/sketches and am a singer/songwriter with Christian band 'Kry'.

Darrell Bate

19 Silverhall Street, Old Isleworth, Middx, TW7 6RF
T (0181) 568 1195 F (0181) 560 9893
I am a trainee actor and mime artist with several years' theatre experience. I teach drama and physical theatre at drama schools, churches and to children.
❖ Actor, mime ■ Secular theatres, churches £ Variable ✸ Variable
✿ No

Karen Beal

2 Church House, Orts Road, Reading, Berks, RG1 3JN
T (01734) 664 209
I am currently working as a theatre in education practitioner and have a particular interest in working with young people.

Beyond the Barricades

See main entry under Dance section.

Bijou Theatre
John D Slater

167 Queensway, Didcot, Oxon, OX11 8SJ T (01235) 812 268
Performances include 'The Gospel According to St Mark', 'Mrs Moses', 'Scarecrow's Holiday', 'Happy Birthday Whatsinaname'. Workshops conducted with adults and children. Also clowning.
❖ Humorous ■ Anywhere £ From £75 ✸ Clear space ✿ Yes

Max Carpenter

'Shalom', Alexandra Road, Crediton, Devon, EX17 2DP
T (01363) 773 957
Many years' experience in Christian theatre as an actor, director and (sometime) writer. Have done 12–15 programmes for TV up till about 1984. Since then concentrated on local church leadership. Now able to specialise again in theatre.
❖ Acting: 2–handers mostly ■ Churches £ Petrol + production costs (if any) ✸ Acting area 30'x20' minimum. Lights an advantage
✿ No

Karen Cavallini

See main entry under Play Writing section.

Marc Cavallini

See main entry under Play Writing section.

Centre Stage
Gary Bastin

The Centre, 18 Winchester Street, Basingstoke, Hants, RG21 7DY
T (01256) 461 430 F (01256) 810 791
Centre Stage communicates biblical truth through short, entertaining dramatic sketches and songs, to children between the ages of five and sixteen.
❖ Short, punchy, funny, modern 'parable' type stories ● 3 people
■ Local primary schools (and some secondary), churches too
£ Expenses if out of town. No set fees ❀ None – we provide all we need except space ○ No

Elaine Chalmers-Brown

24 Yorkshire Place, Warfield Green, Berks, RG42 3XE
T 01344 426 286 F 01344 426 286
Drama workshops, training, compere, actress. Worked in schools, churches, prisons, pubs, missions. Monologues. Produced and directed. Radio presenter and producer.
❖ Drama ● 1, 2 or 3 ■ Anywhere £ To be arranged ○ No

Gerry Cohen-Stone

48 Ethelbert Road, Margate, Kent, CT9 1SB
T (01843) 230 751 E-mail Gerry.Cohen@btinternet.com
Worship/drama workshops for all ages – from a few hours to a week – very low cost – over 20 years' experience – Bible-based drama and songs.
❖ Evangelism and church teaching ● 1 ■ Wherever invited
£ Negotiable low fee + travel expenses ❀ Electric socket, OHP, PA if available ○ No

Covenant Players
Deborah Harder

European Development Office, 70 Park Road, Rushden, Northants, NN10 0LH
T (01933) 413 830 F (01933) 395 753
E-mail 106561.3177@compuserve.com
Covenant Players exists to communicate the Lord Jesus Christ through the medium of drama, serving the Church and society, throughout the world.
❖ Communicative drama ● Teams of 3–4 people @450 worldwide
■ Wherever an audience can gather £ Varies depending on size of user group ❀ Performing area ○ Yes

Susanna Crowther

11a Chatham Street, Southwell, Notts, NG25 0EY
T (01636) 815 661
Four years at drama school in Guildford, 18 years' acting experience. Teach theatre class at a private school and heavily involved in special needs.

Andrew Cullum

56 Yelverton Road, Holbrooks, Coventry, W Midlands, CV6 4AH
T (01203) 689 394 or (0973) 782 067
A one-man show telling the story of Christ through the eyes of his friends and enemies. Fast-moving drama that lingers in the memory.
❖ Classical theatre ■ Small theatres, arts centres, church halls, churches £ Based on £150 per performance ❀ Basic lighting. Stage 12x6ft minimum ○ Yes

Diakonos Physical Theatre
Danny Scott

PO Box 11073 London, SE15 4ZE
T (0181) 299 2021 F (0181) 299 2021
Toured throughout Europe, USA, and Australia: unique style combines theatre, dance, mime, text and poetry. Raw unsanitised confrontation/ tender and sensitive, evocative and penetrative. A professional company.
❖ High energy, abstract, emotive and thought-provoking ● 4 company members/3 performers ■ Professional secular theatre venues, festivals £ £375.00 p/performance + expenses (approx.) ❀ Full PA, lighting rig, 25'x25' stage ✿ Yes

Rose Dick
Pheonix Performing Arts Trust

PO Box 11073, London, SE15 4ZE
T (0181) 299 2021 F (0181) 299 2021
Skills include acting/acting technique, directing and teaching. An experienced theatre/drama teacher and workshop leader with both adults and children.
❖ Theatre/drama ● Solo up to 4 ■ Theatres, schools, churches £ negotiable plus expenses ❀ suitable performance/workshop space ✿ Yes

DRIFT
Alison Booker

St Peter's Vicarage, 29 Warrington Road, Dagenham, Essex, RM8 3JH
T (0181) 983 8198
I work with any age group, training people to 'do' drama through workshops etc. or to 'use' it in evangelism or teaching eg. Sunday school, church.
❖ Teaching – informal, fun. Performance – variable! ■ In churches – special services, away weekends, etc. £ Variable ❀ Large(ish) space ✿ Yes

Dunamis Dance Company

See main entry under Dance section.

Elle M Theatre Company
Emma Govan

10 Inkerman Terrace, Chesham, Bucks, HP5 1QA
T (01494) 786 116 E-mail e.govan@rhbnc.ac.uk
A Christian women's theatre company with a wide-ranging repertoire – cabaret to dramatic meditation. Particularly focusing on female experiences of life and God. Also offer workshops.
❖ Range from cabaret, comedy to dramatic meditation ● 2–3 women ■ Festivals, art centres, colleges, churches £ Fee (negotiable) + expenses ❀ A room/hall with 16'x16' performance space ✿ Yes

Beth Ellis The Garden Cottage, 18 Lonsdale Road, London, W11 2DE
T (0171) 229 6504
Trained RADA – 40 years rep. touring – National Theatre – West End and television. Member of Christians in Entertainment. Speaker on TV, religious broadcasting and Christian conferences.
❖ One woman shows – excerpts from plays or verse etc.
■ Conferences – ACG etc. £ Negotiable ❀ Lighting and sound and operators ✿ Yes

Peter English 9 Carlton Row, Trowbridge, Wilts, BA14 0RT
T (01225) 752 243
Running workshops on aspects of drama including street theatre, drama in worship, play writing, directing and reading in public; festival adjudication; writing of plays and poetry; directing and speaking to groups.

Essential Theatre Company
Ian Richardson
45 Ripon Road, Ansdell, Lytham St Annes, Lancs, FY8 4DS
T (01253) 737 367 F (01253) 735 367
E-mail Andrew_Hardcastle@msn.com
A company of six who work nationally in schools, universities, youth clubs, Christian events, churches on various topics. Specialise in looking at social injustice. Work with all ages.
❖ Plays, sketches, mime, workshops ● Six ■ Churches, schools, universities, conferences £ To be negotiated ❀ To be discussed ✿ Yes

Ian Farthing 102 Latchmere Road, Battersea, London, SW11 2JT
T (0171) 738 99 28 F (0171) 629 1284
Has worked in rep, large and small scale tours; especially work on new plays. Works regularly at the Players' Theatre Music Hall in London.
£ Equity rates

Footprints Theatre Trust
Steve or Janet Stickley
St Nicholas Centre, 79 Maid Marion Way, Nottingham, NG1 6AE
T (0115) 958 6554 F (0115) 952 4624
Currently developing 'Storymine' project – storytelling/storymaking workshops, performances as part of educational and community work.

Bridget Foreman 11 Whitecross Road, York, YO3 7JR
T (01904) 640 408
Actress (stage, radio, TV). Theatre director and writer. Ongoing association with Riding Lights Theatre Company.

drama

Derek Greenwood

Chapel House, Belper Lane End, Belper, Derbys, DE56 2DL
T (01773) 825 250
Writing sketches, plays, entertainments for outreach/teaching use, by my production/training organisation 'Son-Rise Theatre Co'. Designed for street/small audience (to 150) 'in the round'.
❖ Small scale theatre using parable/allegory/entertainments ● To support outreach and teaching (limited availability, up to 8 performers) ■ Derby area – from classroom to village hall and street £ Expenses, both production and travelling ❀ Flat surface and electricity ✿ Yes

Hands + Feet Trust
Jo Pimlott

27 Forest Street, Kirby-in-Ashfield, NG17 7DT
T (01623) 750 978
Drama and creativity in work with young people and schools. Production of resources tackling real issues training and development for church groups.

Harlow Causeway Drama Group 'Living Stones'
Gary Knott

8 Chapel Fields, Harlow, Essex, CM17 9EG
T (01279) 301 892 F (01279) 866 276 E-mail garyknott@compuserve.com
The Harlow Causeway Drama Group has a unique ministry performing drama in mime to music and narration. The group is made up of able-bodied/disabled (learning and/or physical) people and performs at churches and Christian events around the UK
❖ Mime to music/narration (learning/physical disabilities) ● 15 ■ Churches, celebrations, Christian events £ Travelling expenses and gift for ministry ❀ 13 AMP sockets x3 Wheelchair access ✿ No

Julie-Ann Hilton
Jean Marsh
(administrator)

Bible Society, Stonehill Green, Westlea, Swindon, Wilts, SN5 7DG
T (01793) 418 100
'Twelve' is a collection of Scripture-based dramatic monologues, devised by Julie-Ann as a 'stepping stone to evangelism'. She is an Equity member and a postgraduate theology student.
❖ Informal, but professional ● One woman and set/props/costumes ■ Anywhere I can be seen and heard £ £250 (artist fee is £150) payable to Bible Society ❀ A raised platform minimum 12'x9' ✿ Yes

Jakes Ladder Theatre Company
Steve and Jane Evans (Artistic Directors)

5 Alfred Street, Blandford Forum, Dorset, DT11 7JL
T (01258) 454 384
Hailed at '95 Edinburgh Fringe for their own unique brand of physical theatre. Described by 'The Scotsman' as 'very accomplished'.
❖ Fast-moving Brechtian storytelling and sketches in different genres ■ Churches, theatres, festivals £ £70 per half day + travel ❀ Performing area and access to electrical points ✿ Yes

Tony Jasper 29 Harvard Court, Honeybourne Road, London, NW6 1HL
T (0171) 813 4362 F (0171) 435 4246
400+ presentations since 1992, either small/large cast tours re-interpreting major religious figures or movements or cabaret (outreach) songs, sketches etc.
❖ Professional actor/singer ● a) Music drama or b) cabaret
■ Theatres, schools, churches, private houses £ Depending on cast – £100–£625 ○ Yes

Kettle of Fish Theatre

Marc and Karen Cavallini

92 St Donatt's Road, New Cross, London, SE14 6NT
T (0181) 691 9782 F (0181) 691 9782
Entertaining, challenging theatre; regularly commissioned by charities to profile social issues. Community theatre encouraging participation of local people. Available for performances, workshops and writing commissions.
❖ Contemporary theatre ● 2 upwards (depending on production)
■ London and on tour £ By negotiation ❀ Dependent on production ○ Yes

Rob Lacey 101 Welham Road, Furzedown,
London, SW16 6QH
T (0181) 677 4044 Mobile (0378) 386 952
Full time for over 10 years (1st with 'Trapdoor Theatre Co', then solo). Currently touring two full-length solo shows, available for outreach, schools work, workshops and book signings!
❖ Humorous, thought-provoking ● Solo
■ Churches, schools, festivals, conferences, youth situations £ Approx £200 a show + 30p per mile ❀ Tie-clip radio mic for groups over 150 ○ Yes

Keith (Kit) Loring

St MadocYouth Camp, Llanmadoc, Gower, Gwent
T (01792) 386 301 E-mail 101366.2630@compuserve.com
Trainer/enabler, writer, producer, performer drama and music. 'Seeker service' training.
❖ Contemporary music, clowning, poetry, play-writing and drama
■ Conferences, festivals, churches, pubs, clubs, etc. £ From £100 + expenses ❀ Nothing (more or less) to PA, lights, staging ○ Yes

Rose Lunt 65 Old Fosse Road, Odd Down, Bath, BA2 2SP
T (01225) 835 036
God's mobile showcase (fragile, handle with care) offering a word in season in two acts. Act one: 'The Homecoming', a drama. Act two: 'A Tea Rose Afternoon'. Curious? Phone Bath 835 036.
● One-woman review ■ Churches so far! £ Negotiable ❀ We bring the lot as a package ○ No

Linda Mae

23 Foley Road, Ward End, Birmingham, B8 2JT
T (0121) 786 2488
*A variety of performances are on offer for all ages –
from Shakespeare to pantomime, religious drama
to nursery rhyme land, issue-based plays to fun
sketches. Solo performances also available.*
❖ Drama ● Solo or two ■ Schools, churches,
playschemes, youth clubs £ £150–£200 +
expenses ❀ Power point ✿ Yes

**Peter D
McCahon**

See main entry under Clowning Magic section.

**Mosaic
Theatre**
Catherine Francoise

71 Leachcroft, Chalfont St Peter, Bucks, SL9 9LD
T (01753) 882 646 or (0850) 617775 F (01753) 408 089
*Music theatre productions such as 'Women of Faith' which focuses on
lives from biblical times through the ages including religious, royal,
literary and social impacts.*
❖ Music theatre ● 35887 ■ Churches, art centres, theatres,
schools £ Variable ❀ Performance space ✿ Yes

**New
Creations**
Jacqui Frost

Lantern Arts Centre, Raynes Park Methodist
Church, Tolverne Rd, Raynes Park,
London, SW20 3RA
T (0181) 944 5794 F (0181) 947 5152
E-mail 100427 3310@compuserve.com
*Art Centre's productions include 'Godspell' and 'The
Lion, the Witch and the Wardrobe'. Two qualified
teachers – Anna and Jaqui – deliver Bible-based
workshops and shows for schools.*
❖ Short or full length plays, musicals, workshops
● Amateur and professional actors and musicians ■ Lantern Art
Centre and London schools £ Contact for details ❀ Large hall for
schools work ✿ No

**New
Directions
Theatre
Company Ltd**
Robin Meredith

8 Compton Road, Lindfield, Haywards Heath, W Sussex, RH16 2JZ
T (01444) 482 334
*Formed to develop/promote new writing in the dramatic arts, focusing on
work of contemporary relevance and exploring the significance of Christ
to today's world.*

**One Way
Ministries**
Paul Symonds

175 Quarmby Road, Quarmby, Huddersfield,
W Yorkshire, HD3 4FE
T (01484) 460 321
*One Way perform short sketches and songs (if desired), suitable for
church services and outreach events.*
❖ 2–5 minute sketches. Mainly light-hearted with Christian message
● 6 members (ages 13–34) ■ Churches £ Not set fee but would
appreciate at least expenses ❀ Possibly vocal amplification (not for
small venues) ✿ Yes

drama

Mark Payton
Agent: Janet Welch
(0181) 332 6544

11 Whitecross Road, York, YO3 7JR
T (01904) 640 408
Actor, director. Actor in theatre (National Theatre 1995), TV, radio, film (Howards End, 1992), director for Riding Lights Theatre Company

Phoenix Performing Arts Trust
Mary Scott

9 Henley Court, 90 Peckham Rye, London, SE15 4HA
T (0181) 299 2021 F (0181) 299 2021
Phoenix Performing Arts Trust founded on Christian principles, aims to teach, train and encourage those involved in the performing arts to realise their full artistic potential through seminars, workshops and performance.
❖ Physical theatre, mime, modern dance and poetry ● 36008 ■ Nationally and internationally theatre venues £ Equity negotiable ❀ 20x20 performance space, sound system, PA ✿ Yes

Lance Pierson

48 Peterborough Road, London, SW6 3EB
T (0171) 731 6544 F (0171) 731 1858
Range of one-man shows presenting Bible truths for Christians or enquirers of all ages, in worship, mission and entertainment.
❖ One-man shows ● Just me ■ Churches, colleges, festivals £ Scale of fees by negotiation and expenses ❀ Overhead projector and audio cassette amplification ✿ No

Resurrection Theatre Co
Juliet Muttalib

11 Batley Road, Northenden, Manchester, Lancs, M22 4FL
T (0161) 945 5486
Manchester-based professional Christian touring theatre company providing creatve workshops for all ages and support for the teaching of religious education within the National Curriculum.
❖ Biblical theatre ● 7 artists ■ Theatres, schools, churches £ Negotiable ❀ Lighting rig, sound system ✿ Yes

Riding Lights Theatre Company
Janis Smyth

8 Bootham Terrace, York, YO3 7DH
T (01904) 655 317 F (01904) 651 532
RLTC tours a full range of professional community and mainstream productions; producing theatre with a spiritual heart, from the grass roots to the highest level.
❖ Theatre ● 36073 ■ Schools, prisons, theatres, community centres, art centres, churches £ Gifts/donations and expenses ✿ No

Lea Rochelle

9 Chatsworth Close, Maidenhead, Berks, SL6 4RD
T (0162) 826 409
An actress who has been in plays and on TV, doing a variety of roles etc. I also sing.

113

Michael Saffery (Act for Christ)

190 Stowey Road, Yatton, Bristol, Avon, BS19 4QS
T (01934) 834 865
Michael Saffery is gaining an international reputation as a Christian dramatist. Funny, poignant, sometimes unsettling, always deeply powerful – this is drama at its most effective.
❖ Contemporary drama ● Usually solo or team of two – occasionally up to five performers ■ Theatres, schools, churches, streets, prisons, hospitals £ Contact for details ✿ Decent working space; workable lighting; PA with cassette facility ○ No

Danny Scott
Director Pheonix Performing Arts Trust

PO Box 11073, London, SE15 4ZE
T (0181) 299 2021 F (0181) 299 2021
Professional performance artist/teacher/director – physical theatre, mime and poetry; over 12 years' international experience. Relentless energy, hard-hitting and evocative, tender and moving – on stage and in class. Not so much seen/met as experienced!
❖ Post-modern mime and physical theatre (modern dance) ● 35947 ■ Professional secular fringe theatre, television £ Equity rates basic, open to negotiation ✿ Full PA incl. CD, twin cassette, lights, 30'x30' stage ○ Yes

Seeds
Neil Ruckman

24 Meadway Close, New Barnet, Herts, EN5 5LA
T (0181) 364 9652
To encourage creativity in churches, education and prisons through workshops with professional artists.
❖ Varied ● Varied ■ Churches, schools, prisons £ £35 per hour ✿ Minimal or none ○ Yes

Son-Rise Theatre Company
Derek Greenwood

Chapel House, Belper Lane End, Belper, Derbys, DE56 2DL
T (01773) 825 250
Son-Rise Theatre Co is a freelance resource for churches wanting to use the medium of theatre and needing help and ideas to get started or extend their existing activities.

Ava de Souza

7 Evelyn Road, Ham, Richmond, Surrey, TW10 7HU
T (0181) 948 3874
I am small and slim with long dark hair and of mixed Indian and Danish parentage. I have had a wide range of experience in theatre and television. Recent work includes playing Yoko Ono in 'Imagine' at the Liverpool Playhouse, where I received good reviews: 'Ava de Souza is stunning as Yoko Ono'.
■ Theatre, TV, churches, halls, schools £ Basic equity ✿ None

Spice Theatre Co
Anita Clark

Flat 1/2, 375 Dumbarton Road, Partick, Glasgow, G11 6BA
T (0141) 339 9261
Spice Theatre Company use movement, music, text and visuals to create performance work specifically aimed at young people. They are trained professionals and are able to lead workshops.
❖ In your face collaboration ● Trained dancers – actors – teachers ■ Youth venues, festivals, community centres, churches £ Expenses + fee circa £100 a day (performance and workshop) ✿ Sound system and radio mics ○ Yes

Stairs & Whispers Theatre Company
Graham Webb

PO Box 131, Ipswich, Suffolk, IP2 0RF
T (01473) 687 186
Since 1985 have provided original professional Christian theatre with teeth! Full-length show and sketches for all. Workshops undertaken for all levels of experience.
❖ Unique synthesis of physical theatre, mime and drama ● Four full-timers and a van! ■ Churches, theatres, schools, halls £ £200 a day + 30p a mile travelling (discounts for a series of bookings) ✿ Clear flat performing space and power supply ○ Yes

STAMPS (St Andrews and Methodist Players)
Maggy Garton

18 Folders Lane, Bracknell, Berks, RG42 2LP
T (0134) 454 694
Plays and sketches with a Christian message or focus, based on biblical material, for Christian festivals or celebrations, as acts of worship within church services and to fund-raise for charities.
❖ Mainly Bible-based plays ● 12 ■ Local churches £ None ✿ Acting space only ○ No

Theatre Roundabout Ltd
Sylvia Reid and William Fry

859 Finchley Road, London, NW11 8LX
T (0181) 455 4752
Two-person Christian touring theatre presenting challenging shows for churches and adaptations of great literature for theatres and arts centres. 3,500 performances in 35 years.
❖ Dramatic dialogues in a multitude of characters ● Husband and wife ■ Churches, theatres, art societies, schools, colleges £ From £215 + VAT ✿ Simple furniture, 4 spotlights, 1 cassette player, 2 helpers ○ No

Two Across Physical Theatre Company
Bruce Stanley

5 Talbot Avenue, Bristol, BS15 1HE
T (0117) 960 8964
Two Across is a company exploring new media for communicating the gospel through circus theatre, physical comedy and storytelling. Workshops, seminars and performances.
❖ Mime, street show, storytelling, stand-up ■ Anywhere with a high ceiling £ £75 and upwards + expenses ✿ None ○ No

Wedding Songs – Catherine Francoise

See main entry under Classical Music section.

**What 4,
Cutting Edge
Band/Drama
group**

Dave Barker

What 4 Office, Ingles Manor, Castle Hill Ave, Folkestone,
Kent, CT20 2TN
T (01303) 850 950
*What 4 is the youth department of Mission Aviation Fellowship, and
mobilises young people to think and do mission in the UK and overseas.
Their music/dramas are challenging.*
❖ Contemporary, rock, mime, drama ● Youth organisation ■ UK all
over £ Expenses only ❀ Self-contained ✿ Yes

Mary Allen 61 Abingdon Road, London, W8 6AN
T (0171) 937 9192
I have had three books published and am half-way through writing the fourth.

Anne Atkins St Dionis' Vicarage, 18 Parsons Green, London, SW6 4UH
T (0171) 736 2585
I went to Oxford University, then drama school, then worked for a number of years as an actress, before becoming a novelist. Published novels: 'The Lost Child', 'On Our Own'.
❖ Good, especially Shakespeare on the Bible £ 100 ✿ None ○ No

Cherith Baldry 12 Wraylands Drive, Reigate, Surrey, RH2 0LG
T 01737 221 955
Cherith writes fantasy and science fiction – for both adults and children. She tries to convey spiritual truth through the power of the imagination.

Linda Ball *See main entry under Prose section.*

Ian Barclay 35 Marine Avenue, Hove, W Sussex, BN3 4LH
T (01273) 421 628
Author of two crime novels, 'The Dragon's Balk' and 'The Dark Lady'.

Davis Bunn 5 Warfe Lane, Henley-on-Thames, Oxon, RG9 2LL
Mainstream fiction published under pen-name 'Thomas Locke' by Lion. Evangelical fiction under his own name published by Bethany and distributed by Kingsway. Contracted for feature film screenplay.

C P Clarke *See main entry under Poetry section.*

Audrey Constant The Mill Farm House, Trotton, Petersfield, Hants, GU31 5EL
T (01730) 813 654
Children/adult novels. Biographies for classroom work. Articles. Radio.

Jenny Cooke 26 Mornington Road, Cheadle, Cheshire, SK8 1NJ
T (0161) 428 4293
My vision is to see books with Christ in them on every bookstall in England. My 6 published books include: 'The Cross Behind Bars' (1983) and 'Light Through Prison Bars' (1995).

Nick Curry 74 Weydon Hill Road, Farnham, Surrey, GU9 8NY
T (01252) 712 952 Home (01932) 789 681 Work
As a journalist/writer who is starting to see his first words in print, I would like to see my writing change attitudes, shape lives, stir people to act and eventually bring them to Jesus.

Heather Douglass
Heather Gout

9 Pashler Gardens, Thrapston, Northants, NN14 4QF
T (01832) 734 436 F (01832) 734 436
E-mail phlgout@corbybot.demon.net.uk
I write a mixture of fantasy/fabulist fiction and poetry. Currently working on a novel 'The Reunification of Germaine'. Also give an inspirational 2-hour seminar for creative Christians.
❖ Performance poetry/readings ● Solo ■ Small halls, churches, poetry groups £ £50 + expenses per appearance ❀ Amplification in larger venues ○ Yes

Elizabeth Gibson
Lizzie Gibson

105 Reculver Walk, Maidstone, Kent, ME15 8QT
Writer of psychological fiction for women, and the occasional prize-winning poem. Loves to do readings/workshops.
❖ Readings (poetry and fiction) ● 1 ■ Writers and women's groups in South £ Negotiable ❀ OHP ○ No

Revd Carol Hathorne

The Manse, 222 High Street, Pensnett, Brierley Hill, W Midlands, DY5 4JP T (01384) 78438
I am an Anglican woman priest. Author of 'A Ferret in the Vestry' (Pub. Monarch, May 1995). Twenty-five years as a freelance writer (novels and stories).

Veronica Heley

58 Barnfield Road, Ealing, London, W5 1QT
T (0181) 997 4674
Writer and speaker. 38 books published including crime, historical novels, children's and teenage fiction. Book reviews and articles for Christian magazines and for Premier Radio. Events organiser for Fellowship of Christian Writers.
○ No

Sheila Jacobs

15 Godwin Close, Halstead, Essex, CO9 1XA
T (01787) 475 297
Children's fiction, humour, plays, short stories, also articles about Christian living, cults, occult, theology (I have a diploma in theological studies LBC), manuscript criticism, 'ghosting', editing.

Jean S Munro

See main entry under Journalism section.

Lynda Neilands

See main entry under Other section.

Christopher Norris

See main entry under TV / Film / Video / Animation section.

Sue Rann

34 Laurel Grove, Rising Brook, Stafford, ST17 9EF
T (01785) 222 439
I've written poetry and song lyrics; interested in SF/fantasy and Celtic themes; currently writing first contemporary novel, 'Two To The Power of One'.

Noreen Riols La Grange, Rue Pierre Bourdan, 78160 Marly-le-Roi, France
F (00 33) 1 3916 6816
1983–87, 3 books pub. by Hodder & Stoughton. 1990–91, 1 book pub.
by Word (UK). 1992–97, 5 books pub. by Eagle.

Lynda Rose 95 Staunton Road, Oxford, OX3 7TR
T (01865) 768 774 F (01865) 768 774
I am an Anglican priest, writing Christian non-fiction and mainstream
fiction. My first novel 'Kingdom Come' was pub. by Headline in 1996
and my next, 'Heaven's Door', came out in 1997.

Fay Sampson Christie Cottage, Tedburn St. Mary, Exeter, Devon, EX6 6AZ
T (01647) 612 89 F (01647) 612 89
Children's and adults' novels, stories, prayers, fantasy, historical,
contemporary, humorous, SF, – special interests: Dark Age legend and
history, Celtic Christianity. Talks about making books, depicting good
and evil, reworking myth.

Joan
Scowcroft 3/41 Princes Road, Clevedon, N Somerset, BS21 7NQ
T (01275) 879 537
Write fiction and features (also letters) on Christian issues. Published in
New Christian, Ark, Universe, Catholic Herald, Grapevine and others
several times. Write about cats.

Russell
Sherwen *See main entry under Play Writing section.*

Susan Skinner Bieldside, West Furlong Lane, Hurstpierpont, W Sussex, BN6 9RH
T (01273) 835 597
I am a writer, creative writing tutor and calligrapher. Poetry is my
central concern and children's fiction. I have published 2 poetry
collections, 3 children's novels, articles and reviews.

Kenneth C
Steven *See main entry under Poetry section.*

Pam Weaver *See main entry under Journalism section.*

Anno Domini Designs
Adrian Paul Miles

Alexandra Residential Club, 27 Norfolk Road, Birmingham, B15 3PY
An amazing selection of original designs on posters, leaflets, T-shirts and sweatshirts. Available to suit your budget. Top quality. All exclusively marketed by myself.

Communiqué Design Associates
Ross Purcell

32 Morlem Field, Warminster, Wilts, BA12 0BU
T (01985) 217 498
The graphics work that can be undertaken by Communiqué includes: identity design, design for print – brochures, pamphlets, leaflets, promotional material and exhibitions.

Anita Cuttill

See main entry under Contemporary Music section.

Colin T Hale

See main entry under Painting section.

Jireh.co.uk
Andrew J Bruce

2 Old Annandale Road, Kirkella, E Yorks, HU10 7TB
T (01482) 655 453 F (01482) 655 453
E-mail ajb@jireh.co.uk Web site http://www.jireh.co.uk
Jireh.co.uk aims to provide a high quality design service from original concept to finished product. Working with mainly charities and Christian organisations in both traditional media and internet contexts.

Paul Jones – Associates

98 Eden Way, Beckenham, Kent, BR3 3DH
T (0181) 663 3963 F (0181) 663 3964
Helping Christian organisations to communicate effectively through design for print. My work includes corporate identity (design styling and application), magazines and newsletters. Please call for relevant samples.

Paul Jones
0181-663 3963

Message Graphics
Bruce Stanley

5 Talbot Avenue, Bristol, BS15 1HE
T (0117) 960 8964 or (0589) 509 958
Bruce is an experienced and unusual designer, producing radical and communicative work. Contact him for posters, logos, booklets, slides at affordable prices.

Silver Fish Creative Marketing Ltd
Stephen Jones

44c Fermoy Road, Maida Vale, London, W9 3NH
T (0181) 964 8036 or (0181) 960 8224 F (0181) 964 8036
E-mail abo23@dial.pipex.com
A creative marketing agency with a vision to help Christian ministries and businesses communicate more effectively. Also work with secular clients such as BP, BBC and Saudi Airlines.

Adrian St Clair Fewins
Chartered Designer
BA, DipAD, MCSD

28 Delara Way, Woking, GU21 1NY
T (01483) 771 029
Senior lecturer in design and media studies: graphic designer responsible for national packaging and editorial design. Photographic exhibitions: background in architectural design.

120

Paul James Thomas

Craddock House, Craddock Road, Canterbury, Kent, CT1 1YR
T (01227) 766 896
My work consists of fine art etchings on devotional themes, mainly faces looking through the physical to divine the spiritual underneath.

Dimitrios G Tsouris

See main entry under Painting section.

Lindsey Attwood
4C Walter Street, Derby, Derbys, DE1 3PR
T (01332) 361 173 F (01332) 361 173
I am an artist/designer who produces greetings cards and also works to commission. I often integrate calligraphy and illustration using modern and traditional techniques.

Janet Ayers
15c Walnut Way, South Ruislip, Middx, HA4 6AT
T (0181) 841 9573 E-mail jayers@spck.co.uk
A gathering of words, scripture and images perceiving heaven in every object and everyday life, through both collage and drawing, conceptual and figurative.

Steve Beal
2 Church House, Orts Road, Reading, Berks, RG1 3JN
T (01734) 664 209
I am currently a youth and children's worker. I use cartoons, murals and various other art forms as part of my work in schools, churches and the wider community.

Susan Burman
See main entry under Puppetry section.

Steve English
Val English
93 Greystown Avenue, Belfast, Co Antrim, N Ireland, BT9 6UH
T (01232) 629 182
A cartoonist/illustrator currently involved in bringing out people's interest in the Bible (mainly the Gospels) and theology through the use of cartoons.

Colin T Hale
See main entry under Painting section.

Sam Hawkins – Boo Designs Ltd
Woodlands, Fauld Lane, Fauld, Burton-Upon-Trent, Staffs, DE13 9HS
T (01283) 520 502
I am an illustrator-artist and co-produce spiritual greetings with my mother who is a poet. Our company is Boo Designs Ltd.

Lynn Hopwood
40 Walton Road, Woking, Surrey, GU21 5DL
T (01483) 768 328
Work includes: book covers; children's fictional illustrations; banner designs; logos; posters; postcards and greeting cards. Media: collage; watercolour; pen and ink. Very fluid, mostly figurative.

Stephanie I'ons
84 Water Eaton Lane, Kidlington, Oxford, OX5 2PR
T (01865) 842 370 F (01865) 842 870
God's creation is a marvellous insight into his imagination. If I can use my imagination for his glory, then life is all the more enjoyable!

Laurence Pusey
See main entry under Painting section.

Alan Reed
See main entry under Painting section.

**Nanette
Heather Rhee**

BA (Hons)   *See main entry under Painting section.*

John Schwob   Flat 9, 72 Gordon Road, London, W5 2AR
T (0181) 810 5301
Illustrations of buildings usually. 'Realistic' style done in pencil or ink.

**Revd Gordon
L Tubbs**   61 Lichfield Road, Cambridge, CB1 3SP
T (01223) 248 749
Cartoon and whiteboard illustration for street work.

illustration

journalism

Muthena Paul Alkazraji
10a Beckford Gardens, Bathwick, Bath, Avon, BA2 6QU
T 01225 337 320 F 01225 337 320
Freelance journalist and photographer writing arts and entertainment, social affairs and travel articles. My work has been published in the Church Times, Christianity magazine, New Christian Herald, Scotland on Sunday and The Independent.

Dudley Anderson
See main entry under Radio section.

Linda Ball
See main entry under Prose section.

Adrian Barnard
See main entry under Radio section.

Robert Beale
37 Eddisbury Ave, Flixton, Manchester, M41 8GE
T (0161) 748 9999
A sub-editor on the staff of the Manchester Evening News for over 20 years and also its classical music critic.

Julia Bicknell
c/o Arts Centre Group, The Courtyard, 59A Portobello Road, London, W11 3DB
T c/o (0171) 243 4550 F c/o (0171) 221 7689
Freelance BBC Radio/TV news presenter/reporter and interviewer. Launch breakfast presenter, Premier Radio. Chair discussions, debates and interviews at special events e.g. Greenbelt seminars.

Graham Clinton
14 Cedars Road, Hampton Wick, Surrey, KT1 4SE
T (0181) 943 2237
Secretary, International Christian Mensa.

Mike Collins
See main entry under Photography section.

Jenni Costello
Premier Radio, Glen House, Stag Place, London, SW1E 5AG
T (0171) 233 6705 F (0171) 316 1371
Regular presenter/producer of 'The Afternoon Show' on Premier; a music-based show, highlighting many Christian artists in the music business and arts.

Gillian Crow
2 Gardener Place, Biddenham, Bedford, MK40 4QU
T (01234) 354 374 F (01234) 354 311 E-mail crow@kbnet.co.uk
Secretary of the Russian Orthodox Church in Britain; writer for the national and religious press; RE material; Christian books; speaker (talks and courses).

Paul Dakin
33 Pages Hill, Muswell Hill, London, N10 1PX
T (0181) 883 7571 F (0181) 482 9942
Writer, speaker and broadcaster. Editor of 'Compass'. Medical doctor. Author of three books including 'Crossing Cultures'. Interested especially in crosscultural mission, training, and the prophetic.

124

Chris Dunkerley Gilmerton Lodge, North Berwick, E Lothian, EH39 5LQ
T (01620) 880 294 F (01620) 880 294
I am a freelance journalist, specialising in features. Particular areas of interest are crime, travel and religion. I write for 'Scotland on Sunday' and 'The Scotsman'.

Hilary Dyer 130 Rothley Road, Mountsorrel, Leics, LE12 7JX
T (0116) 230 3699 F (0116) 230 3699 E-mail
Hilary@hjdyer.demon.co.uk
Formerly a lecturer in Information and Library Studies. Now retired. An experienced academic writer, Hilary is now turning her hand to Christian writing.

Catherine Francis *See main entry under Contemporary Music session.*

Zafar Francis 20 Myrdle Street, Stepney, London, E1 1EU
Rosemary James T (0171) 423 9422 F (0171) 702 8730
I am a chief correspondent for a Pakistani film and media Urdu newspaper. Also, I write Urdu novels as well as writing dramas for Asian communities. My writings are always based on Kingdom values, focusing on unreached people.

Revd Frederick Grossmith 4 St Helier's Road, Cleethorpes, Lincs, DN35 7LQ
T (01472) 603 258 F (01472) 697 526
Commissioned Christian articles in World War II genre. Author of 5 books and a Hollywood screenplay. Helps churches become more professional through teaching basic journalism.

Martyn Halsall 42 Knowsley Road, Ainsworth, Bolton, Lancs, BL2 5PU
T (01204) 394 171
Professional newspaper journalist since 1970 with an eternal interest in poetry. Guardian staff correspondent and married to Isobel, an Anglican priest.

Revd William B G Mather *See main entry under Painting section.*

Howard McCalla *See main entry under Radio section.*

Jean S Munro Barton Hall, Bullwood Road, Dunoon, Argyll, PA23 7QJ
T (01369) 702 265
I am a freelance journalist. I write for Christian and secular markets. I am a part-time lecturer in creative writing for Glasgow University.

Steve Norman 114 Crosby Road, Northallerton, N Yorkshire, DL6 1AS
T (01609) 777 879
I am currently studying freelance journalism from home and hope to use this in the Christian field. I also present a review slot of CCM on BBC Radio Cleveland.

Benedict Parsons *See main entry under Photography section.*

Sandie Ridgley 'Osbourne House', Norwich Road, Mulbarton, Norwich, Norfolk, NR14 8JP
T (01508) 570 691 F (01508) 570 691
Freelance journalist working for the Christian press (Woman Alive, New Christian Herald, Good News for Norwich) Publicist for Norwich Christian charity – The Magdalene Group which reaches out to prostitutes.

Ian Roberts Photography *See main entry under Photography section.*

Marion Stroud Candle Communications, 42 Brecon Way, Bedford, MK41 8DD
T (01234) 266 001
Marion Stroud has written 15 non-fiction books, mainly relationship- and family-oriented. She speaks to Christian and secular groups on these topics and teaches writing skills.
£ For speaking £50–£75 depending on group + travel expenses
☼ Yes

Pam Weaver 72 Harefield Avenue, Worthing, W Sussex, BN13 1DR
T (01903) 691 775
I write family-based articles, travel articles, about my personal experiences as a Christian, and children's fantasy books (8–12yr). I am also working on an adult saga.

Wendy Whitehead 9 The Lodge, 3 Blackwater Road, Eastbourne, E Sussex, BN21 4JF
T (01323) 638 234
Author, broadcaster, lay preacher. Teacher of journalism. Also 'Spread the Word' workshops designed to encourage outreach and mission through Christian comment columns, press releases, writing your own life story, local hospital/radio etc.

Stella Wiseman
Paul Eggleton
5 Hale Place, Monkton Lane, Farnham, Surrey, GU9 9BY
T (01252) 710 339 F (01252) 710 339 E-mail pe@nhm.ac.uk
Writer/editor specialising in natural history, education and parenting. Writes for children and adults. Editor ACG magazine 'Artyfact'. Author of 'Charles Colson and the Story of Prison Fellowship'. DTP work.

Veronica Zundel *See main entry under Prose section.*

Beyond the Barricades   *See main entry under Dance section.*

Ian Dock   Flat 4 , 296 Chatham Hill, Chatham,
Kent, ME5 7DU
T (01634) 855 772
Sound Vision seeks to aid those attempting to understand the truth of the gospel in a new and dynamic way through mime and movement.
❖ Illusion, mime, creative dance and physical theatre ● Solo ■ Anywhere £ Negotiable
✺ PA tape-playing equipment ☼ No

Gof The Clown   *See main entry under Clowning Magic section.*

Goldmime
Carole A Hemingway
17 Severn Drive, Garforth,
Leeds, LS25 2BD
T (0113) 287 6348
Available for church services, school assemblies, workshops, street work, performances. Our aim is to assist a blind world to see once more through mime ministry.
❖ Mime ministry ● 6 adults, 9 young people ■ Churches, schools, community halls £ Fees negotiable, expenses required ✺ PA system, lights, staging ☼ Yes

Harlow Causeway Drama Group 'Living Stones'   *See main entry under Drama section.*

Jolly Jack the Clown & Emilé the Mime
David Girt
7 Bishopstone, Bradville, Milton Keynes,
Bucks, MK13 7DQ
T (01908) 317 487
The gospel proclaimed through clowning, mime and gospel music for all ages. Workshops in clowning, mime, drama, puppetry and street theatre.
❖ Traditional and contemporary clowning and mime ● Mostly one-man shows ■ Missions, churches, workshops, theatres and other venues £ Negotiable ✺ None – self-contained ☼ Yes

Juggling John
John Hayns

176a Lyham Road, London, SW2 5QD
T (0181) 671 9228 F (0171) 924 6612
E-mail epicentre.mail@ukonline.co.uk
Ranges from fun family entertainment to serious solo mime. Trained at Desmond Jones School of Mime. Act can contain 'message' or not as required. Juggling, balancing, acrobatics, mime, puppetry, fire-eating etc.

❖ Family show, street theatre, or mime to music ● Just me!
■ Family events, parties, cabaret, dinners, schools £ Negotiable
❀ Open air if you want fire stuff. Changing facilities ☼ Yes

Dale Kirk

103 Hartham Road, Isleworth, Twickenham, Middx, TW7 5EY
T (0181) 569 9475
I try to pose questions, suggest ideas and challenge our faith through a performance, combining mime, dance, drama and music.
❖ Energetic combination of mime and dance ■ Churches and community settings £ Approx £100 per day. Negotiable ❀ Stage – minimum 3mx4m ☼ Yes

Rob Lacey

See main entry under Drama section.

Steve Legg

See main entry under Clowning Magic section.

Masterpiece Theatre Company
Juliet Malcolm

4 Morston Drive, Dumpling Hall, Newcastle Upon Tyne,
Tyne & Wear, NE15 7RZ
T (0191) 243 2418 or (0191) 233 2288 F (0191) 233 0499
E-mail juliet@city-church.co.uk
Masterpiece use physical theatre to communicate the message that God is not dead and church is not boring! They also teach workshops and a weekly youth theatre class.
❖ Mime, physical theatre ● 42005 ■ Churches, theatres, schools, open air £ Expenses plus ministry gift (negotiable) ❀ Performance area min 20x12 PA with cassette deck power ☼ No

Peter D McCahon

See main entry under Clowning Magic section.

Mimeistry – Todd & Marilyn Farley
Jacque Hyde
(UK Director)

The Coach House, Woodhill, Congresbury, BS19 5AF
T (01934) 833 652 F (01934) 645 001
E-mail 73671.1707@compuserve.com
International performances combining mime, drama, dance and song. Also offer a structured teaching programme: mime and dance. Practical workshops: mime, dance and drama, seeking excellence in artistic ministry.
❖ Combining mime, drama, dance and song ● Solo, duet and troupe
■ Churches, theatres, schools £ By arrangement ❀ Provided by us: 'theatre' lighting and PA ☼ Yes

Gill Moore

See main entry under Dance section.

John Persson 9 Brookhill Crescent, Wollaton, Nottingham, Notts, NG8 2PU
T (0115) 928 7288 F (0115) 928 7288
Through mime and physical theatre John brings striking visual insights into life and Christianity.
● Solo performer ■ Churches and theatres £ – ❀ PA system with cassette facility plus lighting ✿ No

Danny Scott *See main entry under Drama section.*

Christiane Spivey *See main entry under Dance section.*

The Titanic Brothers 40 Walton Road, Woking, Surrey, GU21 5DL
Dave Hopwood T (01483) 768 328
Lead workshops and perform mime on the streets, in churches, schools and other venues for the purpose of worship, teaching and evangelism.
❖ Mime and physical theatre, some silent, some performed to music and narrative ● Two males (Dave Hopwood and Ken Wylie) who mime plus a singer and narrator ■ Churches, town centres and schools £ £100 per day + travel @ 25p per mile ❀ Good visibility and space ✿ No

Christopher Bevon
Flat 2, St Mild-ed's House, Roserton Street, London, E14 3PG
T (0171) 515 7975 or (01792) 386 308
I am primarily a silversmith, which means that I work on a larger format than jewellery and will typically make cups, jugs, tea sets, cutlery, boxes etc. of silver. I do also work in gold, platinum, copper, bronze, brass and as a designer for production runs for souvenirs, badges etc. in these metals.
❖ Silver smithing

Mary Boddington
The Rectory, 65 Church Avenue, Farnborough, Hants, GU14 7AP
T (01252) 544 754
I work in stoneware making some domestic pottery but am more interested in decorative pieces. Am inspired by nature for form and texture and from ethnic influences for decoration. Local exhibitions considered.
❖ Ceramics

Ruth Boddington
30 Victoria Road, Redhill, Surrey, RH1 6DX
T (01737) 780 043
Calligrapher and lettering artist. Work ranges from one-off pieces on wood or cloth, vellum or paper, to 'graphic' lettering used for reproduction.

Karen Bourne
5 Princes Street, Maidstone, Kent, ME14 1UR
T (01622) 675 477
Trained as a graphic designer, now work as a calligrapher. My style is modern combining lettering on paper/fabric with beading/embroidery to create pictures.

Rebecca Brewin
238b Shirland Road, Maida Vale,
London, W9 3JF
T (0181) 969 0502
Use of theatre techniques in educating all ages on issues of social justice and the importance of central truth. I write drama for churches/conferences and resource material for creative workshops.
● Varies according to need ■ Churches/schools
○ No

David Burns
190 Marsh Lane, Fordhouses, Wolverhampton, WV10 6RZ
T (01902) 560 822
Community artist, potter and lecturer in ceramic design at various colleges/art schools, exhibited in a number of galleries for the last 20 years.

Thomas Collett-White
Dave Newby
53 Pathfield Road, Streatham, London, SW16 5NZ
T (0181) 769 0035
Through a presentation with approx 50 slides of Michelangelo's sculpture, painting and architecture and portraits of leaders in the Renaissance in Italy, I trace his spiritual pilgrimage from Renaissance humanism to his conversion to Christianity.

Jennifer Conway

31 Oxford Road, Mistley, Manningtree, Essex, CO11 1BW
T (01206) 396 274 F (01206) 396 274
I have been engraving glass since 1972. The technique used is that pioneered by John Hutton at Coventry and Guildford Cathedrals etc. Fellow, Guild of Glass Engineers.

Susan M Cook
AMGP

Attimore Hall Barn Studios, Ridgeway, Welwyn Garden City, Herts, AL7 2AD
T Studio (01707) 334848 Home (0171) 2638481
Contemporary spiritual expression in glass. A wide range of commissions in this country and internationally both secular and ecclesiastical. Designs are lyrical and fluid – mainly figurative using representational elements.
✿ Yes

Martin Crampin

'Rose Grange', High Road, Langdon Hills, Basildon, Essex, SS16 6HP
I work with interactive environments and computer multimedia. This incorporates illustrative material, text, video and music.
❖ Interactive multimedia

Alastair Cutting

St John's Vicarage, Church Road, Copthorne, Crawley, W Sussex, RH10 3RD
T (01342) 712 063 F (01342) 712 063 E-mail alastair@cutting.sonnet.co.uk
Anglican minister and arts and media enthusiast, Alastair ran The Nave for 5 years. Involved in pastoral support of artists, and theological basis for arts in the Church. Synths and keyboard player.

Judy Davies

55 St Leonard's Road, East Sheen, London, SW14 7NQ
T (0181) 878 3955
I am a lettering artist and calligrapher. My areas of interest include banner design, book jackets, logos, letterheads, hand-painted signs, invitations and posters.

Deirdre Ducker

91 The Common, Broughton Gifford, Melksham, Wilts, SN12 8ND
T (01225) 783 330 F (01225) 783 330
Theatre set design/costumes. Graphics for print: logos; illustration; fine art – oil paintings.

Footprints Theatre Trust

Storytelling. See main entry under Drama section.

Patricia M Griffin

37 Woodlands Road, Witney, Oxon, OX8 6DR
T (01993) 774 912
I believe that the Word of God should be shown at calligraphy exhibitions whenever relevant. I also teach calligraphy at local AE classes.

John Hardwick

Storytelling. See main entry under Clowning Magic section.

Angus Henderson
44 College Drive, Heacham, Norfolk, PE31 7BY
T (01485) 572 155 F (01485) 571 633 E-mail
Cleartextdesign@Btinternet
Engraving in full lead crystal glass, also designs on T-shirts, textiles and mouse mats.

Jeanny Man
Flat 7, Dunster Court, 103 Worple Road, Wimbledon, London, SW20 8HB T (0181) 455 2779
I believe theatre is about a sense of time and space. In its design, these two elements can be manipulated to achieve what is known as 'theatricality'.

Carolyn A Meer
Eira Reeves
St Just, 5 Highdown Avenue, Worthing, W Sussex, BN13 1PU
T (01903) 266 236
Flowers, foliage, driftwood, fungi, etc. create wonderful visual effects, that become a bridge and enable me to speak about my Christian faith.
❖ Floral designer

Andrea Mitchell
Creative writing tutor. See main entry under Poetry section.

Lynda Neilands
46 Diamond Gardens, Finachy, Belfast, N Ireland, BT10 0HE
T (01232) 619 849
A writer and storyteller, Lynda Neilands is the author of books for adults and children including 'Fifty Five-Minute Stories' – a resource for teachers, parents and children's workers. (Kingsway 1996).
❖ Storytelling ◗ 1 ■ Churches £ Negotiable ❀ Microphone ✺ No

The Netherbow
Donald Smith, Director
John Knox House, 43–45 High Street, Edinburgh, EH1 1SR
T (0131) 556 9579 / 2647 F (0131) 556 7478
Workshops in drama, storytelling and participatory worship; advice on all aspects of the arts in church life in Scotland. Recently the George Mackay Brown 'Scottish Storytelling Centre' has been established to further the revival of oral storytelling in church and community. Also see entry under Services: Art Galleries.

Christopher Norris
Project development. See main entry under TV / Film / Video / Animation section.

Penny Phillips
Ensorspeak Vocal & Presentation Skills Centre, 348 Richmond Road, E Twickenham, Middx, TW2 2DU
T (0181) 844 9390
All aspects of training in communication skills and voice care. One-to-one and group sessions with speakers, actors etc. Consciously clear caring communication is fun!

Shane Rootes
Training seminars. See main entry under Contemporary Music section.

Rosemary Inglis Simpson
Rosemary Simpson

15 The Crescent, Truro, Cornwall, TR1 3ES
T (01872) 276 780
I am a potter interested in raku – have built a raku kiln. I also work in earthenware.

Rosie Smith

85 Berwick Road, Marlow, Bucks, SL7 3AS
T (01628) 478 644
Mixed media artist in residence for Berkshire Education – painting, printmaking and sculpture. Teachers' in-service training; courses such as 'Drawing and painting for the terrified'; children's art weeks; assembly presentations; church workshops including 'Releasing God's creativity'.

Storytelling Project

The Northumbria Community, Nether Springs, Hetton Hall, Chatton, Northd, NE66 5SD
T/F (01289) 388 477
Sponsored by the Bible Society and run by the Northumbia Community, this project intends to create and serve a biblical storytelling community across Britain.
❖ Storytelling performances, workshops, networking and resources
■ Anywhere ❀ Minimal

John Tinnin Mixed Visual Media

7 Princes Crescent, Brighton, E Sussex, BN2 3RA
T (01273) 692 010
The visual images are explicitly Christian in content and are designed to facilitate worship or speak of Christian truth. Currently mixing 2D and 3D imagery.
❖ Mixed visual media

Ian Traynar

54 Ravenswood Road, Redland, Bristol, BS6 6BT
T (0117) 924 3770 E-mail iancma@cix.compulink.co.uk
Speaker and facilitator on the subject of Arts/Artists and a Christian World View – a new and revolutionary counter-culture!
✿ No

Stella Wiseman

DTP work. See main entry under Journalism section.

W Margaret Wright

Stained glass. See main entry under Painting section.

133

Evelyn W P Ansell
93 Lake Road, Hamworthy, Poole, Dorset, BH15 4LF
T (01202) 682 359
I have not had art training. God led me to paint 3–5 years ago, whilst suffering from ME. Most paintings are Spirit-led.

Lyn Armigate
8 Homestead Close, Cossington, Leicester, LE7 4UN
T (01509) 814 768
Qualified teacher. Teaches adults and runs courses in watercolour painting. Floral work including still life and gardens. Also works in oils.

Robert Bailey
Joy and Maynard Hall
Beech House, Curthwaite, Wigton, Cumbria, CA7 8BG
T (01228) 710 347
I paint landscapes and cathedrals. I see my work as worship and a mirror of God's character. I also organise group exhibitions.

Olwen Ballantine
The Rectory, Churchover, Rugby, Warks, CV23 0EH
T (01788) 832 420
I aim to release the imagination in Christian growth by running guided exhibitions of my paintings, collages and textiles and workshops/ retreats, encouraging creative worship.

Alison Berrett
23 Summerfield, New Hinksey, Oxford, Oxon, OX1 4RU
T (01865) 240 736
I am essentially interested in natural forms from land/seascape to the figure. I explore change and metamorphosis within these themes.

Pat Betts
Hunters Lodge, North Road, Bathwick, Bath, BA2 6HP
T (01225) 464 918
I have been painting and drawing using a variety of media for the last twenty years, based in Bath.

Paul Bloomer
8 Cygnet Lane, Pensnett, Brierley Hill,
W Midlands, DY5 4DL
T (01384) 70708
Painter/printmaker – a graduate from the Royal Academy schools. I try to express a biblical world view visually in a way that is relevant to contemporary society. I paint murals for churches – and can give talks on Christian art.

Eleanor Bowen
17 Gilesgate, Durham, Co Durham, DH1 1QW
T (0191) 383 1441
I am a visual artist (combined media). Studio: Newcastle. Associate lecturer in Fine Art, University of Sunderland. I also publish poetry.

Mark Brooke
The Stables, Healey House, Huddersfield,
W Yorks, HD4 7NR
T (01484) 661 440
Mark aims to produce pictures which are life-communicating and life- enhancing. His delight in portraying the everydayness and ordinariness of life certainly produces memorable images.

Ursula Brooke
Brewery House, South Stoke, Bath, BA2 7DL
T (01225) 833 153
I run art prayer groups. People find permission to hand over their own, in favour of God's point of view. Art skills unnecessary. Quiet Day, 8 in group.

Fiona Burr
13b Grafton Mews, London, W1P 5LG
T (0171) 916 8106
I work on stained glass/painting commissions. I regularly exhibit my work. I have also experience working with homeless/underprivileged groups in a variety of settings, both here and in South America.

Dan Clouts
Henrietta Clouts
869 High Road, North Finchley, London, N12 8QA
T (0181) 446 1469
I paint landscapes, still lifes and portraits in pastel. I have been represented in numerous one-man and group shows in England and Finland.

Thomas Collett-White
See main entry under Other section.

Robert William Cox
10 Chantry Road, Kempston, Bedford, Beds, MK42 7QU
T (01234) 853 298
Robert Cox is director of Art at Bedford Modern School. He is a painter, printmaker (linocuts A1 size) with a Christian message. A committed Christian.
✿ Yes

Susan Cox
17 Copley Way, Tadworth, Surrey, KT20 5QS
T (01737) 356 103
I paint large-scale strong coloured narrative works. I work part-time as a registered art therapist with children and adults.

Barbara Dawe
23 Byron Road, Aylesbury, Bucks, HP20 7LU
T (01296) 29889
Our search for God can be superficial, like looking at cardboard packaging. Beneath the surface may be turmoil but here Jesus died for us.

Tracey Dawning
80 Southbridge Road, Croydon, Surrey, CR0 1AE
T (0181) 688 5873
My work involves 'picture making' using mixed media. Bodies of work usually have a theme. My work is extremely varied, depending on the concept.

Olivia Downey
93 Coombe Road, New Malden, Surrey, KT3 4RE
T (0181) 942 0525
Figurative painter/drawer. Constant elements in work are light, line, the figure. Drawing extends to installed wall-drawings.

Ruth Ducker
Deirdre Ducker

91 The Common, Broughton Gifford, Wilts,
T (01225) 782 958 E-mail james_q@dircon.co.uk
I paint large abstracted landscapes, and also have experience in illustration, design and model-making for animation.

Elyse L Forty

20 Tor Haven, Abbey Road, Torquay, Devon, TQ2 5NB
T (01803) 212 885
Retired art teacher renewing my skills after two eye operations. Scenes in North India after a 'Himalayan retreat'.

Julia Gascoigne Palmer

Ashmore, The Square, Rowledge,
Surrey, GU10 4AA
T (01252) 792 633
I work primarily in oils, most drawing mediums – pencil, charcoal, pastel, crayon and ink, as well as collage. I have always had a major preoccupation with colour – my subject matter alternating between landscapes and still life.

Jane Gabbatiss

6 Washbourne Close, Brixham,
S Devon, TQ5 9TQ
T (01803) 853 905
I paint on silk with dyes which I make into banners, waistcoats, scarves, flags and ribbons.

Kate Green

7 The Orchard, Aldenham Road, Elstree, Herts, WD6 3AJ
T (01923) 852 204
I am a figurative painter. I document my love, life and faith in paint. The edges of my pictures are often irregularly shaped. (Represented: Boundary Gallery).

Philip Grieve

17 Windsor Avenue, Holywood, N Ireland, BT18 9OG
T (01232) 422 141 E-mail u9122346@queens_belfast.ac.uk
Dabble in graphic design. Majority of work acrylic/watercolour paintings and black & white pen drawings.

Colin T Hale

20 Robert Street, Dudley,
W Midlands, DY3 2AY
T (01902) 671 412
As a painter I seek to express my love of structure, pattern and light in the local landscape, to the glory of God. Illustration and graphic design commissions accepted also.

Gerda Haynes – van der Bijl

3 Peace Cottages, Badley Hall Road, Great Bromley, Nr Colchester, Essex, CO7 7UX
T (01206) 230 825
I have been painting landscapes and flowers etc. for about 6 years. Recently I started something completely different, 'Paintings about Hope'; about feelings and emotions, but also about hope and a way out – The way out.

Janice Henley   1 Water Road, Gornal Wood, Dudley, W Midlands, DY3 2NH
T (01384) 821 161
I paint murals to commission in hospitals and currently in a Christian pub. Also landscape and genre paintings.

Paul Hobbs   Gores Cottage, Manor Yard, Combe Hay,
Bath, BA2 7EG
T (01225) 840 635
Painting and sculpture in both conceptual and abstract styles, using unusual media to address topical or newsworthy subjects from a Christian perspective. Talks, workshops and exhibitions.
✿ Yes

Cynthia James   44 Avon Close, Little Dawley, Telford, Salop, TF4 3HP
T (01952) 591 354
In the Renewal, God has given me a vision for the arts in the Church. I have recently begun to paint prophetic, inspirational pictures.

Leokadia
Ulrike Schnaubert   42 Croydon Road, Reigate, Surrey, RH2 OPQ
T (01737) 248 304
Leokadia studied in the Netherlands at the Academy of Art in Groningen 1985–1990. She makes large oil paintings and small prints and illustrations about people, Bible stories etc.

Paul John Lewis   Star Fish Studio, Frensham Garden Centre, The Reeds, Frensham, Surrey, GU10 3BP
T (01252) 794 023
My work includes landscapes, portraits and imaginative themes e.g. 'The Cloud Triptych' centring around the Lamb of God. Others include 'Jacob and the Angel' and 'Gethsemane'.

David Lloyd Griffith   35 Glan Y Fedw, Betws Yn Rhos, Abergele, Clwyd, LL22 8AP
T (01492) 680 630
Full-time artist, working mainly on landscape themes in oil. All work is broadly figurative and is inspired by N Wales scenery. Also hoping to develop interest in biblical themes for near future.

Shona MacDonald   *See main entry under Worship Music section.*

Mary Mallon   *See main entry under Sculpting section.*

Terry Mart   The Rectory, Glyn-y-Marl Road, Llandudno, Gwynedd, LL31 9NS
T (01492) 583 579
I am a painter working mainly in landscape and seascape which include architectural details.

Revd William B G Mather

The Vicarage, 35 Church Street, Littleover,
Derby, DE23 6GF
T (01332) 767 802
Vicar, journalist, painter: exhibitions in oils,
watercolours, pastels; work in private collections;
variety of conference and speaking engagements;
Council of Reference: Arts in Mission; member of
Arts Centre Group.

Gondolas, courtesy Mr
Adrian Llewellyn-Evans,
Bristol

Peter N Millward

The Chestnuts, Coton, Nr Whitchurch, Salop, SY13 2RA
T (01948) 880 770
Peter is a full-time artist/evangelist involved in church and streetwork,
producing pictures which illustrate the gospel. His work is available as
prints.

Kyoko Nishimura

3 Crescent House, 113–115 Worple Road, London, SW20 8JD
T (0181) 947 5556
I paint with mixed medium, using mainly colour as a way of expressing
my inner feeling, as well as in response to God's beautiful creation.

Rosemarie Oehler

Arts for Relief and
Missions, Inc.

5623 N Bernard Street, Chicago, Illinois, 60659 USA
T (00 1) 312 588 3881 F (00 1) 312 588 3969
Rosemarie Oehler uses fine art in evangelistic ministry. With
'Reconciliation' as a theme, the 14–year focus on East and West Europe
is now on inner-city ministry.

Tom Oldham

Yew House, Newbiggin-on-Lune, Kirkby Stephen,
Cumbria, CA17 4NS
T (015396) 23312
III year BA Fine Artist. I have used film to question people's reactions to
life and death. I now am studying the beauty of a flower through
painting.

James R Parfitt

45c Roland Gardens, London, SW7 3PQ
T (0171) 370 5389
Have exhibited from early 1970s at RA Summer Exhibition. Don't
exhibit regularly now. Hold one-man shows when enough work and
accept small landscape and portrait commissions. Would be interested in
greater variation of work.

Laurence Pusey

8 Victoria Terrace, Leeds, W Riding, LS3 1BX
T (0113) 245 1382
A painter and evangelist. He divides his time between
marketing prints of his landscapes and life studies and
chaplaincy work at Leeds University. Takes teams to
India preaching and healing.

Alan Reed
Alan or Susan Reed

17 Cheviot View, Ponteland ,
Newcastle-upon-Tyne, NE20 9BP
T (01661) 871 800
I produce watercolour paintings and limited edition prints of towns and cities. I regularly exhibit my work and also undertake commissions of other subjects.

Nanette Heather Rhee
BA (Hons)

22 Leonard Avenue, Otford, Sevenoaks,
Kent, TN14 5RB
T (01959) 524 964
Recently studied advanced painting course at Maidstone, 'Transcriptions' using William Blake, Samuel Palmer's 'Valley of Vision, Shoreham'. Pilgrimage to Holy Land (photographs). Card issued for the British Museum (Drawing Prints) Room.

Colin Riches

See main entry under Sculpting section.

Nicola Roberts
Trevor Barton

13 Camden Avenue, Pembury, Nr Tunbridge Wells, Kent, TN2 4PQ
T (01892) 822 932
I love the colours and shapes in creation and I see my work as a means of praising God for his gifts to us.

Kiran Sharma

Newington Court, 1 Collins Road, Islington, London, N5 2UF
T (0171) 226 3626
My work gains most of its inspiration from looking at nature, the figure and other artists; focusing on rhythm.

Rosie Smith

See main entry under Other section.

Dimitrios G Tsouris

'Tregudda', West Hill, Wadebridge, Cornwall, PL27 7EW
T (01208) 816 421
A symbolist artist interpreting social themes in a contemporary idiom. Graphic design for CDs, cassettes. Company/business brochures, leaflets. Speaker on the 'Arts and a Biblical Perspective' and 'Arts Mandate'.

Alison Waite

58 Park Road, Witney, Oxon, OX8 5EW
T (01993) 708 874 F (01993) 708 874
Freelance artist/art tutor working in watercolour, pen & wash, oils, acrylics – landscapes, flowers, portraits – murals, posters, creative Scripture interpretation.

Sheilah Ward Ling

13 High Wickham, Hastings, E Sussex, TN35 5PB
T (01424) 425 192
Sheilah Ward Ling is an actress, writer and painter in which the painter predominates. She has exhibited in solo and group shows and sold work in England and abroad.

Samantha Willes
74 Weydon Hill Road, Farnham, Surrey, GU9 8NY
T (01252) 712 952
My work which includes drawing, painting and metalwork, is mainly concerned with the celebration and wonder of God's creation.

Paula-Marie Wray
11 Wilsmere Drive, Northolt, Middx, UB5 4JA
T (0181) 423 4815
I have completed a BA(Hons) degree in art, which gave me the opportunity to exhibit my own work. I have undertaken various commissions including wedding invitations and drawings/paintings.

Charlotte Wright
Questers, The Common, Berkhamsted, Herts, HP4 2QB
T (01442) 871 927
My paintings are mainly landscapes usually relating to the fells of my native Cumbria and involving the themes 'Fire by Night' and 'Cloud by Day' derived from the Exodus story.

W Margaret Wright
18 Upper Town Road, Greenford,
Middx, UB6 9JE
T (0181) 575 1340
Senior citizen. Lifelong interest, painting, sculpture, drawing, recently stained glass. Work: outcome of need to express faith, hope, witness to a living God and Saviour through joy in his creation.

Muthena Paul Alkazraji
See main entry under Journalism section.

Austin's Photography
Frank Michael Austin
St Silas' Church, Hesters Way Road, Cheltenham, Glos, GL51 OSE
T (01242) 233 177
I cover all aspects of photography and am willing to travel. Playgroups, parties and schools a speciality, legal and insurance work also covered.

Simon P Baker
1 Redland Way, Aylesbury, Bucks, HP21 7RJ
T (01296) 434 143 Mobile (0374) 937 348
Photo/illustrator: illustration, photography and graphics. Specialising in AV. Presentation using multimedia.

Mike Collins
8 Abbeydale Drive, Mansfield, Notts, NG18 4TL
T (01623) 464 646 F (01623) 428 575
My mission is to praise God through photograpy, capturing the life, colour, light, people and architecture of his Church through my work, 'Images of Praise'.

Anita Cuttill
See main entry under Contemporary Music section.

Mike Gough
66 Rushden Gardens, Clayhall, Ilford, Essex, IG5 0BP
T (0181) 550 0957 F (0171) 255 1443
E-mail 101444.3347@compuserve.com
'You are the first generation raised without religion. We are all creatures with religious impulses, where do these impulses flow in a world of TV dinners, malls and jets?' D Coupland, 'Life after God', 1994.

Jean Havilland
5 Harwood Close, Tewin, Herts, AL6 0LF
T (01438) 717 744 Mobile (0836) 330 500 F (01438) 717 744
I have been a photographic model for 25 years and for the last seven years have been working in photo-journalism. I work as a photographer (celebrity photo calls mainly).

Stephen Owen
Whipley Studio, Bramley, Guildford, Surrey, GU5 0LL
T (01483) 278 309 F (01483) 278 309
Using photography to tell a story, I work unobtrusively, recording events as they unfold. Weddings a speciality, capturing the unusual with a different approach. Enquiries welcome.

Benedict Parsons
Priors House, The Court, Croft Lane, Crondall, Nr Farnham, Hants, GU10 5QF
T (01252) 851 137 Mobile (0468) 105 785
F (01252) 851 137
Photojournalism, professional photography; news, exhibitions, commercial. Ecumenical clientele include Spring Harvest, Keswick Convention, CRE, 'Independent', 'Church Times', thirty further publications.

Ian Roberts Photography

4 Greenway Gardens, Chippenham, Wilts, SN15 1AJ
T (01249) 660 907
Competent, creative photographer, available for concerts, music, drama or dance, conferences or any event, any size anywhere in UK. Available for social events, weddings, church anniversaries etc.
✿ Yes

Matt Roper

4 Abbey Road, Mansfield, Notts, NG18 3AF
T (00 55) 91 522 7314 F (00 55) 91 522 3325 E-mail paz@ax.apc.org
Matt works with abandoned and abused children in the Brazilian Amazon. Through writing and photo journalism he aims to communicate issues of poverty and injustice.

Claire Schwob

Flat 9, 72 Gordon Road, London, W5 2AR
T (0181) 810 5301
Portraits, reportage, illustration, exhibitions, still photos, publicity.

Paul Stanier

Natural World Photography, Croston Barn House, Croston Barn Lane, Nateby, Preston, Lancs, PR3 0JL
T (01995) 603 954 or (0370) 338 818 F (01995) 600 585
I work to reveal a spiritual aesthetic as well as a physical aesthetic and often illustrate this through abstraction. I am a professional landscape photographer.

Woodland Photographic
Andrew Sandars

The Dowager Cottage, Woodland Park, Wrington Road, Congresbury, Bristol, BS19 5AN
T (01934) 833 864 or (0860) 682 847
F (01934) 832 783 E-mail 101366.3352 @ Compuserve.com
I shoot both commercial and social photographs. I work in medium and large format and have a photographic library of West Country topics.
✿ Yes

Paul Alexander   *See main entry under Drama section.*

**Elizabeth Anne
Bristow**   *See main entry under Worship Music section.*

**Karen
Cavallini**   92 St Donatts Road, New Cross, London, SE14 6NT
T (0181) 691 9782 F (0181) 691 9782
*Experienced writer, librettist, actor and singer. Qualifications include
BEd and cert performance, also attended Bart Gavigan's Advanced
Screenwriters' course. Work performed on stage and TV. CV available.
Commissions welcomed.*
£ Negotiable ☼ Yes

Marc Cavallini   92 St Donatts Road, New Cross, London, SE14 6NT
T (0181) 691 9782 F (0181) 691 9782
*Experienced professional freelance director, writer and workshop leader.
Writing work includes major commissions for charities profiling
HIV/AIDS, drugs education and mental health issues. Particular
expertise in Forum and Verbatim theatre.*
£ Negotiable ☼ Yes

Ann Clifford   Fox House, High Street, Cobham, Surrey, KT11 3EB
T (01932) 865 036 F (01932) 860 373
*A full member of the Writers' Guild of Great Britain. My work has been
performed in many venues both nationally and internationally,
including the West End Fringe.*

Penelope Ellis   4 Burton Bank, Yeate Street, London, N1 3EP
T (0956) 881 351 or (0171) 225 6927
*Focus is on personal and social issues grappling with the struggle and
suffering in the world: drama that is inspired by real events/experiences.*
❖ A variety poetic/abstract/thematic ● Group of us write together
■ Church venues £ To negotiate ❀ No ☼ No

Peter English   *See main entry under Drama section.*

**Essential
Theatre
Company**   *See main entry under Drama section.*

**Kettle of Fish
Theatre**   *See main entry under Drama section.*

play writing

Jayne Kirkham 'Hillside', 68 Cressingham Road, Reading, Berks, RG2 7JR
T (0118) 975 5704 E-mail
JAYNE.KIRKHAM@termapart.demon.co.uk
Full-scale plays and musicals covering wide range of biblical and social themes, using wide range of theatrical styles. Lots of colour, spectacle and serious bits, and parts for everyone!
£ Expenses, commissions welcomed ✿ Yes

Rob Lacey *See main entry under Drama section.*

Linda Mae *See main entry under Drama section.*

Mosaic Theatre *See main entry under Drama section.*

New Directions Theatre Company Ltd
Robin Meredith
8 Compton Road, Lindfield, Haywards Heath, W Sussex, RH16 2JZ
T (01444) 482 334
Production facility to encourage/develop Christian writing in dramatic arts, challenging the writer to explore the significance of Christ's teaching in the reality of today's world.

Russell Sherwen
Anne Sherwen
Correnden, 32 Dry Hill Park Road, Tonbridge, Kent, TN10 3BU
T (01732) 353 381
'Sometime in their Lives' full length play being considered; 'Idyll in Ithaca', a one-act play published by New Playwrights Network. 'He didn't want to go to Paris' published by Adelphi, a long short story. Poem from the Portuguese published in anthology 'Aspects of Faith', Arrival Press.

Son-Rise Theatre Company *See main entry under Drama section.*

Barbara Sumner 15 Tolworth Road, Surbiton, Surrey, KT6 7TA
T (0181) 397 7806
After six years' professional theatre with a variety of Christian and secular companies I am developing my work in script-writing and directing.

Chris Antcliff
BA (Hons)

126 Melton Road, Stanton-on-the-Wolds,
Keyworth, Nottingham, NG12 5BQ
T (0115) 937 2966
*Since 1981, I have written poetry. This has
grown to include performance poetry and poetry
workshops. I've also had poems published in
local and national publications.*
❖ Highly charged ● Select poems appropriate
for each occasion ■ Locally, but have gone
wider, with help as disabled £ No fees,
grateful for help with transport ❀ PA if in
large room ✿ Yes

**Peter
Brassington**

53 Rickmansworth Road, Pinner, Middx, HA5 3TJ
T (0181) 429 0358
*Young, balding poet expressing through humorous, accessible verse that
Jesus is real, but so is life. I still have problems, questions, fears... and
hope.*
❖ Poet and speaker ● Just me and possible moral support of one
■ Missions, church socials, CUs £ Full travel expenses plus gift
appropriate to venue ❀ An audience✿ Yes

C P Clarke
Carlos Clarke

59 Harvesters Close, Isleworth, Middx, TW7 7PS
T (0181) 755 1049 or (0378) 290 918
*A performance poet whose work is both Christian and non-Christian,
and also the author of many short stories.*
❖ Performance poetry ● Solo ■ Churches, conferences, outreach
events £ Expenses plus gift ❀ PA ✿ No

Hazel Collins

28 Pound Road, East Peckham, Tonbridge, Kent, TN12 5BE
T (01622) 872 135
*I am an amateur poet – have had 3 poems published (2 by Triumph
House) in mixed anthologies. Very involved with Methodist Church in
East Peckham.*
✿ No

**Geoffrey
Daniel**

Reed's School, Sandy Lane, Cobham, Surrey, KT11 2ES
T (01932) 869 017 F (01932) 869 046
*Teacher, 42, married – writes haiku, sonnets, free verse etc. Bible study
and meditations. Published in 30+ Magazine and anthologies. Can
tutor, run writing groups, preach or lead in worship.*
✿ No

**Heather
Douglass**

See main entry under Fiction Writing section.

**Jocelyn S
Downey**

93 Coombe Road, New Malden, Surrey, KT3 4RE
T (0181) 942 0525 E-mail jdowney@hgmp.mrc.ac.uk
*Scientist. Published in 'Loose Change' (Poetry now) and 'Candlelights'
(Forward Press). Writing extends to prose.*

Hilary Elfick   74 Middle Street, Brockham, Betchworth, Surrey, RH3 7HW
T (01737) 845 154 F (01737) 845 154
Ex BBC Religious Education Dept. Books: 'Folk & Vision' (Hart Davis);
'The Horse Might Sing' (poems), 'Travelling Light' (play), 'Unexpected
Spring' (poems), 'Going Places' (poems – Envoi Press). Ex head
English/6th form tutor (including residential). I am a performing poet
who teaches poetry skills and conducts courses on meditation and
writing.
❖ Informal ● Self ■ Schools, halls, libraries, community centres,
churches, cathedrals, etc. £ £75 for 1/2 day workshop, £80 per
performance. £120–£140 full day ✿ None ☼ Yes

Malcolm Evans   *See main entry under Contemporary Music section.*

Faith C Gage   8 Wheatfield Road, Stanway, Colchester, Essex, CO3 5YJ
T (01206) 766 424
I am a widowed mum and physiotherapist who has written several
books of poetry with a Christian flavour, including sad, seasonal,
humorous and children's specialities.

Elizabeth Gibson   *See main entry under Fiction Writing section.*

Ray Givans   26 Kingsland Park, Gilnahirk, Belfast, BT5 7FB
T (01232) 485 952
Published in mainstream poetry outlets, since 1980. Second collection
presently under consideration. Given many readings.

Marion Irene Goodwin   5 Waterham Road, Easthampstead, Bracknell, Berks, RG12 7NE
T (01344) 642 440
I have had 16 poems published, 2 being in 'International Society of
Poetry' and 'Poetry in Print', local paper for winning a Certificate of
Excellence and have been accepted in American Comp.

Roger Hampton   'Junetone' , Tiled House Lane, Pensnett, Dudley, W Midlands, DY5
4LW T (01384) 571 684
Single, 31. The struggles of being a Christian, prayers, people I meet,
inspire me!? Pub'ished in anthologies.

Mary Hathaway   *See main entry under Prose section.*

Ken Hodgson   *See main entry under Dance section.*

Shona MacDonald   *See main entry under Worship Music section.*

Paul Mangan   *See main entry under Sculpting section.*

Phil Andrews McGovern   9 Kite Hill, Eaglestone, Milton Keynes, Bucks, MK6 5BL
T (01908) 242 485
Committed to poetry as worship. Devises chants and liturgy for experimental services. With wife, composer Nicola Ellis Andrews regularly has songs included in programmes of contemporary classical music.

Marlene Meilak   115 Millfield, Creekmoor, Poole, Dorset, BH17 7XB
T (01202) 387 209
Poetry was a new 'gift' given to me at fifty plus. Now many of my poems are set to music to become worship songs.

Andrea Mitchell   63 King Edward Crescent, Horsforth, Leeds, W Yorkshire, LS18 4BE
T (0113) 258 0236
Poems in major literary magazines. Readings in public libraries. Songwriter in several genres: folk, blues, worship, children's. Creative writing tutor in issues of faith and creativity. Postal tuition service.

Evangeline Paterson   8 Oakhurst Terrace, Benton, Newcastle-Upon-Tyne, NE12 9NY
T (0191) 266 2311
Three major poetry collections, fourth pending. Poet's handbook. Founding editor Other Poetry magazine. Readings and workshops.
❖ Poetry readings, workshops ■ Poetry groups, festivals, church groups £ Negotiable ❀ Microphone if needed ✿ Yes

Lance Pierson   *See main entry under Drama section.*

Sandra Robinson – Boo Designs Ltd   Woodlands, Fauld Lane, Fauld, Burton-Upon-Trent,
Staffs, DE13 9HS
T (01283) 520 502
I am a poet and illustrator, and co-produce spiritual greeting cards with my son who is an illustrator-artist.

Shane Rootes   *See main entry under Contemporary Music section.*

Rosemary   *See main entry under Worship Music section.*

Guy Ross
H G R Williamson   39h Cumberland Street, London, SW1V 4LU
T (0171) 834 1430
Have been writing poetry since about 7 years old. I love communicating with economy and simplicity.

Coral Rumble   8 Fielding Road, Maidenhead, Berks, SL6 5DE
T (01628) 74169
Works independently and for the Poetry Society. Workshops for all ages. Much published. Contributes to anthologies, including Lion and OUP books. Broadcasting experience. Judges poetry competitions. In-service training for teachers.
❖ Adaptable to venue and purpose of event. ● Me! ■ Schools, clubs, pubs, churches... £ Schools £105+ expenses. Other venues negotiable ❀ Microphone and spotlight, small PA ✿ Yes

Mary Shepherd
Schrödinger Publications, c/o 6 Greenway, Berkhamsted, Herts, HP4 3JD
T (01442) 866 484 F (01442) 866 484
From cosmic washing machines to quantum love, Mary Shepherd's poetry celebrates the bittersweet experience that is life, and the invisible force that sustains it.
❖ From lively humour to thoughtful meditation ● Performance poet (and sometimes accompanying guitarist) ■ Churches, colleges, evangelistic events £ Expenses + £50 fee (negotiable) ❀ Radio mic. (and mic/amplification for guitarist) ✿ Yes

Russell Sherwen
See main entry under Play Writing section.

Kenneth C Steven
18 Cathedral Street, Dunkeld, Perthshire, PH8 0AW
T (01350) 727 359 F (01350) 728 606
Professional writer of prose and poetry concerned particularly with the wild world, and with the relationship between the land and its people.
✿ Yes

Steve Stockman
'The Sett', 49a Derbyvolgie Ave, Belfast, BT9 6FP
T (01232) 661 739 F (01232) 669 909
E-mail 101500.1614@compuserve.com
Poetry of a non-academic kind that throws depth charges to the soul. Lyrically, I have written songs with Sam Hill, Iain Archer and others. Have read at Summer Madness, Greenbelt and pilot on radio, not funny!
❖ Poetry and chat ● Me ■ Conferences, festivals, radio, anything £ Negotiable ✿ Yes

Vivienne Tsouris
See main entry under Dance section.

Wendy Whitehead
See main entry under Journalism section.

Linda Ball 9 Kirby Place, Temple Cowley, Oxford, OX4 2RX
T (01865) 395 273 E-mail 100544.1253 @ compuserve.com
Experienced freelance writer/ghost writer/journalist. Four non-fiction books published. First novel out April '97. Particularly interested in mission (lived in Asia for 10 years).

Trevor Barton c/o 18 Embley Close, Calmore, Totton, Southampton, Hants, SO40 2QX
T (01703) 869 301
Modern English and creative writing graduate/published poet. Writer of short, creative prose. 'Rehumanising', 'Healing' creativity? Ecofriendly? Prophetic creativity? Postmodern-aware technophobe romanticist? Oh yes!

C P Clarke *See main entry under Poetry section.*

Anne Coomes 2 Festival Drive, over Alderley, Macclesfield, Cheshire, SK10 4SQ
T (01625) 584 028 F (01625) 582 297
Former journalist for Church of England, now freelance writer specialising in biographies and 'ghosted' autobiographies of Christians.

Geoffrey Daniel *See main entry Poetry section.*

Marion Field 14 Frailey Hill, Maybury, Woking, Surrey, GU22 8EA
T (01483) 772 881
Freelance writer. Articles published in a variety of magazines (Christian/secular). David Thomas Award 1993 (best self-published non-fiction book). Second book (biography) accepted by Highland Books.

Roger Hampton *See main entry Poetry section.*

Mary Hathaway 62 Castle Road, Weddington, Nuneaton, Warks, CV10 0EW
T (01203) 340 895
I write prose, poems, meditations, prayers, alternative forms of worship and children's fiction. I have had 16 books published (including one out in May) with 3 publishers in a total of 16 languages.

Christine Leonard Birches, 51 Browning Road, Fetcham, Surrey, KT22 9HN
T (01372) 458 850
I like writing true stories about people, also fiction based on truth and 'ghosting' for others. I've had seven books published, plus poems, articles, short church histories etc.

Revd William B G Mather *See main entry under Painting section.*

Lynda Neilands *See main entry under Other section.*

Lance Pierson   *See main entry under Drama section.*

Kathleen   7 St John Road, Wroughton, Swindon, Wilts, SN4 9ED
White   T (01793) 812 081
Ten teenage biographies published, one book of fables, many articles and book reviews, many poems published or broadcast, several radio broadcasts.

Stella Wiseman   *See main entry under Journalism section.*

Christine   12 Oak Hill, Surbiton, Surrey, KT6 6DY
Wood   T (0181) 399 7354
I have had 20 books published, 18 children's books and 2 auto-biographical. I have also written numerous articles for British and American magazines.

Douglas C   12 Oak Hill, Surbiton, Surrey, KT6 6DY
Wood   T (0181) 399 7354
While I have written many articles (over 30 years), my main work is historical biographies of Christians. Bishop Latimer, John Wycliffe and Oliver Cromwell. 'Such A Candle' (Latimer) still in print.

Veronica   72 Wilton Road, Muswell Hill, London, N10 1LT
Zundel   T (0181) 883 1448 F (0181) 444 7740 E-mail ed@cityscape.co.uk
I have written Bible reading notes, compiled anthologies of prayers and poems, a book about relationships, and led workshops on writing, the Bible and feminism.

Jim Bailey, Kingdom Creative   *See main entry under Worship section.*

Susan Burman   7 Church Street, Mears Ashby, Northampton, NN6 0DN
T (01604) 811 682
A biblical marionette puppet theatre demonstrating Bible stories to the junior age group. The theatre is transportable and uses scenery, lighting and music. Also used for adult workshops/demonstrations.
❖ Puppet theatre ● One 'man' show
■ Schools and churches £ £20 for first performance – after that £10 ✿ Darkened room and power point ✿ Yes

Revd Stuart Holt   23 Castle Grove, Portchester, Fareham, Hants, PO16 9NY
T (01705) 321 425
Visits schools and churches, presenting Bible stories through puppetry and music. A writer and film maker. Leads church holiday clubs/parish weekends.
❖ Evangelism/performance ● Church educational puppetry
■ Schools/churches £ £175/day, £125/presentation ✿ None
✿ Yes

Life-givers Puppet Theatre
Shirley Ely   17 Foundry Lane, Earls Colne, Essex, CO6 2SB
T (01787) 223 089
We are a puppet team ministering to young children right up to senior citizens to bring the Good News of Jesus in a fresh way.
❖ Appropriate for venue/gospel ● 6–9 people from Baptist church
■ Churches, schools, fetes, etc. £ Petrol expenses ✿ Electricity
✿ No

Little People Puppets
Judith Simmons   12 Burwash Close, East Preston, Nr Littlehampton, W Sussex, BN16 1DP T (01903) 786 018
Puppet ministry. Talks and 'hands on' puppet shows with a message. Any puppet made to order from life-size 'wide mouth' animals. Biblical characters in cloth or papier maché.
❖ Puppet shows ● One ■ Church meetings, Sunday schools £ £15 upwards + travel – 50 mile radius only ✿ Powerpoint, table, 2 chairs ✿ No

Dudley Anderson 11 Trevithick Close, Stourport-on-Severn, Worcs, DY13 8AN
T (01299) 822 413
I am a freelance radio presenter/interviewer and produce for two radio stations in South Africa. I specialise in music interviews and personal testimonies. My work includes voice-overs, DJ and journalism.
❖ Worship leading ● 1 ■ Church worship £ Travel costs ❋ PA, guitar, and backing tracks ♢ No

Adrian Barnard 93 Queen Street, Worthing, W Sussex, BN14 7BH
T (01903) 233 958 F (01903) 233 958
E-mail 101704 3241@compuserve.com
Independent radio and audio producer; radio interviews, packages; talking newspapers; radio presenter; script writing. Clients include FEBA Radio, Herald House Ltd, Challenge Publishing, Focus Radio, Waves, March for Jesus.

The Big Picture *See main entry under Contemporary Music section.*

Jeff Bonser PO Box 124, Westcliff on Sea, Essex, SS0 0QU
T (01702) 348 369 F (01702) 348 369
I am General Secretary of the Churches' Advisory Council for Local Broadcasting and offer help and advice for Christians interested or involved in radio/TV.

Janette Caiels 26 Mavis Court, 4 Raven Close, Colindale, London, NW9 5BJ
T (0181) 203 3130
Researcher, Premier Radio 1995; producer/presenter, FEBC radio, Philippines, 1995; organiser/broadcaster, Radio Cracker, 1991; Asst Editor, BBC TV news/current affairs, 1989/90; reporter/features writer, local newspapers, 1981/82; DIPHE.

Tony Jasper *See main entry under Drama section.*

Jay Knox 12 Townley Road, East Dulwich, London, SE22 8SR
T (0181) 693 4454
I am a freelance radio producer and journalist, working mainly on overseas development and environment issues. I also work as a programme presenter.

Howard McCalla BBC Three Counties Radio, 'Gospel Focus' on 'Black Mix', PO Box 3CR, Luton, Beds, LU1 5XL
T (01582) 441000 F (01582) 401467
Radio journalist/presenter – Gospel Focus every Sunday around 9.30pm for twenty minutes – 103.8FM, 95.5FM or 104.5FM.

Nick Page *See main entry under TV / Film / Video / Animation section.*

Graham A Pollitt c/o GCHE, FCH Campus, Swindon Road, Cheltenham,
Glos, GL50 4AZ
T (01242) 532 967
A member of Assoc. of Christians in local broadcasting and Christians in European broadcasting.

Resurrection Theatre Co *See main entry under Drama section.*

Coral Rumble *See main entry under Poetry section.*

William Shaw c/o Dedham Oak Cottage, Coles Oak Lane, Dedham,
Essex, CO7 6DN
BBC Radio journalist and producer: keen to bridge the gap between the Church and the media.

Roger Stamp 29 Riseley Road, Maidenhead, Berks, SL6 6EP
T (01628) 20697
Radio journalist and presenter. Media consultant. Ten years' experience in secular broadcasting for BBC and commercial radio. Audio tape copying service.

Jason Young 86 Park View Road, Tottenham, London, N17 9DP
T (0181) 801 7592
Prior to becoming a Christian back in 1987, I used to use my voice for radio plays. Now, I use it to communicate the gospel.
❖ Narrating – voice over, storytelling, etc. ■ The International School of Filming £ £50 basic fees plus travelling costs ❀ Recording equipment ○ Yes

**Thomas
Collett-White**   *See main entry under Other section.*

Iain Cotton   4 Coronation Villas, Tunley, Nr Bath, BA3 1DZ
T (01761) 472 768
Wood and stone and metal and... carving, constructing, assembling images of God's glory in creation; still falling but being redeemed. Earthy, quirky eloquent, crafted, commissions!

Susan Hadley   16 Washington Street, Chichester, W Sussex, PO19 3BN
T (01243) 774 142
With a 1st class honours in Art & Design; Susan Hadley is a sculptor who works in stone, clay and bronze. Her sculptures reflect all aspects of life and the Christian content comes naturally. (She spends 6 months sculpting and 6 months teaching.)
■ I give sculpture workshops ✿ Yes

Mary Mallon   73 Glebe Road, Crookes, Sheffield,
S Yorkshire, S10 1FB
T (0114) 266 5422
Minister's wife, sculptor, painter, and grandmother – this is me. My most recent work has been the result of meditating upon Christ's resurrection – the brokenness of life and the hope to come.

Paul Mangan   68 Philipsburgh Terrace, Marino,
Dublin 3, Eire,
T (01 833) 54 79
Usually 3-dimensional non-figurative abstract work using the scriptures as inspiration. Sculpture reflecting the wonder of creation by 'the Sculptor of all sculptors'.

Marbleous
Haydn Sheppard   Wick Court, Court Lane, Wick, Bristol, BS15 5RB
T (0117) 937 4480
Restoration and reproduction of marble and stone architectural/ sculptural pieces. Specialising in limited edition objet d'art and furniture works.

**Network
Crafts**
Alex Thomson   27 Bisley Road, Cheltenham, Glos, GL51 6AB
T (01242) 517 637
Network Crafts makes available resources, to enable mostly unwaged persons to develop their creative skills through wood carving and turning.

**Jono Retallick
– Artist**   100 West Street, Flat B, Farnham, Surrey, GU9 8SH
T (01252) 717 625 F (01252) 718 104
My work involves using mixed media and found objects to create inter-active sculpture on the theme of relationships with both my God and others.

Colin Riches
Wydcombe Manor, Whitwell, Nr Ventnor,
IOW, PO38 2NY
T (01983) 730 961
Colin Riches is a freelance sculptor working for commission and exhibitions. He regularly lectures and runs workshops including at Greenbelt, Spring Harvest, and in schools, colleges and HM Prisons.

Laurence Tindall
11 Shophouse Road, Bath, BA2 1EB
T (01225) 318 479 or 874 779
I tell Bible stories in sculpture. These stories are being forgotten and need retelling in a fresh way.

Isabel Wheeldon
5 Roxholme Road, Leasingham, Nr Sleaford,
Lincs, NG34 8LF
T (01529) 303 502
Figurative wire sculpture – including the Crucifix. Also metal garden features – including water features, wind chimes, candle lanterns etc. Appropriate quotes from the Bible/hymns are engraved or written into the work.

Gayle Willson
A J Willson
Rose Cottage, Pipers Lane, Alley Green, Luton, Beds, LU1 4DS
T (01582) 840 517
The work I do is created through patiently building piece by piece. Each rooster is individual, like in life.

W Margaret Wright
See main entry under Painting section.

Alex Aldous 2 Bramston Close, Oundle, Peterborough, Northants, PE8 4DP
T (01832) 273 824
I run a part-time gentleman's accessories business. I hire out wedding items and evening wear (waistcoats, spats, etc.) as well as a wedding car. I am also interested in various other art forms and organise arts events in schools and churches.

Gillian Arnold 19 Queensway, Carrickfergus, N Ireland, BT38 7LA
c/o Helen Arnold T (01960) 351 406
After completing a fashion/textiles degree in Liverpool, I have continued producing (primarily from factory resources) wall hangings, mainly for architectural/stage settings.

Aura 6 Marshside Close, Edmonton, London, N9 8LQ
Janet Edwards T/F (0181) 245 4182
I am a colour and image consultant who works with Christian groups or individuals who are interested in having a particular look for a photo shoot or concert.

Sharon Blackman 53 Storr Gardens, Hutton, Brentwood, Essex, CM13 1HT
T (01277) 231 961
Textile artist, specialising in using dyes, appliqué – very contemporary designs. Runs workshops and creativity days in various churches – encouraging people to be creative in presentation.

Christian Banners 9 Chestnut Court, Chestnut Lane, Amersham, Bucks, HP6 6ED
T (01491) 727 528
Priscilla Nunnerley *Two books available on banner-making. The first is a handbook. The second is about overseas banners. Talks given locally.*

Patricia Eastwell C/o Hilltop Banners, 54 Elizabeth Way, Stowmarket,
Suffolk, IP14 5AX
T (01449) 674 730
Textile hangings on commissioned basis. Postal gift range of small banners. Speaking engagements with aid of banner making. Completed 'Way of The Spirit' and 'Prophetic Bible Teaching' (Kingdom Faith Ministries).
❖ Speaker and visual aid of banner making ● 1 £ Travel expenses + love offering for charity. ✿ Yes

Judith Eaton 66 Whitehill Lane, Selly Oak, Birmingham, B29 4QF
T (0121) 478 3871
My work has been mostly in fashion, design, theatre costume, and as a textile artist. Started to design banners and run workshops in 1990.

Yvonne Anne Forman 24 Cambridge Road, Stamford, Lincs, PE9 1BN
T (01780) 752 746
Aiming to be as environmentally friendly as possible, I combine recycled materials (e.g. plastics) with natural fabrics to produce new and exciting textiles which range from miniature to large scale.

Yvonne Gill
Diana Snelling
(Member of ACG)

45 Ravensdale, Kingswood, Basildon, Essex, SS16 5HU
T (01268) 533 848
Self-employed fashion designer.

Diana Haswell

22 Princethorpe Road, Sydenham, London, SE26 4PF
T (0181) 778 7707
Individually designed vestments and liturgical textiles (stoles, chasubles, altar frontals etc.) Made to suit individual requirements and special situations.

Ruth Hodgson

10 Highland Croft, Beckenham, Kent, BR3 1TB
T (0181) 658 0972
Specialising in wedding jewellery, crosses and other items: one-off designs – unique technique of knitting wire with beads, spectrum of colours/metals. Available to order

Carole Kane

58 Eglington Street, Portrush, N Ireland, BT56 8DY
T (01265) 823 266 Mobile: 040 273 9826
I make stitched hand-made paper pieces based on the themes of ecclesiastical architecture and creations.

Amanda King

63 May Road, Twickenham, Middx, TW1 6RJ
T (0181) 898 9268 or (0973) 425 376 F (0181) 898 9268
A freelance fashion designer, also working in illustration. Clients include: Motorola, British Telecom, Looks, More magazine, Paperchase, and most high street fashion shops.

Louise Mabbs

18 Sumburgh Road, Balham,
London, SW12 8AL
T (0171) 223 2752
A textile artist/teacher for over 10 years, recently several commissions have had religious themes. Mathematical/ optical/ colour/ 30 techniques feature in other pieces.

Cassandra Postema

141 Cleveland Street, London, W1P 5PH
T (0956) 124 893 F (0171) 387 2593
Recycled one-off pieces to wear, available at Camden Canal market. Textile design involves prints on knitted fabrics sold throughout New York, Europe and Japan.

Ready to Assemble
Gaynor Burrett

5 Alfred Street, Westbury, Wilts, BA13 3DY
T (01373) 858 334
Original designs for ecclesiastical banners, vestments and altar drapes, supplied in ready-to-assemble packs.

Debi Retallick – Textile Artist

100 West Street, Flat B, Farnham, Surrey, GU9 8SH
T (01252) 717 625 F (01252) 718 104
My work is a celebration of creation. I am concerned with 'the manipulation of surface quality', colour and design concepts.

Nanette Heather Rhee

BA (Hons)

See main entry under Painting section.

Rosemary

See main entry under Worship Music section.

Annette Smith

45 Newtown, Hullavington, Chippenham, Wilts, SN14 6EL
T (01666) 837 215 F As above by arrangement
E-mail cliff.smith@ukonline.co.uk
I make decorative and functional hangings etc. in the ancient, tactile, colourful medium of handmade felt. Workshops given. Also charcoal/pastel drawing.

Rachel Stevenson

Alex Stevenson

The Grove, 27 Manor Street, Ardwick Green, Manchester, M12 6HE
T (0161) 273 1637 F (0161) 273 1641
One of my main inspirations is the appreciation of colour and the thoughts and feelings expressed through it.

Marlene Wylie

88a De Vere Gardens, Ilford, Essex, IG1 3EE
T (0181) 554 3765
Commission-based printed textiles work. T-shirts, banners, etc. Fabric for upholstery and curtains designed and printed.

Paul Alexander   *See main entry under Drama section.*

Julian Boote   117 Church Road, Acton, London, W3 8PY
T (0181) 992 9107
A graduate BA in film and drama, art and art history, Julian writes scripts, performs in and directs plays/films, and illustrations/designs cover art.

Russell Boulter   53 Napier Road, London, N17 6YG
T (0181) 885 4773 F (0181) 885 4773
E-mail 101576,3511 @ Compuserve
I am an actor who has worked extensively in theatre, TV and radio. I have also done a good deal of presenting, West End, RSC, BBC and ITV!
■ Theatre, TV, radio £ Equity minimum ✿ Yes

Richard Bramall
Michael Ladkin PM
Suite 1, Ground Floor, 1 Duchess Street , London, W1N 3DE
T (0181) 892 3926 or (0585) 821 467
Freelance producer/director of TV/film drama. Worked in industry for 25 years as above. Experience of all types of production both fiction and non fiction.
❖ 29 St Stephen's Gardens = agent ✿ Yes

Robert Brown   55 Chatsworth Gardens, Acton, London, W3 9LP
T (0181) 993 9883 F (0181) 752 1141
I am a television editor and occasional producer/director who has worked exclusively in broadcast television. Ex-BBC, now freelance. Documentary specialist.

Karen Cavallini   *See main entry under Play Writing section.*

Marc Cavallini   *See main entry under Play Writing section.*

Adrian Crofts   15 Chatfield Road, Cuckfield, Nr Haywards Heath,
W Sussex, RH17 5BB
T (01444) 457 797
Creating animations for computer games since 1994 using softimage software. Struggling and hoping to find some way to serve God – perhaps film/media?

Stephen Daltry   8 Tavistock Avenue, Walthamstow, London, E17 6HR
T (0181) 531 5362
I am a professional composer who writes and performs piano pieces of a classical nature and gives talks on film music, my major work.
❖ Classical/contemporary music ● Solo performer ■ Recording studios and theatres and churches £ £80 negotiable ❀ Piano and TV, VCR, amplification ✿ Yes

tv / film / video / animation

159

Sally Day

c/o 203 Canterbury Road, Bapchild, Sittingbourne,
Kent, ME10 4UL
T (01795) 425 227
Scriptwriter, researcher, production assistant, runner. Various TV and film productions experience. Writing aimed at secular audiences. Genres include drama, comedy, action and fantasy.

Gary Dell

The Willow, 138 Cock Lane, High Wycombe, Bucks, HP13 7EA
T (01494) 817 136 Mobile (0468) 848526 F (01494) 817 620
E-mail gary.dell@virgin.net
Freelance assistant producer for studio and outside broadcast programmmes – multi-camera directing; single camera producing/ directing; VT directing (inserts/compilations/highlights). Currently AP on 'Morning Worship' (ITV).

Ian Farthing

See main entry under Drama section.

Ben Forde

c/o Drumcree House Ltd, PO Box 46, Newtownards, N Ireland,
BT22 2AF T (01247) 862 198
A retired detective after 32 years in the Police in N Ireland, now sharing the Christian gospel with all ages in word and song. 'This is my story, this is my song.' Shares his experiences of police work and God's working in the lives of others.
❖ Country gospel. Backing tracks and guitar ■ Church and assorted community groups all ages £ No fee. Expenses appreciated ✪ Yes

Funktion Junktion

See main entry under Contemporary Music section.

grace

See main entry under Worship Music section.

A Haastrup
Sina Haastrup

Flat 2, 23 Regina Road, Ealing, London, W13 9EG
T (0181) 567 0520 F (0181) 567 0520
E-mail 100645.2153@compuserve.com
After 10 years in the BBC as assistant film editor, I have set up my own consultancy, making documentary programmes.

Keith Hopper

3rd Millennia Productions Ltd, 43 Terrington Hill, Marlow,
Bucks, SL7 2RE
T (01628) 484 777
Film/video cameraman. Freelance, following 30 years with BBC. Now operating 3rd Millennia Productions to resource Christian video.

Tony Jasper

See main entry under Drama section.

Steve Legg

See main entry under Clowning Magic section.

160

Katrina Moss Lakewood, Heathfield, Cobham, Surrey, KT11 2QY
T (01372) 844 484
E-mail KatrinaJM@aol.com
I am a freelance script writer and have worked as a production manager on three BBC 1 documentaries during 96/97, organising shoots in South Africa, USA, Switzerland and Ireland.

Christopher Norris 22c Belfort Road, London, SE15 2JD
T (0171) 639 7981 F (0171) 639 7981
Television – e.g. You're Booked [LWT], Identified Flying Objects [C4/ Discovery], Rivers of the World [BBC]. Project development – e.g. World Book Day, River 2000. Also – published author, SEEDS (chairman), ACG (director), FRSA (1996).

Nick Page Thatched Cottage, Otford Hills, Sevenoaks, Kent, TN15 6XL
T (01959) 523 740 F (01959) 525 011 E-mail nickpage@xc.org
Presenter, interviewer, film narrator, voice-over artist, theatre/film reviewer, continuity announcer, producer. Work has included BBC TV, ITV, BBC Radios 2/4, BBC local and various independent stations.

PC+
Paul Clowney 55 Drayton Green, London, W13 0JD
T (0181) 991 0029 F (0181) 997 8894 E-mail pcplus@mailbox.co.uk
Design and print for page and screen. Animation, CD ROM development with many projects for Christian charities.

Resurrection Theatre Co *See main entry under Drama section.*

Olave Snelling 8 Berkeley Place, London, SW19 4NN
Freelance TV and radio producer.

'Spider' Webb
Iain Webb 1 Oldershaw Mews, Maidenhead, Berks, SL6 5HB
T (01628) 33011 F (01628) 784 157
Big screen video, one man show!! (only one in the UK) up to 25 feet wide. Gospel message like no other!! Repent and be 'saved'.

Shan Stephens c/o St Stephens, Canonbury Road, Islington, London, N1
Multi-skilled video producer-director. Promotional videos, multicamera directing. Working in corporate video suite, cable TV and fringe theatre.

tv / film / video / animation

Paul Turner   Logos Media Projects, 4 Sedgely, Ashfield Park, Standish,
Lancs, WN6 CBZ
T (01257) 427 530
Scriptwriter and producer of over 40 religious, educational and corporate videos. Also journalist, contributing features on arts, leisure and media to national magazines.
✿ No

Ally!
Alastair
Hetherington

62 Angerton Avenue, Shiremoor, Newcastle on Tyne,
Tyne & Wear, NE27 0TU
T (0191) 251 2519
I am a solo, contemporary folk artist – guitar and vocals – and use my music to help powerfully and vividly portray who God is.
❖ Contemporary folk/protest ● Solo ■ Church events, prison ministry, festivals £ Very negotiable, usually just travel expenses
❀ 1 mic and 1 line in a suitable PA, usually I bring my own ✿ Yes

Dudley Anderson

See main entry under Radio section.

Colin Andrews

1 Midland Close, Harrow Way, Basingstoke, Hants, RG21 3LD
T (01256) 527 10 F (01256) 381 685 E-mail colin@arsm.co.uk
In recent years I have played saxophone with various bands/worship groups, at major Christian conferences, including Spring Harvest. Recording experience.
❖ Rock/pop ● Me ■ Local church, celebrations, national events
£ Depends on distance. Expenses only ❀ A band to play with! ✿ No

Bernie Armstrong

37 Graemesdyke Avenue, London, SW14 7BH
T (0181) 549 5531 Mobile (0973) 265 940
F (0181) 549 5531
Songwriter and worship leader, vocals, guitar, keyboards. Session musician – recorded 4 albums.(Formerly New Beginnings/CHO.)
❖ Adult-oriented worship (AOW) ● Solo
■ Churches £ POA ❀ PA System ✿ Yes

Jim Bailey, Kingdom Creative

Elim Centre, 45 Rowlands Road, Worthing, W Sussex, BN11 3JN
T (01903) 211613 or 0973 206625 F (01903) 211613
Anointed and professional family worship and evangelism resource. Jim is the originator and founder of Kingdom Kids. He ministers at Spring Harvest and other Bible weeks.
❖ Contemporary family worship and evangelism ● 1–3 people
■ Churches, halls, schools, theatres, Bible weeks £ Available on request ❀ Bring own PA, lights and stage set ✿ Yes

Gill Beard

133 Epsom Road, Guildford, Surrey, GU1 2PP
T (01483) 569 067
A Christian song writer and singer. I lead worship at St Saviours, Guildford and am Director of Music for the Archbishop of Canterbury's Teaching Missions.
❖ Worship ● Myself and accompanist ■ Anywhere/churches £ On application ❀ PA for voice, keyboard, guitar ✿ Yes

Beyond Jordan
Howard Cross

'Tehillah', 19 Chisledon Close, Haydock, St Helens, Merseyside, WA11 0FE
T (01744) 26954 F (01744) 26954
Contemporary worship/light rock band – appealing to all ages – incorporating dance and drama with a message if required – we are your servants.
❖ Contemporary worship/light rock ● 8 ■ Churches, church halls, outside, schools £ Love offerings ❀ Own set up supplied ✿ Yes

David Blaylock

23 Hillside Avenue, Swindon, Wilts, SN1 4LS
T (01793) 611 140
Worship leader in local church and have led town-wide inter-church celebrations.

Christine Brand

See main entry under Classical Music section.

Elizabeth Anne Bristow

69 Smith Lane, Bradford, W Yorks, BD9 6DD
T (01274) 496 775
Teacher and artist able to give workshops and performances in creative worship, including children's and healing groups, incorporating music, dance, drama, artwork and writing to encourage the full use of the creativity of the whole people of God.
❖ Creative ● 1 ■ Church £ Donation ❀ Piano, tape recorder ✿ No

Brown Bear Music
Ian Mizen

55 Avignon Road, Brockley, London, SE4 2JT
T (0171) 635 8355
Brown Bear Music seek to bridge the gap between worship music and contemporary. They are equally at home leading a worship service as they are playing in London's clubs and nightspots.
❖ Contemporary – indie/rock music ● 5 ■ Clubs/youth events/pubs/colleges £ £250 (negotiable) ❀ None ✿ Yes

Susan Burman

See main entry under Puppetry section.

Dave Childs

5 Rievaulx Close, Morton-on-Swale, Northallerton, N Yorkshire
T (01609) 773 171
A singer-songwriter and worship leader currently used as worship leader in church and has a recent release available.
❖ Contemporary worship ● Dave plus Karen, Norman on backing vocals ■ Churches £ Expenses only (gift optional) ❀ 2 mics and small PA ✿ Yes

Tom Clelland

40 White Hart Mansions, The Parade, Margate, Kent, CT9 1ET
T (01843) 298 558
Prophetic, original songwriter. Ex pub singer called out by God. Folk/country style. Looking to expand ministry. Experience local churches 5 years worship leader.
❖ Christian folk/country style ● Single/duo with wife, occasionally with other musicians ■ Churches £ To be arranged ✿ Yes

**Gerry
Cohen-Stone** *See main entry under Drama section.*

**Christine
Cottingham**
LGSM LTCL *See main entry under Classical Music section.*

Credo 10 New Street, Stamford, Lincs, PE9 1ES
Dorothy Chambers T (01780) 754 641
4-piece, middle-of-the-road gospel band. 2 female vocalists, keyboard, guitar/vocalist (male). Concerts, worship leading plus 60s/70s secular programme. Recent TV appearances. Together 10 years.
❖ Eclectic – MOR pop/folk, specialising in vocal harmonies ● 4 and occasional guest instrumentalists ■ Churches, village halls, barbecues, pubs, open air, schools £ Expenses + donation ❀ At least one square pin socket ✿ Yes

**Paul Ian
Critchley** 32 Chatterley Street, Burslem, Stoke-on-Trent, Staffs, ST6 4HL
T (01782) 827 262
Sensitive worship sessions, available on my own with keyboard or with a full band when needed.
❖ Praise and worship ■ Churches, youth clubs, open air £ £50 + expenses (£100 with band) ❀ Reliable power source ✿ No

**Maggie Croft/
Alison Holmes** *See main entry under Contemporary Music section.*

**Martin
Crowley** 41 Waterfield Green, Tadworth, Surrey, KT20 5HY
T (01737) 355 872 E-mail mcrowley@uk.b_r.com
Solo singer/guitarist – performing a collection of original songs which give a personal testimony of Christian experience. Approx 1–1.5 hour set.
❖ Acoustic songs of a 'ballad/folk' style ● Solo act (but can provide backing group) ■ SE/SW England £ £30 per hour + expenses ❀ PA system suitable for guitar/vocals ✿ Yes

**Neil
Cruickshank** 30 Park Avenue, Chelmsford, Essex, CM1 2AB
T (01245) 287 112
Lead worship in churches and networked events (e.g. March for Jesus), teach worship, huge pool of musicians and dancers, run worship and creativity courses.

Clive Davenport
35 Portland Crescent, Longsight, Manchester, M13 0BU
T (0161) 224 0764
Musician/songwriter. Has worked extensively in mission situations and multi-media events. Includes lights and PA and optional video in his presentation. Training for musicians and in music technology.
❖ Song – various styles – often with sequencers ■ Schools, churches, youth clubs, universities £ Negotiable. Rough guide £100 (one-off event); £50/day for a week ❀ 2x13 amp sockets and blackout for lights and video ✿ Yes

d.votion
Steve Smithson
34 Astley Road, Chorley, Lancs, PR7 1RR
T (01257) 277 232 or (0973) 511 087
d.votion are experienced musicians and worship leaders who are available to support your special event or encourage your church with original and established material.
❖ Contemporary worship ● 6-piece band ■ Churches and special events £ Expenses + negotiable fee ❀ Basic plan of venue would be useful ✿ Yes

Elastic Band
Ros Oswald
17 Kandahar, Aldbourne, Marlborough, Wilts, SN8 2EE
T (01672) 540 619 F (01672) 540 619
Interactive worship for children and young people enabling attendees to sing, play, move and dance along with us and the band.
❖ Pop – folk – rock ● Min 8, max everyone who wants to take part ■ Wiltshire £ Travel expenses only ❀ Power for amplification ✿ Yes

Malcolm Evans
See main entry under Contemporary Music section.

Excursion
Belinda Patrick
YWAM, Highfield Oval, Ambrose Lane, Harpenden, Herts, AL5 4BX
T (01582) 463 215 F (01582) 463 305
We lead worship for conferences and youth events. We also train worship teams and seek to mobilise young people into missions.
❖ Contemporary, various styles ● 6 ■ Churches, conferences, camps £ Travel expenses + gift ❀ Negotiable ✿ Yes

Face to Face
See main entry under Contemporary Music section.

Andrew Flannagan and Peter Ryan
See main entry under Contemporary Music section.

Dave Flowers
10 Sycamore Road, Hythe, Southampton, SO45 5EJ
T (01703) 848 245
Acoustic guitarist/singer with backing CD, portraying God's love, healing and forgiveness, with lyrics that speak encouragement to Christians.
❖ Worship ballads ● Solo ■ Churches, coffee mornings, outreach events, festivals £ Travelling expenses and donations if poss ❀ PA if possible, but have one if needed ✿ Yes

grace
Jonny Baker

38 Airedale Road, Ealing, London, W5 4SD
T (0181) 567 6926 E-mail 100750.1422 @ Compuserve.com
grace is an alternative worship service. We are willing to help others re-imagine worship and have a range of musicians and artists to help in this process.
❖ Laid back clubby worship ● Variable ■ Regular service in Ealing, events like Spring Harvest £ Negotiable ✿ Yes

Iver Grimstad
Iver or Patricia
Grimstad

53a Cleaver Square, Kennington,
London, SE11 4EA
T (0171) 735 2902(h) or (0171) 820 1508(w) F (0181) 692 3068
E-mail 100747,2217@compuserve.com
Main focus of my music is to lift people into a place of worship, as well as challenging them to turn to Christ and to serve him passionately.
❖ Contemporary, folk,ballads and worship
● 35947 ■ In churches £ Negotiable ❀ PA unless very small gathering ✿ Yes

Robin Hagues

See main entry under Classical Music section.

Ruth Hays

8 The Grove, Idle, Bradford, W Yorkshire, BD10 9JS
T (01274) 619 725
I lead worship, playing keyboard and guitar usually at my own church as part of a team, but am available to play elsewhere occasionally.

Julian Heming

12 Ilfracombe Way, Lower Earley, Reading, Berks, RG6 3AQ
T (0118) 926 8242 F (0118) 926 8242 E-mail
jheming@meto.gov.uk
Bass player with 15 years' experience of both live and studio work with professional musicians and national worship leaders in the UK and abroad.
❖ Contemporary, jazz, worship music ● Pardon? ■ Wherever God wants me to £ Negotiable ❀ Own personal equipment ✿ Yes

Graham Hepburn

See main entry under Classical Music section.

Paul Heyman
Jan Heyman

26 Mavis Court, Raven Close, Colindale, London, NW9 5BJ
T (0181) 203 3130
Electric violin worship concert in varied Jewish and Christian styles. testimony includes kidney failure experiences; why I believe in God; and why I am Messianic Jewish.
❖ Worship songs, Jewish and Christian ● 1 and backing CD
■ Churches, halls, functions £ £150 + expenses (support at lower fee) ❀ CD player, basic PA for DI violin and vocal mike ✿ Yes

Brian Hoare
1 Central Buildings, Westminster, London, SW1H 9NH
T (0171) 222 8010 F (0171) 233 0323
Trained as music teacher, now a Methodist minister. Writer of hymns and songs (words and music), published in many contemporary books. Leader of music/worship workshops.
✿ Yes

Phil Holburt
See main entry under Contemporary Music section.

Peter Holland
98 Prestbury Road, Macclesfield, SK10 3BN
T (01625) 425 279
Christian musician(keyboard) with many years experience of Anglican organist and free-church worship. Musical director. Both liturgical and modern rhythmical worship styles available. Currently leading 7-piece band at Pentecostal church.

Alison Holmes
See main entry under Classical Music section.

Ira Jackson
PO Box 376, Folkestone, Kent, CT19 6GJ
T (0973) 184 398
I have a vision to see souls saved and music restored to its rightful place that God intended. Ira is Minister of Music for His Kingdom Ministries.

JNR MACK
See main entry under Contemporary Music section.

Andy Langton
Stratton Lodge, Becket's Lane, Nailsea, Bristol, BS19 2LT
T (01275) 854 300 F (01275) 854 300
Committed worship leader with a rock style; used to ministering in a charismatic setting releasing open worship and the gifts of the Spirit, especially among young people.

Cid Latty
King's Trust , PO Box 3916, London, SE19 1QE
T (0956) 258 460 F (0181) 761 8207
Worship leadership for churches and Christian organisations, mentoring and training for worship musicians and top quality music arrangement and printing for songwriters is what we do best.

Geraldine A Latty
Nick Hodges
52 Pine Road, 'Treetops', Brentry, Bristol, BS10 6RT
T (0117) 949 6458 F (0117) 951 4244
I have been involved in leading worship at Spring Harvest, Baptist Assembly, etc. Involved in music at local church and have also given workshops on improvisation/gospel music, here and abroad.
❖ Gospel, soul, blues ■ Churches, seeker services £ £100 per day (if attached to workshop), otherwise negotiable ❀ Mic, PA with backing track facilities ✿ No

Philip Lawson Johnston
307 Woodstock Road, Oxford, Oxon, OX2 7NY
T (01865) 515 417 F (01865) 54104
I lead worship and write worship songs, travelling to churches and fellowships – teaching at seminars and leading services. I am also a freelance glass engraver working mainly to commission.

Peter Lewis 22 Marlborough Rise, Aston, Sheffield, S31 OET
Long-established ministry in music and word serving churches, schools and anyone/anywhere seeking a Christian to entertain, educate and/or evangelise/enthuse/enliven/encourage.
❖ Simple singable, tuneful, congregational songs and hymns
■ Churches, schools, halls £ Yes ❀ Good performing, leading space ✿ No

Phil Lewthwaite 62 John Street, Moor Row, Nr Whitehaven, Cumbria, CA24 3JB
T (01946) 813 633
Combining largely original with nationally known material, I minister in church settings seeking to encourage the body of Christ. I also have much experience in children's and young people's work.
❖ MOR Light rock ● 1 ■ Churches £ Expenses and love gift if possible ❀ None – provide own equipment ✿ Yes

Loose Goose *See main entry under Contemporary Music section.*

Bradley Luff 7 Coburg Place, South Woodham Ferrers, Essex, CM3 5LY
T (01245) 321 080
Married with two children. Youth/worship leader of 'The King's Church', South Woodham Ferrers. Singer/songwriter of worship songs, outreach songs and poems.
❖ Country rock – humour ■ Churches, halls £ Travel expenses
❀ Electricity ✿ No

Shona MacDonald 6 Bryson Road (3F3), Edinburgh, EH11 1EE
T (0131) 221 0295
My work is Celtic-flavoured, linking my own roots with those of the Christian faith through great messengers such as Moses and Job. I also sing blues gospel material
❖ Celtic, blues, gospel ● Solo ■ Scotland
£ Expenses ❀ Good microphone ✿ Yes

Alison Maclure Green Pastures Retreat and Training Centre, Corehouse Estate, Sandilands, Nr Lanark, ML11 9TY
T (01555) 664 711 F (01555) 664 711
Solo vocalist – uses songs that aim to encourage and challenge believers, and witness to non-believers in various settings, including celebrations and leading worship.
❖ Worship, contemporary ● Solo vocals, plus guitar/band accompaniment ■ Church services, women's groups, celebrations, etc. £ Usually expenses – depends on travelling distance ❀ PA system ✿ No

Paul Mangan *See main entry under Sculpting section.*

Andrew Maries
c/o Keynote Trust, Townhaven, Pound Square, Cullompton, Devon, EX15 1DN
T (01884) 34389 F (01884) 34389

Ian Marriott
2 Bridgefield Close, Banstead, Surrey, SM7 1LR
T (01737) 216 894
I am a semi-professional drummer working with contemporary and worship bands/musicians. Available to work with the same for worship sessions, concerts, etc.
❖ Contemporary (rock, pop, etc) and worship ■ Churches, clubs, functions, suites £ Negotiable ❀ Space for drum kit ✿ Yes

Mike & Jon
Mike Walters
105 Mulgrave Road, Cheam, Sutton, Surrey, SM2 6JS
T (0181) 661 2456
A guitar-based worship band leading contemporary praise and worship for churches or church-based organisations (availability mainly on Sunday evenings in South London/Surrey area).
❖ Contemporary praise and worship ● Two guitars including lead vocalist ■ Churches and church/school halls £ Expenses only ❀ OHP and screen; PA an advantage ✿ Yes

Andrea Mitchell
See main entry under Poetry section.

Peter Moran
26 Glebe Lane, Buckden, Huntingdon, Cambs, PE18 9TG
T (01480) 811 336 F c/o (01277) 234 401
A Roman Catholic Christian. I am a worship leader and liturgy animator with Sion Community for evangelism. Working in mission and parish renewal.

Network
David Morsley
1 New Close, Cop Hill, Slaithwaite, Huddersfield, W Yorkshire, HD7 5XA T (01484) 844 935 F (01484) 847 372
Serving local churches we are an evangelistic lively band using semi-professional equipment. Our music is contemporary praise and ideal for group worship and ministry/healing.
❖ Worship, praise and meditation ● Bass/guitar/keyboard/drums/vocalist/flute ■ Churches evangelistic meetings £ Free ❀ Space ✿ Yes

Network Music
David Wayte
33a The Crescent, Stanley Common, Ilkeston, Derbys, DE7 6GL
T (0115) 944 1819
Network Music is a critiquing and support group for Christian songwriters, both performance work and worship. For more information, contact us at the above address.

New Forest Fire
Dave Flowers/
Russell Dyer

The Pentecostal Church, Hardley Green, Hardley,
Southampton, SO45 3NN T (01703) 243 306
Funk/rock praise and worship band, very experienced and committed to praising God in a fun/powerful way.
❖ Praise and worship ● Piano, bass, drums, 2 guitars, backing vocals ■ Churches, youth events, festivals £ Expenses only ❀ None: we have PA and lights ✿ Yes

New Horizons Choir
Andrew King

16 Braemar Gardens, West Wickham, Bromley, Kent, BR4 OJW
T (0181) 777 8523
Evangelical mixed voice choir singing sacred music that is easy listening and entertaining, but also spreading the light of the gospel to God's glory.
❖ Easy listening sacred music ● Mixed voice choir,70 ■ Southern England £ No charge ❀ – ✿ Yes

The Now
Belinda Patrick

YWAM, Highfield Oval, Harpenden, Herts, AL5 4BX
T (01582) 463 215 F (01582) 463 305
Belinda and the band lead worship for conferences and youth events. They also train worship teams and seek to mobilise young people into missions.
❖ Contemporary, various styles (funk, rock, groove) ● Band of 8 people ■ Conferences, churches £ Negotiable ❀ Varies – (decent PA with 16 channel mixer) ✿ No

Richard O'Conor

31 Clarendon Road, Holland Park, London, W11 4JB
T (0171) 229 3198
Co-ordinator of sound and worship teams at St Barnabas' Church in Kensington (Anglican, HTB plant) for eight years. Worship leader. Co- founded 'Loose Goose', am a singer/songwriter/ businessman/run small song publishing/ recording company 'Loose Goose Music'.
❖ Vineyard/folk/rock ● Solo or full band – 5 ■ St Barnabas Church, Kensington/charity and Christian outreach events £ Negotiable after expenses ❀ Venue – dependent on solo or full band ✿ Yes

Oasis
Chris Rogers

22 Sovereign Way, Moseley, Birmingham, B13 8AT
T (0121) 449 3661
We are an instrumental group with a variety of styles and line-ups, also performing with singers. We are evangelistic in outlook.
❖ Varied: meditational, roots gospel ● Instrumental group: rhythm guitar, lead guitar, bass, keyboard, violin ■ Church services, programmes, evangelistic events £ Expenses only for gospel events ❀ 1–4 microphones into PA depending on line-up ✿ No

The Ocracy
Richard Cleaves

The Manse, Highbury Congregational Church, Priory Walk, Cheltenham, Glos
T (01242) 522 050
Alternative worship events. Sanctified dance worship on 2nd Saturdays, live band celebrations on 4th Saturday. With big screen visuals, smoke, lights. 8–10pm @ Highbury Congregational Church, Cheltenham.

John Pantry 2 Conifer Close, Alresford, Essex, CO7 8AW
T (01206) 824 257 F (01206) 824 257
I am a singer/songwriter called to encourage and stir up people for God.
❖ Songs for reflection and worship ■ Churches, town halls, theatres
£ Travel + gift ✹ Carry own keyboard and PA ☼ Yes

Jan Payne 48 Impington Lane, Impington, Cambridge,
Cambs, CB4 4NJ
T (01223) 233 577 F (01233) 233 577
E-mail jan@djbpayne.easynet.co.uk
*Jan is a professional musician, initially an oboist
by training. She now specialises in directing
music for worship, giving training, and is
available for classical concerts, private events
etc.*
❖ Traditional, classical to modern worship
● Myself (and accompanist as needed)
■ Where invited £ Negotiable but cover travelling minimum
✹ Power point ☼ Yes

**Julian A
Perkins** The Tehillah Trust, 49 S. Mary's Park, Nailsea, BS19 2RP
T (01275) 855 988 (day) (01275) 858 650 (eve)
F (01275) 855 988
*A contemporary singer/songwriter/worship leader/speaker; a qualified
psalmody leader; formally music director for Kingdom Faith Ministries;
Good News Crusade. Currently with Charles Sibthorpe at Living Waters
Church.*
❖ Contemporary worship music ● Solo or husband and wife (band
provided if required) ■ Camps, conferences, churches, celebrations
£ Negotiable ✹ PA system preferred ☼ Yes

**Angela
Pinnington** 2 Milton Road, St Mark's, Cheltenham, Glos, GL51 7ES
T (01242) 232 852 (after 4pm weekdays)
*A Christian for 20 years, single parent, singer/songwriter working with
small groups (talks illustrated with songs) or in worship/celebration with
theatre group/drama*
❖ MOR/folk sound ● Solo artist (possibility of duo coming up)
■ Locally (mostly) – don't have own transport £ Expenses ✹ PA if
required for size of room/hall/church ☼ No

Paul Poulton *See main entry under Contemporary Music section.*

**PRISM (Praise
In St Mary's)**
Lynda Frith 'Arran', Bishops Court, Maidenhead, Berks, SL6 4EX
T (01628) 21044
*We give presentations on biblical themes, frequently using original
words and music composed by Linda Frith, our leader. We have material
suitable for all ages.*
❖ Varied. A lot of original material ● Group of singers and
instrumentalists ■ Churches, church halls, schools, etc. £ None
asked for unless abnormal expenses incurred ✹ Piano/keyboard –
but can supply own ☼ Yes

Pure Silk *See main entry under Contemporary Music section.*

Nigel Ratcliffe 100 Linden Road, Coxheath, Maidstone, Kent, ME17 4RA
T (01622) 741 110 F (01622) 564 100
Musical director of worship bands for local, regional, national events; runs YMCA youth performing arts group; plays keyboards and co-writes worship songs; musical arrangement/production.
❖ Contemporary Christian music ■ Church £ Up to £12/hour depending on venue, etc. ❀ Normal PA (can supply for smaller venues) ✿ Yes

Timothy Rawe *See main entry under Architecture section.*

Paul & Sharon Reid *See main entry under Contemporary Music section.*

Geoff & Judith Roberts Brenchley, 8 Hamilton Road, Sidcup, Kent, DA15 7HB
T (0181) 302 0733
Serving the Church in songwriting and music. Based at Sidcup Community Church.

Andrew Rogers 20 Dunsuivnish Avenue, Portstewart, County Derry, N Ireland, BT55 7EP
T (01265) 834 300 F (01265) 834 300
Worship leading with a 'prophetic edge'. Prayer concerts combining worship and prayer for revival based on the five elements of the 'Lord's Prayer'.
❖ Acoustic rock Celtic jazz ● Usually 4 plus other local musicians ■ Church services, festivals, concerts £ Offering (no set fee) ❀ PA suitable for venue ✿ Yes

Rosemary
Rosemary Hall 29 Lacy Drive, Wimborne, Dorset, BH21 1AY
T (01202) 883 461
Singer songwriter with own guitar accompaniment, backing when available on trumpet, keyboard and drums. Songs have evangelistic, worshipful and prophetic content, linked with poetry and prophetic pictures.
❖ Praise and worship, easy listening ● 35886 ■ Churches, community centres £ No fee but gifts welcome ❀ One microphone ✿ Yes

Sarah Ross Tun 2 Limewood Close, Ealing, London, W13 8HL
T (0181) 997 1805
A singer and actress. I have trained and worked in a variety of styles. Greatest interest is in film and one great love is to sing – be it jazz, gospel or worship.
❖ Gospel, old jazzy, musical theatre, worship, American folk ● Independent ✿ Yes

worship music

Rugby Methodist Praise & Worship Band
Joe Bean

104 Bath Street , Rugby, CV21 3JD
T (01788) 547 347 E-mail JBEAN28876@aol.com
Church-based praise and worship band engaged in celebration style events to put Jesus on the throne of people's lives and provide an opportunity for him to minister to their needs.
❖ Worship band – fairly modern ● 6 adult members – guitar, keyboard, vocals, etc. ■ Rugby and surrounding churches £ Nil ✿ 13 amp socket outlet – OHP and screen ✿ No

Joan Russell

c/o 67 The Avenue, Camberley, Surrey, GU15 3NF
T (01276) 21469
Musical director, experienced choral conductor, singer (soprano), pianist, flautist, keen composer and arranger.
❖ Classical/modern ■ To be the Bath/Avon area £ Negotiable ✿ No

S'dANCE
Daniel Bowater

113 Yarborough Crescent, Lincoln, Lincs, LN1 3NE
T (01522) 541 570 F (01522) 541 570
E-mail 101325.1602@compuserve.com
S'dANCE produce and perform sanctified dance music for worship at Christian clubs, raves, festivals and at colleges etc. Singers, dancers, MC, DJ, etc.
❖ Contemporary dance e.g. house, rave ● Average 5 (but varies) ■ Own events, colleges, festivals £ Guide price only £250 + expenses. We are flexible ✿ PA, microphones, lighting ✿ Yes

Sanctuary
Rachel MacDonald

34 Chatburn Park Drive, Brierfield, Nelson, Lancs
T (01282) 699 447
Worship and ministry group using both contemporary and traditional material, with the emphasis on intimacy with God, contemplation and meditation. Also using dance where appropriate.
❖ Acoustic-based worship and ministry ● 4–6 piece group (plus technician) ■ Churches etc. £ Travel costs/PA hire/donation ✿ Good quality PA system (can provide own) ✿ No

Shalom
Nicholas J Manvell

20 West End, Melksham, Wilts, SN12 6HJ
T (01225) 706 931
Shalom is a small, recently formed group specialising in modern (Kendrick style) worship music.
❖ Praise and worship music ● 11 in number (9 singers and 2 musicians) ■ Churches £ Expenses – general travelling ✿ 1x13 amp plug with 30' of 'stage' ✿ No

Silhouettes of Christ
Varina Kellman

c/o Bonneville Christian Centre, 12 Poynders Road, Clapham, London, SW4 8MY
T (0956) 824 671
Gospel steelband. To enable young Christians to play an active role within the church and through this be able to spread the gospel, build relationships with one another and most important, devote our time and efforts to our Lord Almighty!

The Fiona Simpson Band See main entry under Contemporary Music section.

David Snowdon Hawthorn Cottage, New Road, Bream, Lydney, Glos, GL15 6HJ
T (01594) 563 400
I have a lot of experience of leading worship in church meetings or outreach events, as well as playing guitar and bass in worship/outreach bands to professional level.
❖ Praise and worship, and some contemporary music ● Solo, or with small group if necessary ■ Local mission, outreach, wherever asked £ Expenses and a consideration for time off work if necessary ✿ A decent PA system if more than 50 people ☼ Yes

Julie Steventon 23 Oxford Square, Watchfield, Nr Swindon, Wilts, SN6 8TB
T (01793) 783 385
Worship leader/songwriter/performer leads worship in own church, and locally includes own songs. Wants to glorify Jesus, has a heart for hurting people. Writes/stages musicals.
❖ Contemporary worship ● Solo or with a band ■ Churches mostly, celebrations £ Expenses + optional love gift ✿ Own PA but no lights or OHP ☼ Yes

Andy Strong 100 Edgeworth, Yate, Bristol, BS17 4YP
T (01454) 319 503
Songwriter and worship leader with guitar and haircut for large or small events.
❖ Folk ● Solo or small band ■ Schools, churches, youth events £ Negotiable ✿ PA system ☼ No

Neil Thompson
Revd Neil Thompson 'Aldersgate', 5 High View Close, Farnborough, Hants, GU14 7QD
F (01252) 544 823
I am a Methodist minister, previously a working musician, now involved in developing music/drama groups in churches. Published works include musical plays 'Child of Fire' and 'From the Heart'.

William Thompson EMS Audio, PO Box 100, Bangor, N Ireland, BT19 7AW
T (01247) 274 411 F (01247) 274 412
E-mail 100577.3317@compuserve.com
Leads worship at home church, Kings Fellowship, Bangor; in demand as MD for large events such as, Songs of Praise, Spring Harvest celebrations; writes contemporary worship material.

Tongues of Fire
Chris Woolgar 22 Portland Place, Epsom, Surrey, KT17 1DL
T (01372) 724 938
Lighting a fire in the Christian community! We glorify God through the quality of our music and we bring spiritual refreshment to all God's children.
❖ Contemporary worship music and suitable secular music ● Drums, guitars, keyboard, sax and vocals ■ Virtually anywhere – church, shopping centres, theatres £ Negotiable ✿ Sound amplification which we can provide ☼ No

Lydia Watson 19 Silverhall Street, Old Isleworth, Middx, TW7 6RF
T (0181) 568 1195 F (0181) 560 9893
I am a trained actress/singer with 10 years' performing experience, including West End. I sing professionally for weddings and funerals and perform solo worship songs.
❖ Worship songs ● Solo or together with husband ■ Churches, weddings, funerals £ Negotiable ❀ Pianist or sound system ☼ Yes

Clive Wayland 16 Linnet Drive, Westcott, Aylesbury, Bucks, HP18 0PB
T (0956) 815 240
I work full-time for Crusaders and am also 'worship leader' at my church. Approx 20 years' experience of this and youth-related work/worship.
❖ Contemporary ● Me and occasional backing band ■ Churches, youth events £ Expenses + 'gift' ❀ Own PA ☼ No

Virginia White *See main entry under Dance section.*

Chris Woolgar 22 Portland Place, Epsom, Surrey, KT17 1DL
T (01372) 724 938
I am a singer/songwriter, guitarist and flautist. As well as leading worship, I try to encourage a heart for worship in others.
❖ Gentle and sensitive ■ Churches and smaller venues £ Negotiable
☼ No

Jan Woolgar 22 Portland Place, Epsom, Surrey, KT17 1DL
T (01372) 724 938
I use my voice to glorify God. I sing in choirs, worship bands and solo and at weddings and funerals.
❖ Worshipful with feeling ■ Theatres, street work, churches
£ Travelling expenses ❀ Amplification depending on location ☼ No

Charlotte Wright *See main entry under Painting section.*

Bryn Yemm
Ann Yemm Severn House, 79 St Helen's Road, Abergavenny, Gwent, NP7 5YA
T (01873) 855 581 F (01873) 857 335
Britain's biggest-selling gospel artiste. Crusades undertaken. India, South America, Tell Wales, radio and TV around the world.
❖ Easy listening ■ Theatres, churches and crusades
£ Negotiable/love offerings ❀ Own Bose sound system and crew
☼ Yes

Services

art galleries

The Nave John Witcombe. The Nave at St Margaret's, Uxbridge, Middx, UB8 1AB
T (01895) 812 193 F (01895) 812 194
A church-based arts centre hosting a regular programme of events (speakers and performing arts), which contribute to the cultural and spiritual life of the community.

The Netherbow Donald Smith, 43–45 High Street, Edinburgh, EH1 1SR
T (0131) 556 9579 / 2647 F (0131) 556 7478
Arts centre with studio theatre, gallery, café and museum located on Edinburgh's Royal Mount. Owned and managed by the Church of Scotland. Also see entry under Artists: Other.

artist support groups

ACG – Arts Centre Group Ltd Ian Farthing, Administrator, The Courtyard, 59A Portobello Road, London, W11 3DB
T (0171) 243 4550 F (0171) 221 7689
E-mail acg@dial.pipex.com
The ACG is a national association of Christians working professionally in arts and media. We aim to encourage and support members through a range of events and publications.

Arts in Mission Hermione Thompson, 193A Norwood Road, London, SE24 9AF
E-mail HermioneT@aol.com
Aims to encourage, enable and equip Christians within the full spectrum of the arts and to assist the whole Church in mission and catalyse synergy between them.

Fellowship of Christian Writers Mr D Jolley, 76 Sarum Crescent, Wokingham, Berks, RG40 1XF
Our vision is to see quality writing in every area of the media, either overtly Christian or shaped by a Christian perspective, reaching the widest range of people across the UK and beyond.

audio / video recording

ARM – Audio & Recording Ministries Anthony Hubble. 79 Haycroft Drive, Gloucester, GL4 6XX
T (01452) 418 418 Mobile 0378 999 980 F (01452) 418 418
Live PA and/or recording for concerts, conferences. A complete audio service for churches, Christian organisations, musicians. Suppliers of sound installations and hearing aid loop systems.

CVG Television
Andy Price, First House, 1 Sutton Street, Birmingham, B1 1PE
T (0121) 622 1337 F (0121) 622 3080
E-mail.101501.2752@compuserve.co
Christian production company with over ten years' experience in all forms of programme making. Ring for brochure or free advice.

Callister Communica-tions Ltd
John Callister, 88 Causeway End Road, Lisburn,
Co Antrim, BT28 2ED
T (01846) 673 717 F (01846) 673 652
A film, TV, video production and facility company established in 1990 by former BBC film editor/producer. Beta SP crews and Avid off/on-line editing.

Christian Copyright Licensing Ltd
Chris Williams, PO Box 1339, Eastbourne, E Sussex, BN21 4YF
T (01323) 417 711. F (01323) 417 722
E-mail 100631.364@compuserve.com
Issues the copyright licence for churches, schools and organisations giving instant access to reproduce the words of 120,000 hymns and worship songs from 1,200 catalogues for non-commercial purposes.

CN Productions
Christopher Norton, 5 Little Way, Moortown, Leeds, LS17 6JN
T (0113) 269 3930 F (0113) 266 2075
E-mail 100275,366@compuserve.com
CN Productions is a music production company, with publishing and licensing as important adjuncts to its main activities. Midi data and television music also.

Creative Audio
John Ellis, 170 Holly Road, Aldershot, Hants, GU12 4SG
T (01252) 343 840 F (01252) 343 840
We are a small, friendly, professional, experienced Christian staff. Advice/sales of pro audio equipment. Established over 15 years yet we still enjoy rock 'n roll! (And most other music forms).

CrossView Audio Visual
Terry Smith, PO Box 22, Felixstowe, Suffolk, IP11 9EU
T (01394) 270 110 F (01394) 270 110
E-mail CROSSVIEW@compuserve.com
The production of top quality videos for evangelism – particularly for those on a tight budget.

Clive Davenport
35 Portland Crescent, Manchester, M13 0BU
T (0161) 224 0764
Musician/evangelist. Digital recording studio with sync to video. Small 1kW PA system and lights. Training in music technology, worship, performance, etc.

services

The Digital Audio Co

Dave Aston & Jon Blamire, 3 Carleton Business Park, Skipton, N Yorkshire, BD23 2AA

T (01756) 797 100 F (01756) 797 101

Established editing and mastering facility run by Christians. Can arrange CD manufacture. Specialists in audio from location to post- production at broadcast standard. We have worked with James, D:ream, Level 42, Grimethorpe Colliery Band, New English Orchestra. Work on 'Thief Takers', 'Famous Five', documentaries for TV. Audio post- production for television at broadcast standard. Recently involved with 'The Governor', 'Famous 5', 'Touch of Frost' and various documentaries for ITV and C4.

Edenfield Communications

Michael Jakins, 2 South View Place, Bath, BA3 2AX

T (01761) 414 992 F (01761) 411 805

E-mail michael@donns.telme.com

Edenfield Communications specialise in the hire or permanent installation of sound systems for all public events, especially in churches or other Christian events. Outdoor events a speciality.

Forward Vision Communications Ltd

David Furmage, 10 Claverdon Close, Solihull, W Midlands, B911QP

T (0121) 711 7500 Mobile (0585) 949 900 F (0121) 711 7600

E-mail action@forward vision.co.uk

Producing videos and multi-media content for Christian organisations of ALL sizes: promotional, music, youth, training, evangelism, conference inserts. Clients: Operation Mobilisation, Bible Society, CPAS, Bill Drake, Nelson Word, Coventry Diocese.

Longview Training & Video Services

Ken Acton, 72 Marlow Road, High Wycombe, Bucks, HP11 1TH

T (01494) 526 930 F (01494) 526 930

Mobile video recording of live performances using up to three professional cameras. Audio conference recording duplication with on the spot duplication. Video production.

Pathway Productions

Laurence Wareing, 22 Colinton Road, Edinburgh, EH10 5EQ

T (0131) 447 3531 F (0131) 452 8745

E-mail pathway@dial.pipex.com

Video and audio production company specialising in religious and charitable programming. Many years' experience. TV studio/edit suite and sound studio/control room available. Professional and friendly crew. Competitive rates.

Reelife Recordings

Phil Burt, Laverick Hall, Lancaster, LA2 6PH

T (01524) 811 282 F (01524) 811 959

Specialist in conference, convention recording and duplication. PA installation, 16-track studio, supply of audio equipment, cassette copiers, blank and copied cassettes.

Sarner International Ltd

Studios: Sharon McDowell, Sales: David Dempsey, 32 Woodstock Grove, London, W12 8LE

T (0181) 743 1288 F (0181) 749 7699

Sarner is a specialist audio-visual systems and presentations company which also operates recording studios and post-production facilities. 25-year track record, clients worldwide.

Scripture Union Sound & Vision Unit
Mike Jiggins, 207–209 Queensway, Bletchley, Bucks, MK2 2EB
T (01908) 856 000 F (01908) 856 111
E-mail mikej@scriptureunion.org.uk
Scripture Union produce Christian audio and video programmes primarily as resource materials for church and other groups, and individuals. They can also provide a production service for other Christian organisations.

Sound Supplement
Nick Page, Thatched Cottage, Otford Hills, Sevenoaks,
Kent, TN15 6XL
F (01959) 525 011 E-mail nickpage@xc.org
Independent radio producer – features, interviews, religious news, quizzes. Work has included London Broadcasting Co, Premier Radio, various BBC and Independent local radio, Christian stations.

Simon Jones
31 Henthorn Road, Clitheroe, Lancs, BB7 2LD
T (01200) 442 245 Mobile 0973 625 665 F (01200) 442 245
E-mail capelin@argonet.co.uk
Freelance broadcast sound recordist, also offering complete CD and cassette album record and manufacture service for any musical genre in studio or on location.

cd / audio / video / tape duplication

ARM – Audio & Recording Ministries
Anthony Hubble, 79 Haycroft Drive, Gloucester, GL4 6XX
T (01452) 418 418 Mobile 0378 999 980 F (01452) 418 418
Live PA and/or recording for concerts, conferences. A complete audio service for churches, Christian organisations, musicians. Suppliers of sound installations and hearing aid loop systems.

CVG Television
Andy Price, First House, 1 Sutton Street, Birmingham, B1 1PE
T (0121) 622 1337 F (0121) 622 3080
E-mail 101501.2752@compuserve.com
Christian production company with over ten years' experience in all forms of programme making. Ring for brochure or free advice.

Christian Copyright Licensing Ltd
Chris Williams, PO Box 1339, Eastbourne, E Sussex, BN21 4YF
T (01323) 417 711 F (01323) 417 722
E-mail 100631.364@compuserve.com
Issues the copyright licence for churches, schools and organisations giving instant access to reproduce the words of 120,000 hymns and worship songs from 1,200 catalogues for non-commercial purposes.

Forward Vision Communications Ltd
David Furmage, 10 Claverdon Close, Solihull, W Midlands, B91 1QP
T (0121) 711 7500 Mobile (0585) 949 900 F (0121) 711 7600
E-mail action@forwardvision.co.uk
Producing videos and multi-media content for Christian organisations of ALL sizes: promotional, music, youth, training, evangelism, conference inserts. Clients: Operation Mobilisation, Bible Society, CPAS, Bill Drake, Nelson Word, Coventry Diocese.

Lifestyle Designs
Carleton David Watts, The Studio, No. 1 Myrtle Hill, Pontardulais, Swansea, SA4 1RS
T (01792) 884 758 F (01792) 884 758
E-mail 101620,1404@compuserve.com
'Visionary/creative' artwork for CD, cassette, video covers, including computer-designed graphics and professional illustration. Also production of high quality T-shirts and promotional product.

Longview Training & Video Services
Ken Acton, 72 Marlow Road, High Wycombe, Bucks, HP11 1TA
T (01494) 526 930 F (01494) 526 930
Mobile video recording of live performances using up to three professional cameras. Audio conference recording duplication with on-the-spot duplication. Video production.

Reelife Recordings
Phil Burt, Laverick Hall, Lancaster, LA2 6PH
T (01524) 811 282 F (01524) 811 959
Specialist in conference, convention recording and duplication. PA installation, 16-track studio, supply of audio equipment, cassette copiers, blank and copied cassettes.

Selecta Sound
John Snailes, 5 Margaret Road, Romford, Essex, RM2 5JH
T (01708) 453 424 F (01708) 455 565
Audio cassette duplication and compact disc supply, studio supply, digital audio and video supply.

conference centres

Action Centres UK Ltd
Dave Bliss, Pioneer Centre / Forest Lodge Conference Centre, Cleobury Mortimer, Nr Kidderminster, Worcs, DY14 8JG
T (01299) 271 217 F (01299) 270 948
Action Centres UK provide residential conference and activity centres, part of NAYC, a Christian youth-based organisation. En suite, standard and camping/caravan facilities and meeting venues.

Adelaide's
Andrew Shearman, 209 Bath Street, Glasgow, G2 4HZ
T (0141) 248 4970 F (0141) 226 4247
Adelaide's is a ministry of Adelaide Place Baptist Church and comprises a cafe, guesthouse nursery and auditorium. The auditorium is ideal for hosting concerts, drama, musicals, and workshops or seminars.

Ashburnham Christian Trust
Mark Burlinson, Ashburnham Place, Nr Battle, E Sussex, TN33 9NF
T (01424) 892 244 F (01424) 892 243
E-mail enquirie@ashburnham.org.uk
Conference and prayer centre welcoming individuals and groups. Landscaped grounds and woods together with award-winning catering and a caring community team.

Blaithwaite Christian Centre
DL Bowie – Centre Manager, Blaithwaite House, Wigton, CA7 0AZ
T (01697) 342 319 F (01697) 342 319
Blaithwaite Christian Centre – situated close to Northern Lakes, provides catered or self-catering accommodation for groups of 15 to 100 persons. Full details and brochure from Centre Manager.

Carberry
Jock Stein, Carberry Tower, Musselburgh, EH21 8PY
T (0131) 665 3488 F (0131) 653 2930
A Christian conference centre whose programme includes events making connections between faith and the arts, national life, etc.

Cliff College Conference Complex
Maurice Houghton, Cliff College, Calver, Sheffield, S30 1XG
T (01246) 582 321 F (01246) 583 739
Modern conference complex offering flexible facilities for groups small and large, catering and self-catering, with space for meetings of up to 600, accommodation for 186.

Ellel Ministries
Brian Benford, Pierrepont, Churt Road, Frensham,
Surrey, GU10 3DL
T (01252) 794 060 F (01252) 794 039
Residential and day conference centre with 500-seat auditorium. Numerous venues in one location, set in extensive peaceful grounds with riverside walks and recreational facilities. Close to M3, M4 and M25.

Falkirk Christian Centre
John Todd (Secretary), 'Ardenlea', 37 Saltcoats Drive, Grangemouth, Stirlingshire, FK3 9JR
T (01324) 483 178
Facilities available, 100-seat hall, coffee lounge, with fully-equipped kitchen situated in town centre. Near bus and rail stations.

First Conference Estate plc
Peter Anderson, The Hayes Conference Centre, Swanwick, Alfreton, Derbyshire, DE55 1AU
T (01773) 602 482 F (01773) 540 841
Residential conference centre for groups of 6–400 people. Single rooms, twin and family rooms. En suite accommodation. Full board package. Three conference halls.

Glenfall House Trust
Gareth Morgan, Glenfall House, Mill Lane, Charlton Kings, Cheltenham, Glos, GL54 4EP
T (01242) 583 654 F (01242) 251 314
Christian residential conference house, sleeps 46, 28 bedrooms (20 en suite), excellent food, lovely decor, civic award for restoration, peaceful setting. 3 miles Cheltenham, 1 hour Birmingham, Oxford, Bristol.

Hothorpe Hall
Brian Dunning, Hothorpe, Theddingworth, Leics, LE17 6QX
T (01838) 880 257 F (01838) 880 979
A Christian conference centre providing residential accommodation for up to 140 people. Quiet rural location, yet within 10 miles of M1, M6 and A14.

Ice House Christian Centre
The Revd ET Carter, Victor Street, Grimsby, Lincs, DN32 7QN
T (01472) 349 917 F (01472) 349 244
800-seat concert hall, bookstore and resource centre, Bible World – a dramatic visual aid that makes the Bible come to life! Inc: a huge 26ft model of Israel.

Mid Wales Christian Holiday & Conference Centre
David Morgan, Cefn-Lea Park, Dolfor, Newtown, Powys, SY16 4AJ
T (01686) 625 275 F (01686) 626 122
Leisure complex and holiday centre set in the heart of Wales gradually and tastefully developed during the last 18 years. Set in 50 acres of beautiful and peaceful hilly countryside. Facilities include sports hall, play rooms, park, football, pitch & putt, golf, fishing, walking etc. Main hall seats 500.

NET School of Ministry
Tom Gould, Wirral Christian Centre, Leasowe Road, Moreton, Wirral, Merseyside, L46 3RE
T (0151) 605 1240 F (0151) 606 0051
Bible college with a particular emphasis on teaching within the area of creative arts. Major subjects: music/worship, drama/dance. Electives: singing, creative writing.

Oak Hall, Otford Manor
Ian & Judy Mayo, Oak Hall, Otford, Kent, TN15 6XF
T (01732) 763 131 F (01732) 763 136
Our beautiful manor house is available for conferences up to 80. Oak Hall serves and expeditions visit many parts of the world with Christian friendship and excellent evening Bible talks.

Quinta Conference Facilities
Peter Bevington, Quinta Hall, Weston Rhyn, Oswestry, Salop, SY10 7LR
T (01691) 773 696 F (01691) 774 687
Provide self-catering conference and holiday accommodation for Christian groups 10–240 (catering options available). Sports hall/theatre seating around 350.

counselling service for artists

ACG – Arts Centre Group Ltd
Ian Farthing, Administrator, The Courtyard, 59A Portobello Road, London, W11 3DB
T (0171) 243 4550 F (0171) 221 7689
E-mail acg@dial.pipex.com
The ACG is a national association of Christians working professionally in arts and media. We aim to encourage and support members through a range of events and publications.

Ampleforth Youth Net-Work (AYNW)
David Wright, 25 Coney Grey Spinney, Flintham, Nr Newark, Notts, NG23 5LN
T (01636) 525 176
We are an open community of charismatic Christians founded in the Catholic tradition. We hope our prayer/music days will enrich your life in Jesus.

The Five Gables Charitable Trust
Geraldine Booker, 136 Wish Hill, Willingdon, Eastbourne, E Sussex, BN20 9HL
T (01323) 509 002
We are a counselling organisation and we offer a variety of approaches, disciplines and creative methods in working with individuals and groups.

UCCF Arts/Media Relay Worker Project
Mike Gough, UCCF London Office, c/o YMCA Regional Office, 16–22 Great Russell Street, London, WC1B 3LR
T (0171) 255 1443 F (0171) 255 1443
E-mail 101444.3347@compuserve.com
This project supports and encourages Christian arts/media students working in an area which rejects God set against a Christianity that doesn't understand creativity. Organises gatherings (Interface), exhibitions, workshops, retreats.

drama tutorial / workshops

Christian Dance Fellowship of Britain
Angela Courtney, 25 Scardale Crescent, Scarborough, N Yorkshire, YO12 6LA
T (01723) 377 320 F (01723) 503 399
CDFB promotes Christian religion through the ministry and art of dance, to glorify God and extol Jesus.

NET School of Ministry
Tom Gould, Wirral Christian Centre, Leasowe Road, Moreton, Wirral, Merseyside, L46 3RE
T (0151) 605 1240 F (0151) 606 0051
Bible college with a particular emphasis on teaching within the area of creative arts. Major subjects: music/worship, drama/dance. Electives: singing, creative writing.

Radius
Christ Church and Upton Chapel, Kennington Road, London, SE1 7QP
T (0171) 401 2422
Radius was founded in 1929 to encourage all drama which throws light on the human condition and to help the churches to use such drama for Christian understanding and communication.

Seeds
Neil Ruckman, 30 Grosvenor Avenue, Barnet, Herts, EN5 2BZ
T (0181) 364 9652 F (0181) 364 9652
To encourage creativity in churches, education and prisons through workshops with professional artists. Current areas of specialism include worship, storytelling, forum theatre and performed readings.

UCCF
Arts/Media
Relay Worker
Project

Mike Gough, UCCF London Office, c/o YMCA Regional Office, 16–22 Great Fussell Street, London, WC1B 3LR
T (0171) 255 1443 F (0171) 255 1443
E-mail 101444.3347@compuserve.com
This project supports and encourages Christian arts/media students working in an area which rejects God set against a Christianity that doesn't understand creativity. Organises gatherings (Interface), exhibitions, workshops, retreats.

events venues

Action
Centres UK
Ltd

Dave Bliss, Pioneer Centre/Forest Lodge Conference Centre, Cleobury Mortimer, Nr Kidderminster, Worcs, DY14 8JG
T (01299) 271 217 F (01299) 270 948
Action Centres UK provide residential conference and activity centres, part of NAYC, a Christian youth-based organisation. En suite, standard and camping/caravan facilities and meeting venues.

Adelaide's

Andrew Shearman, 209 Bath Street, Glasgow, G2 4HZ
T (0141) 248 4970 F (0141) 226 4247
Adelaide's is a ministry of Adelaide Place Baptist Church and comprises a cafe, guesthouse, nursery and auditorium. The auditorium is ideal for hosting concerts, drama, musicals, and workshops or seminars.

Ellel
Ministries

Brian Benford, Pierrepont, Churt Road, Frensham, Surrey, GU10 3DL
T (01252) 794 060 F (01252) 794 039
500-seat auditorium. Full catering facilities and residential accommodation available. Ideal for 'Alpha' and church groups. Set in extensive peaceful grounds with riverside walks and recreational facilities. Close to M3, M4 and M25.

The Emery
Theatre

The Revd D Hill, Trinity Centre, 119 East India Dock Road, Poplar, London, E14 6DE
T (0171) 987 1794 F (0171 537 4979
The Emery Theatre is Methodist Church's own theatre in the East End of London. Professional and amateur theatre. 100-seat studio theatre.

Greenbelt
Festivals

Sue Plater or Nancy Butcher, The Greenhouse, St Luke's Church, Hillmarton Road, London, N7 9JE
T (0171) 700 6585 Tickets & Info (0171) 700 1335
F (0171) 700 5765
Annual Christian arts festival held over the August bank holiday weekend. Includes all artistic disciplines and over 80 seminars and workshops on politics, art, faith, etc.

Ice House
Christian
Centre

The Revd ET Carter, Victor Street, Grimsby, Lincs, DN32 7QN
T (01472) 349 917 F (01472) 349 244
800-seat concert hall, bookstore and resource centre, Bible World – a dramatic visual aid that makes the Bible come to life! Inc: a huge 26ft model of Israel.

Quinta
Conference
Facilities

Peter Bevington, Quinta Hall, Weston Rhyn, Oswestry,
Salop, SY10 7LR
T (01691) 773 696 F (01691) 774 687
Provide self-catering conference and holiday accommodation for Christian groups 10–240 (catering options available). Sports hall/theatre seating around 350.

The Nave

John Witcombe, The Nave at St Margaret's, Windsor Street,
Uxbridge, Middx, UB8 1AB
T (01895) 812 193 F (01895) 812 194
A church-based arts centre hosting a regular programme of events (speakers and performing arts), which contribute to the cultural and spiritual life of the community.

graphic design studios

AWM
Graphics

Richard Lackey, PO Box 4006, Worthing, W Sussex, BN13 1AP
T (01903) 215 345 F (01903) 215 456
E-mail 74674.631@compuserve.com
AWM Graphics use their graphics, multi-media and computer skills and resources to aid organisations and national churches in outreach to Muslims of the Arab world.

Bridge
Communica-
tion & Design

Simon P Baker, 1 Redland Way, Aylesbury, Bucks, HP21 7RJ
T (01296) 434 143 Mobile (0374) 937 348
Illustration, photography and graphics. Specialising in AV presentation using multimedia.

Callister
Communica-
tions Ltd

John Callister, 88 Causeway End Road, Lisburn,
Co Antrim, BT28 2ED
T (01846) 673 717 F (01846) 673 652
A film, TV, video production and facility company established in 1990 by former BBC film editor/producer. Beta SP crews and Avid off/on-line editing.

Campsie Litho
Ltd

Norman McNeish, 51 French Street, Glasgow, G66 3JH
T (0141) 554 5225 F (0141) 556 3459
We offer a one-stop service from graphic design to production of leaflets, booklets, brochures and books.

Lifestyle Designs
Carleton David Watts, The Studio, No. 1 Myrtle Hill, off Tyn-y-Bonau Road, Pontardulais, Swansea, SA4 1RS
T (01792) 884 758 F (01792) 884 758
E-mail 101620,1404@compuserve.com
'Visionary/creative' artwork for CD, cassette, video covers, including computer-designed graphics and professional illustration. Also production of high quality T-shirts and promotional product.

Nuprint
Joanne Butler, 30b Station Road, Harpenden, Herts, AL5 4SE
T (01582) 713 133 F (01582) 461 552
Graphic design, colour reproduction, electronic imaging and print production of brochures, books, catalogues, magazines, reports and accounts, corporate productions and promotional literature.

Pinnacle Creative
Chris Wisdom, 17 Clarendon Villas, Hove, E Sussex, BN3 3RE
T (01273) 821 887 F (01273) 770 878
E-mail 100755.2121@compuserve.com
We are a graphic design and video production company working with a variety of Christian and secular artists on commercial and non-commercial projects.

Positive Design
Martyn Brown, 25 Elm Road, Stroud, Glos, GL5 4NU
T / F (01453) 765 727
We WILL make the difference for your marketing campaign. Corporate ID, marketing and promotional material, direct mail, exhibitions and advertising. Design, print and project management.

Wingfinger
Bill Phelps, 15 Queen Square, Leeds, LS2 8AJ
T (0113) 245 0469 F (0113) 244 4688
E-mail bill@wfinger.demon.co.uk
22 years of design and print. Clients include: Tear Fund, Riding Lights, CPAS, Anglican Renewal Ministries and over 80 major university and town missions.

management / agencies

Bible Society
Robin Noad, Stonehill Green, Westlea, Swindon, Wilts, SN5 7DG
T (01793) 418 100 F (01793) 418 118 E-mail noadr@bfbs.org.uk
Bible Society is committed to enabling the Church to engage with and develop understanding of Scripture through the creative arts within contemporary culture.

Christian Arts Promotion Ltd Glastonbury
Catherine Van Zoen, CAP Booking Office, 15 Meadow Close, Street, Somerset, BA16 0UD
T (01454) 319447 F (01454) 319447
Gospel promotion through Christian performing artists. Concerts throughout the South West, our main festival is on the 3rd Saturday of July in Glastonbury.

Connections Personal Management Ltd

David Bemment, PO Box 1941, Dunmow, Essex, CM6 1YP
T (01371) 874 544 F (01371) 874 544
E-mail 106066.3276@compuserve.com
Management agency for professional Christian entertainers including Cannon & Ball, Paul Jones, Mary Millar, Pam Rhodes, Dana and many more.

Crystal Sound Gospel Concerts

Gordon Tyerman, 13 Oakwood Gardens, Knaphill, Woking, Surrey, GU21 2RX
T (01483) 488 972
Contemporary Christian concert promotion and advice for those people setting up in concert promotion.

DIO – Dominion International Opera

David Ashmore-Turner, PO Box 62, Woodford Green, Essex, IG9 5NY
T (0181) 281 0318 E-mail turner75A@delphi.com
DIO is a new interdenominational Christian charitable trust which aims to reach people with the gospel using the medium of opera. The work of DIO has been enthusiastically received by Christian leaders and professional artists alike, as it bridges a gap between Church and community in an exciting and stimulating way.

Mission through Music

Colin Woodcock, PO Box 6, Prudhoe, Northd, NE42 6YY
T (01661) 831 030 Mobile 0973 919 477 F (01661) 831 030
Mission Through Music is a registered charity. We arrange, organise and co-ordinate Christian concerts, conferences and seminars in the north-east region. We support music and teaching ministries in this country and abroad.

Shorehill Arts

Nick Page, Thatched Cottage, Otford Hills, Sevenoaks, Kent, TN15 6XL
T (01959) 523 740 Mobile 0410 295 332 F (01959) 525 011
E-mail nickpage@xc.org
Management of events, tours, conferences, concerts, dramatic presentations,'one-person' shows, multi-media Bible conferences. Work includes 1997 'Adrian Plass alternative Christmas Party' – London. 1998 'Surprised by Joy' – international tour.

Visual Ministries

Junior Spence, 82 Nevill Road, Stoke Newington, London, N16 0SX
T (0171) 241 1901 or (0956) 559 729 F (0171) 241 1901
An organisation specialising in the promotion of British gospel music. Founded in 1990, it has long been established as one of the top gospel organisations in the UK in the field of music promotion, artists management and general consultancy.

miscellaneous

Ampleforth Youth Net-Work (AYNW)
David Wright, 25 Coney Grey Spinney, Flintham, Nr Newark, Notts, NG23 5LN
T (01636) 525 176
We are an open community of charismatic Christians founded in the Catholic tradition. We hope our prayer/music days will enrich your life in Jesus.

Angel Studios
Linda Pettican, 7 Angel Studios, Armitage Bridge Mills, Huddersfield, Yorkshire, HD4 7NR
T (01484) 667 777
1. Art Courses – full year programme of weekly classes – e.g. water colour, mixed media. 2. Prophetic arts – Christian artists exploring the prophetic in painting, music etc.

Peter Bye
14 Avenue Elmers, Surbiton, Surrey, KT6 4SF
T (0181) 390 5896
Musical consultant. Career has spanned such diverse work as writing for, and conducting, the Royal Philharmonic Orchestra and accompanying, in cabaret, the world yo-yo champion.

Catholic Communications Centre
39 Eccleston Square, London, SW1V 1BX
T (0171) 233 8196 F (0171) 931 7497
The CCC provides a national resource for the local church in England and Wales. It offers training and production facilities to enable Catholics and other Christians to communicate effectively through the media. Training includes: radio, TV, public speaking, journalism, etc.

Christian Copyright Licensing Ltd
Chris Williams, PO Box 1339, Eastbourne, E Sussex, BN21 4YF
T (01323) 417 711 F (01323) 417 722
E-mail 100631.364@compuserve.com
Issues the copyright licence for churches, schools and organisations giving instant access to reproduce the words of 120,000 hymns and worship songs from 1,200 catalogues for non-commercial purposes.

Christian Dance Fellowship of Britain
Angela Courtney, 25 Scardale Crescent, Scarborough, N Yorkshire, YO12 6LA
T (01723) 377 320 F (01723) 503 399
CDFB promotes Christian religion through the ministry and art of dance, to glorify God and extol Jesus.

Crystal Sound Gospel Concerts
Gordon Tyerman, 13 Oakwood Gardens, Knaphill, Woking, Surrey, GU21 2RX
T (01483) 488 972
Contemporary Christian concert promotion and advice for those people setting up in concert promotion.

Alastair Cutting
Alastair Cutting, St John's Vicarage, Church Road, Copthorne, Crawley, W Sussex, RH10 3RD
T (01342)712 063 F (01342) 712 063
E-mail alastair@cutting.sonnet.co.uk
Anglican minister and arts and media enthusiast. Alastair ran The Nave for 5 years. Involved in pastoral support of artists, and theological basis for arts in the Church. Synths, keyboard player.

Revd William C Denning
William Denning, Maypole Farm, Thornbury, Bristol, BS12 1LE
T (01454) 411 133 E-mail 106411.1613@compuserve.com
Methodist minister; runs creativity workshops related to spirituality, worship, growth, using a multi-media approach.

The Digital Audio Co
Dave Aston & Jon Blamire, 3 Carleton Business Park, Skipton, N Yorkshire, BD23 2AA
T (01756) 797 100 F (01756) 797 101
Established editing and mastering facility run by Christians. Can arrange CD manufacture. Specialists in audio from location to post-production at broadcast standard. We have worked with James, D:ream, Level 42, Grimethorpe Colliery Band, New English Orchestra. Work on 'Thief Takers', 'Famous Five', documentaries for TV. Audio post-production for television at broadcast standard. Recently involved with 'The Governor', 'Famous 5', 'Touch of Frost' and various documentaries for ITV and C4.

Emprint
Mr KB Empett, 9 Harbour Street, Whitstable, Kent, CT5 1AG
T (01227) 274 952
General printers specialising in Christian work including magazines and books. Established over 25 years.

Free Copyright Commission
Mr C McVie, 1 Oldersham Mews, Maidenhead, Berks, SL6 5HB
T (01628) 33011 F (01628) 784 157
E-mail 100700.3553@compuserve.com
Churches and artists in UK and EEC. Publishing, printing, recording, filming, etc. free of any restrictions, 'God gives freely', let's copy, right!

Genesis Arts Trust
Nigel Goodwin, Gary Collins, Lisa Vallance, 6 Broad Court, Covent Garden, London, WC2B 5QZ
T (0171) 240 6980 F (0171) 240 6973
GAT exist to encourage the integration of faith, art and life. We give lectures, run workshops, artists' breakfasts, student meetings and one-to-one counselling and support.

Greenbelt Festivals
Sue Plater or Nancy Butcher, The Greenhouse, St Luke's Church, Hillmarton Road, London, N7 9JE
T (0171) 700 6585 Tickets & Info. (0171) 700 1335
F (0171) 700 5765
Annual Christian arts festival held over the August bank holiday weekend. Includes all artistic disciplines and over 80 seminars and workshops on politics, art, faith, etc.

Northumbria Bible College
Dr D Smith, 52 Castle Terrace, Berwick Upon Tweed, Northd, TD15 1PA
T (01289) 306 190 F (01289) 306 190
A training college focusing on mission in the modern world with particular options for reflection on the interface between theology and the arts.

Michael Paterson
24 Adamsrill Close, Faversham Avenue, Enfield, Middx, EN1 2BP
T (0181) 360 8898
Artist/conservator: have cleaned pictures in churches, a convent and St Alban's Cathedral. Exhibited in the provinces and at the Alpine Club, London 1994. Freelance lecturer, National Trust etc.

Penny Phillips
Penny Phillips, 44 Craneford Way, Twickenham, Middx, TW2 7SE
T (0181) 892 9302 F (0181) 744 9396
All aspects of training in communication skills and voice care. One-to-one and group sessions with speakers, actors, etc. Consciously clear caring communication is fun!

Rodger – A division of ROLAND (UK) Ltd
Sean Montgomery, Atlantic Close, Swansea, SA7 9FS
T (01792) 702 701 F (01792) 799 644
E-mail 100067.3415@compuserve.com
From single manual to four manual digital organs to classic keyboards, Rodger's classical organs can offer a musical instrument for every situation and budget.

Sue Shepherd
Thornfield, 3 Lee Road, Heptonstall Road, Hebden Bridge, W Yorkshire, HX7 6BB
T (01422) 844 657
I repair and service brass and woodwind musical instruments, as well as mechanical keyboards and percussion such as harmoniums. American organs and xylophones. (Not ordinary pianos or drum kits!)

Theology Through the Arts
Jeremy Begbie, Ridley Hall, Cambridge, CB3 9HG
T (01223) 741 072 F (01223) 741 079 E-mail jb215@cam.ac.uk
TTTA aims to discover and demonstrate ways in which the arts can contribute a) towards a renewal of Christian theology, b) to a sensitive and rigorous engagement of Church and culture and c) to generate new methods of Christian education for use in the Church and the wider community.

Ian Traynar
54 Ravenswood Road, Redland, Bristol, BS6 6BT
T (0117) 924 3770 E-mail iancma@cix.compulink.co.uk
Speaker and facilitator on the subject of arts/artists and a Christian world view – a new and revolutionary counter-culture!

UCCF Arts/Media Relay Worker Project
Mike Gough, UCCF London Office, c/o YMCA Regional Office, 16–22 Great Russell Street, London, WC1B 3LR
T (0171) 255 1443 F (0171) 255 1443
E-mail 101444.3347@compuserve.com
This project supports and encourages Christian arts/media students working in an area which rejects God set against a Christianity that doesn't understand creativity. Organises gatherings (Interface), exhibitions, workshops, retreats.

Vineyard Christian Fellowship
Max Carpenter, 'Shalom', Alexandra Road, Crediton, Devon, EX17 2DP
T (01363) 773 957
New fellowship; strong 'feel' for and appeal to the arts (fine & performing). Many in church with performance experience/training in dance/TV/production/writing.

music publishing companies

CN Productions
Christopher Norton, 5 Little Way, Moortown, Leeds, LS17 6JN
T (0113) 269 3930 F (0113) 266 2075
E-mail 100275,366@compuserve.com
CN Productions is a music production company, with publishing and licensing as important adjuncts to its main activities. Midi data and television music also.

RtH Publishing Ltd
Cid Latty, 13 Paget Road, Wolverhampton, W Midlands, WV6 0DS
T (01902) 310 360 F (01902) 310 360
RtH Publishing provides copyright protection especially for worship songwriters; demo recording appraisals and music publishing information and help.

music tutorial / workshops

Chime
Mr RJ Hubbard, 16 Straight Road, Lexden, Colchester, Essex, CO3 5BT
T (01206) 564 216 F (01206) 560 014
E-mail 100420.244@compuserve.com
CHIME works in an ecumenical framework to foster co-operation between organisations involved in training and resourcing church musicians, and to make information available to the public.

Christian Dance Fellowship of Britain
Angela Courtney, 25 Scardale Crescent, Scarborough, N Yorkshire, YO12 6LA
T (01723) 377 320 F (01723) 503 399
CDFB promotes Christian religion through the ministry and art of dance, to glorify God and extol Jesus.

Christian Music Ministries
Gloria Close, 325 Bromford Road, Hodge Hill, Birmingham, B36 8ET
T (0121) 783 3291 F (0121) 785 0500 E-mail roger@cmm.org.uk
Christian Music Ministries resource churches, schools, bookshops and individuals through teaching, leading workshops, musicals, courses and mail order catalogue; dealing with publishing, recording and marketing of Roger Jones' music.

CN Productions
Christopher Norton, 5 Little Way, Moortown, Leeds, LS17 6JN
T (0113) 269 3930 F (0113) 266 2075
E-mail 100275,366@compuserve.com
CN Productions is a music production company, with publishing and licensing as important adjuncts to its main activities. Midi data and television music also.

Clive Davenport
35 Portland Crescent, Longsight, Manchester, M13 0BU
T (0161) 224 0764
Musician/evangelist. Digital recording studio with sync to video (opening end of 1996). Small 1kW PA system and lights. Training in music technology, worship, performance, etc.

The Harmony Trust
David Williams, Harmony House, 23 Marnham Road, Torquay, Devon, TQ1 3QW
T (01803) 324 850
Harmony is available for advice/information on music in worship and to share in worship events/services, mainly in the South Devon area.

Chris & Linda Mitchell
3 Delamere Road, Earley, Reading, RG6 1AP
T (01734) 267 754 F (01734) 267 754
E-mail cmitchell@worldscope.net
Worship leading training resource. We've led gatherings from 10 to 1,500 people here and abroad. Workshops/seminars: creativity; arts and prophecy; singing; musical skills.

NET School of Ministry
Tom Gould, Wirral Christian Centre, Leasowe Road, Moreton, Wirral, Merseyside, L46 3RE
T (0151) 605 1240 F (0151) 606 0051
Bible college with a particular emphasis on teaching within the area of creative arts. Major subjects: music/worship, drama/dance. Electives: singing, creative writing.

Vineyard School of Worship
John de Jong, PO Box 490, Manchester, M60 1ET
T (0161) 834 9565 F (0161) 839 7667
E-mail 101357.244@compuserve.com
Our aim is to provide training to equip people to become better worshippers. Initially we are concentrating on foundational courses (theology, values and practices) combined with practical courses to build up musical skills.

production companies

CVG Television
Andy Price, First House, 1 Sutton Street, Birmingham, B1 1PE
T (0121) 622 1337 F (0121) 622 3080
E-mail 101501.2752@compuserve.com
Christian production company with over ten years' experience in all forms of programme making. Ring for brochure or free advice.

Callister Communica- tions Ltd
John Callister, 88 Causeway End Road, Lisburn,
Co Antrim, BT28 2ED
T (01846) 673 717 F (01846) 673 652
A film, TV, video production and facility company established in 1990 by former BBC film editor/producer. Beta SP crews and Avid off/on-line editing.

Clearwater Communica- tions
Don Sanders, 163 Marshall Lake Road, Solihull,
W Midlands, B90 4RB
T (0121) 744 3122 Mobile (0378) 502 243 F (0121) 744 1722
Production of evangelistic video/tv programmes, including reconstructed testimonies and children's stories for TV and video cassette distribution in UK and Europe.

CN Productions
Christopher Norton, 5 Little Way, Moortown, Leeds, LS17 6JN
T (0113) 269 3930 F (0113) 266 2075
E-mail 100275,366@compuserve.com
CN Productions is a music production company, with publishing and licensing as important adjuncts to its main activities. Midi data and television music also.

CrossView Audio Visual
Terry Smith, PO Box 22, Felixstowe, Suffolk, IP11 9EU
T (01394) 270 110 F (01394) 270 110
E-mail CROSSVIEW@compuserve.com
The production of top quality videos for evangelism – particularly for those on a tight budget.

The Digital Audio Co
Dave Aston & Jon Blamire, 3 Carleton Business Park, Skipton,
N Yorkshire, BD23 2AA
T (01756) 797 100 F (01756) 797 101
Established editing and mastering facility run by Christians. Can arrange CD manufacture. Specialists in audio from location to post production at broadcast standard. We have worked with James, D:ream, Level 42, Grimethorpe Colliery Band, New English Orchestra. Work on 'Thief Takers', 'Famous Five', documentaries for TV.

Forward Vision Communica- tions Ltd
David Furmage, 10 Claverdon Close, Solihull, W Midlands, B91 1QP
T (0121) 711 7500 Mobile (0585) 949 900 F (0121) 711 7600
E-mail action@forwardvision.co.uk
Producing videos and multi-media content for Christian organisations of ALL sizes: promotional, music, youth, training, evangelism, conference inserts. Clients: Operation Mobilisation, Bible Society, CPAS, Bill Drake, Nelson Word, Coventry Diocese.

International Films
Nigel Cooke, PO Box 201, West Malling, Kent, ME19 5RS
T (01732) 874 784 F (01732) 874 785 E-mail interfilm@aol.com
Film and video producer of own. Commissions ONLY. Offices of CEVMA (Christian European Visual Media Association).

Lamplight Productions
Mark Howe, 3C Horton View, Banbury, Oxon, OX16 9HP
T (01295) 275 708
Production and crewing for broadcast and other video projects. In-house facilities comprise standard and widescreen betacam shooting.

Pathway Productions
Laurence Wareing, 22 Colinton Road, Edinburgh, EH10 5EQ
T (0131) 447 3531 Mobile (0831) 618 633 F (0131) 452 8745
E-mail pathway@dial.pipex.com
Video and audio production company specialising in religious and charitable programming. Many years' experience. TV studio/edit suite and sound studio/control room available. Professional and friendly crew. Competitive rates.

Right Way Up
John Renfrew, 18 While Road, Sutton Coldfield, B72 1ND
T (0121) 355 5439 F (0121) 321 2359
E-mail rwu@compuserve.com
Slides, computer graphics and production. Management for tours and events. Need someone to pull off your grand idea?

Sarner International Ltd
Studios: Sharon McDowell, Sales: David Dempsey, 32 Woodstock Grove, London, W12 8LE
T (0181) 743 1288 F (0181) 749 7699
Sarner is a specialist audio-visual systems and presentations company which also operates recording studios and post-production facilities. 25-year track record, clients worldwide.

Sound Supplement
Nick Page, Thatched Cottage, Otford Hills, Sevenoaks, Kent, TN15 6XL
T (01959) 523 740 Mobile (0410) 295 332
F (01959) 525 011 E-mail nickpage@xc.org
Independent radio producer – features, interviews, religious news, quizzes. Work has included London Broadcasting Co, Premier Radio, various BBC and Independent local radio, Christian stations.

South Asian Concern
Deepak Mahtani, PO Box 43, Sutton, Surrey, SM2 5WL
T (0181) 770 9717 F (0181) 770 9747
E-mail 100126.3641@compuserve.com
SAC produces worship music that is culturally relevant and enables South Asians to worship Jesus Christ.

Tandem TV & Film Ltd
Terry Page, 10 Fargrove Avenue, Hemel Hempstead, Herts, HP1 1QP
T (01442) 61576 F (01442) 219 250
Production of films and videos for Christian and corporate clients.

Telling Pictures   David Martin or Peter Cockburn, 6 Waitemeads, Purton,
Nr Swindon, Wilts, SN5 9ET
T (01793) 770 171 Mobile 0836 556 509 F (01793) 770 171
Specialists in quality religious and educational programmes for video distribution and broadcast. Strong track record. International awards.

record companies

B & H Sound Services   Ian Dunkley, The Old School Studio, Growland Road, Eye,
Peterborough, PE6 7TN
T (01733) 223 535 F (01733) 223 545
Sound and recording facilities for conferences, shows, concerts and roadshows. Fully equipped 24-track recording studio and on location recording facilities.

CN Productions   Christopher Norton, 5 Little Way, Moortown, Leeds, LS17 6JN
T (0113) 269 3930 F (0113) 266 2075
E-mail 100275,366@compuserve.com
CN Productions is a music production company, with publishing and licensing as important adjuncts to its main activities. Midi data and television music also.

Funky Monk Music   Mr R Gregory, 67 Shaw Green Lane, Prestbury, Cheltenham,
Glos, GL52 3BS
T (01242) 526 002
Funky Monk Music is a record company which releases Christian dance music (e.g. house, techno, garage, rave, etc.) for use in worshipping God.

Newid Record Label   Mark Lowe, 27 Great Western Terrace, Llanelli, Dyfed SA15 2ND
T (01554) 750 276 F By request (01554) 750 276
E-mail 100654.1070@compuserve.com
A record label resourcing the Church to worship in both English and Welsh and to promote Welsh talent within the nation.

Plankton Records   Simon Law, 236 Sebert Road, Forest Gate, London, E7 0NP
T (0181) 534 8500
Christian record company for 'Fresh Claim' and other evangelistic artists.

South Asian Concern   Deepak Mahtani, PO Box 43, Sutton, Surrey, SM2 5WL
T (0181) 770 9717 F (0181) 770 9747
E-mail 100126.3641@compuserve.com
SAC produces worship music that is culturally relevant and enables South Asians to worship Jesus Christ.

recording studios

Ark Studio
John J Staff, 42 Alexandra Road, Ashingdon, Rochford, SS4 3HD
T (01702) 544 881 F (01702) 544 881
A small studio with basic facilities. Ideal for talks/interviews and duos.

CN Productions
Christopher Norton, 5 Little Way, Moortown, Leeds, LS17 6JN
T (0113) 269 ?930 F (0113) 266 2075
E-mail 100275 366 @ compuserve.com
CN Productions is a music production company, with publishing and licensing as important adjuncts to its main activities. Midi data and television music also.

Clive Davenport
35 Portland Crescent, Longsight, Manchester, M13 0BU
T (0161) 224 C764
Musician/evangelist. Digital recording studio with sync to video. Small 1kW PA system and lights. Training in music technology, worship, performance, etc.

The Digital Audio Co
Dave Aston & Jcn Blamire, 3 Carleton Business Park, Skipton, N Yorkshire, BD23 2AA. T (01756) 797 100 F (01756) 797 101
Established editing and mastering facility run by Christians. Can arrange CD manufacture. Specialists in audio from location to post-production at broadcast standard. We have worked with James, D:ream, Level 42, Grimethorpe Colliery Band, New English Orchestra. Work on 'Thief Takers', 'Famous Five', documentaries for TV.

Eastside Studio
Dave Keegan, please phone in first instance, Hull, East Yorks
T (01482) 807 512
16-track studio including top of the range sequencing facility. Ideal for rock, pop, dance, solo or spoken word.

ffg
David Pick, Bredow Fields, Elkington Road, Bredon, Tewkesbury, GL20 7HE
T (01684) 772 664 F (01684) 772 902
Recording studio, residential in country location. Record and audio-visual post-production. Music composition and production.

Simon Jones
31 Henthorn Road, Clitheroe, Lancs, BB7 2LD
T (01200) 442 245 Mobile 0973 625 665 F (01200) 442 245
E-mail capelin@argonet.co.uk. Web http://argonet.co.uk/capelin
Freelance broadcast sound recordist, also offering complete CD and cassette album record and manufacture service for any musical genre in studio or on location.

KSM Recording Studios
Ken Smith, 89 Carrick Knowe Avenue, Edinburgh, EH12 7DE
T (0131) 315 2118
16-track studio, 2 music rooms and large control room. Recording facilities, in-house production and session work provided, coffee and Jaffa Cakes.

Lime Tree Studios
Stephen Pitkethly, Lime Tree Barn, Welgate, Mattishall, Dereham, Norfolk, NR20 3PJ
T (01362) 858 015 F (01362) 858 016 E-mail limetree@paston.co.uk
Professional studio with 24-track analogue. Sadie digital editing/ mastering. Macintosh logic sequencing. Large live area. Rest room with kitchen. Large garden. Residential. Countryside setting. Call for brochure.

Pathway Productions
Laurence Wareing, 22 Colinton Road, Edinburgh, EH10 5EQ
T (0131) 447 3531 F (0131) 452 8745
E-mail pathway@dial.pipex.com
Video and audio production company specialising in religious and charitable programming. Many years' experience. TV studio/edit suite and sound studio/control room available. Professional and friendly crew. Competitive rates.

Reelife Recordings
Phil Burt, Laverick Hall, Halton, Lancaster, LA2 6PH
T (01524) 811 282 F (01524) 811 959
Specialist in conference, convention recording and duplication. PA installation, 16-track studio, supply of audio equipment, cassette copiers, blank and copied cassettes.

Sarner International Ltd
Studios: Sharon McDowell, Sales: David Dempsey, 32 Woodstock Grove, London, W12 8LE
T (0181) 743 1288 F (0181) 749 7699
Sarner is a specialist audio visual systems and presentations company which also operates recording studios and post-production facilities. 25-year track record, clients worldwide.

Scripture Union Sound & Vision Unit
Mike Jiggins, 207–209 Queensway, Bletchley, Milton Keynes, Bucks, MK2 2EB
T (01908) 856 000 Mobile 0378 152 246 F (01908) 856 111
E-mail mikej@scriptureunion.org.uk
Scripture Union produce Christian audio and video programmes primarily as resource materials for church and other groups, and individuals. They can also provide a production service for other Christian organisations.

scenery set production and hire

Sarner International Ltd
Studios: Sharon McDowell, Sales: David Dempsey, 32 Woodstock Grove, London, W12 8LE
T (0181) 743 1288 F (0181) 749 7699
Sarner is a specialist audio-visual systems and presentations company which also operates recording studios and post-production facilities. 25-year track record, clients worldwide.

sound and lighting hire

ARM – Audio & Recording Ministries
Anthony Hubble, 79 Haycroft Drive, Gloucester, GL4 6XX
T (01452) 418 418 Mobile 0378 999 980 F (01452) 418 418
Live PA and/or recording for concerts, conferences. A complete audio service for churches, Christian organisations, musicians. Suppliers of sound installations and hearing aid loop systems.

B & H Sound Services
Ian Dunkley, The Old School Studio, Growland Road, Eye, Peterborough, PE6 7TN
T (01733) 223 535 F (01733) 223 545
Sound and recording facilities for conferences, shows, concerts and roadshows. Fully equipped 24-track recording studio and on location recording facilities.

B & H Sound Services – Northern
Andy Baker, Aizlewoods Mill, Nursery Street, Sheffield, S3 8GG
T (0114) 282 3152 F (0114) 282 3179
Provision of PA, lighting, staging, etc., for audiences of 20 to 20,000+, hire or installation. Ring for free quotes at competitive prices.

Creative Audio
John Ellis, 170 Holly Road, Aldershot, Hants, GU12 4SG
T (01252) 343 840 F (01252) 343 840
We are a small, friendly, professional, experienced Christian staff. Advice/sales of pro audio equipment. Established over 15 years yet we still enjoy rock 'n roll! (And most other music forms).

Crystal Clear Audio
Michael Webb, 141a Downham Road, Islington, London, N1 3HQ
T (01923) 445 918
Crystal Clear Audio exists to serve Christian organisations principally by providing high quality sound amplification with competent engineers at an affordable price.

Clive Davenport
35 Portland Crescent, Longsight, Manchester, M13 0BU
T (0161) 224 0764
Musician/evangelist. Digital recording studio with sync to video. Small 1kW PA system and lights. Training in music technology, worship, performance, etc.

Edenfield Communications
Michael Jakins, 2 South View Place, Midsomer Norton, Bath, BA3 2AX
T (01761) 414 992 F (01761) 411 805
E-mail michael@donns.telme.com
Edenfield Communications specialise in the hire or permanent installation of sound systems for all public events, especially in churches or other Christian events. Outdoor events a speciality.

LSS – Lighting & Sound Services
Phil Johnson, 'Ashfield', 126 Chester Road, Helsby, Cheshire, WA6 0QS
T (01928) 723 502 F (01928) 725 012
Sound, lighting and staging for sales and hire. Complete packages for conferences and missions.

Re: creation Sound Ltd Mark Trigg, 107 Stanstead Road, Forest Hill, London, SE23 1HH
T (0181) 699 6000 Mobile 0973 381 917 F (0181) 291 6764
E-mail re_creation=sound@compuserve.com
Provider of a professional sound service, including hire, sales, training and advice. We cater for events of all sizes, conferences, music and theatre.

Sarner International Ltd Studios: Sharon McDowell, Sales: David Dempsey,
32 Woodstock Grove, London, W12 8LE
T (0181) 743 1288 F (0181) 749 7699
Sarner is a specialist audio-visual systems and presentations company which also operates recording studios and post-production facilities. 25-year track record, clients worldwide.

Seal Christian Arts Resources Michael Clements, 66 Connaught Road, Fleet, Hants, GU13 9QY
T (01252) 628 451 Mobile 0378 168 843
We design, hire, install and operate lighting (up to 80kW) and sound systems (up to 6kW) plus special effects for all types of arts events.

Solar Sound Keith Thom, 125 Brediland Road, Linwood, Paisley,
Renfrewshire, PA3 3RX
T (01505) 320 765 Mobile 0585 726 626
PA hire for live music events/rallies or youth services.

WorldWide Christian Productions Ltd Ian Lidstone, Elmleigh, Back Lane, Kingston Seymour,
Bristol, BS21 6UZ
T (01275) 342 728 or (0802) 312 544 F (01275) 340 144
WWCP is a Christian-based company very much in the mainstream of the professional sound and lighting business. Our recent experience has brought us contracts with people like: Vauxhall, Mercedes-Benz, David Bellamy, ECO '95, Ray Bevan and Barratt Homes.

tv / film / video recording studios

CVG Television Andy Price, First House, 1 Sutton Street, Birmingham, B1 1PE
T (0121) 622 1337 F (0121) 622 3080
E-mail 101501.2752@compuserve.com
Christian production company with over ten years' experience in all forms of programme making. Ring for brochure or free advice.

Catholic Communica- tions Centre 39 Eccleston Square, London, SW1V 1BX
T (0171) 233 8196 F (0171) 931 7497
The CCC provides a national resource for the local church in England and Wales. It offers training and production facilities to enable Catholics and other Christians to communicate effectively through the media. Training includes: radio, TV, public speaking, journalism, etc.

CN Productions

Christopher Norton, 5 Little Way, Moortown, Leeds, LS17 6JN
T (0113) 269 3930 F (0113) 266 2075
E-mail 100275,366@compuserve.com
CN Productions is a music production company, with publishing and licensing as important adjuncts to its main activities. Midi data and television music also.

Coburn Television Productions

Peter Coburn, 20 Quantock House, Fore Street, North Petherton, Bridgwater, Somerset, TA6 6TN
T (01278) 663 498 Mobile 0836 556 509 F (01278) 663 498
Betacam SP component 2D, 3D editorial facilities. Beta SP shooting, crews, directors and producers. Discounted rates for Christian and charitable projects. Work includes: broadcast, satellite, charities, Christian, corporate, educational + conference.

Forward Vision Communications Ltd

David Furmage, 10 Claverdon Close, Solihull, W Midlands, B91 1QP
T (0121) 711 7500 / Mobile: (0585) 949 900 F (0121) 711 7600
E-mail action@forwardvision.co.uk
Producing videos and multi-media content for Christian organisations of ALL sizes: promotional, music, youth, training, evangelism, conference inserts. Clients: Operation Mobilisation, Bible Society, CPAS, Bill Drake, Nelson Word, Coventry Diocese.

Lamplight Productions

Mark Howe, 30 Horton View, Banbury, Oxon, OX16 9HP
T (01295) 275 708
Production and crewing for broadcast and other video projects. In-house facilities comprise standard and widescreen betacam shooting.

Pathway Productions

Laurence Wareing, 22 Colinton Road, Edinburgh, EH10 5EQ
T (0131) 447 3531 F (0131) 452 8745
E-mail pathway@dial.pipex.com
Video and audio production company specialising in religious and charitable programming. Many years' experience. TV studio/edit suite and sound studio/control room available. Professional and friendly crew. Competitive rates.

Pinnacle Creative

Chris Wisdom, 17 Clarendon Villas, Hove, E Sussex, BN3 3RE
T (01273) 821 887 F (01273) 770 878
E-mail 100755.2121@compuserve.com
We are a graphic design and video production company working with a variety of Christian and secular artists on commercial and non-commercial projects.

The Digital Audio Co

Dave Aston & Jon Blamire, 3 Carleton Business Park, Skipton, N Yorkshire, BD23 2AA
T (01756) 797 100 F (01756) 797 101
Audio post-production for television at broadcast standard. Recently involved with 'The Governor', 'Famous 5', 'Touch of Frost' and various documentaries for ITV and C4.

Simon Jones

31 Henthorn Road, Clitheroe, Lancs, BB7 2LD
T (01200) 442 245 Mobile 0973 625 665 F (01200) 442 245
E-mail capelin@argonet.co.uk
Freelance broadcast sound recordist, also offering complete CD and cassette album record and manufacture service for any musical genre in studio or on location.

services

Share the vision

If you share **Arts in Mission's** vision there are three important ways in which you can be more closely involved.

1 Partnership schemes
The first is to support **Arts in Mission's** work financially. Through one of three partnership schemes, your gifts can further the production of the directory, help run conferences and retreats for artists, and enable artists who could not otherwise benefit to attend conferences or retreats.

- Why not become an **Encourager of Arts In Mission**? It's £25 + a year.
- Why not become a **Friend of Arts in Mission**? It's £100 + a year.
- Why not become a **Benefactor of Arts In Mission**? It's £1000 + a year.

2 Fund-raising and practical input
The second way you could be involved is by becoming a fund-raiser or offering a venue for **Arts in Mission** fund-raising events.

3 Prayer support
Essential support is needed, too, from people who will pray for **Arts in Mission's** members and ministry.

Through each type of involvement you could play a vital part in the growth of **Arts in Mission's** work. Please return the form to the address below to show the way(s) in which you would like to share the vision and increase Christian participation in and communication through the arts.

Please tick appropriate box(es):

1 Partnership schemes
I would like to become
[ ] an **Encourager of Arts in Mission** (£25+ a year)
[ ] a **Friend of Arts in Mission** (£100+ a year)
[ ] a **Benefactor of Arts in Mission** (£1000+ a year)
[ ] I would like to help an artist to attend a conference/retreat with a financial contribution
[ ] Please send me a covenant form
I enclose a cheque/postal order for £_____ made payable to Arts in Mission

2 Fund-raising and practical input
[ ] I would like to help with fund-raising
[ ] I am willing to offer a venue for fund-raising events
[ ] I am willing to offer my services as an artist to help with fund-raising

3 Prayer
[ ] I would like to support Arts in Mission in prayer

Name (Mr/Mrs/Miss/Ms/Revd/Dr_____

Address_____

_____

Postcode _____ Telephone _____

Fax _____ E-mail _____

Church_____

Like to know more?
Please send me more information about

_____

_____

Arts in Mission

Arts in Mission. 193A Norwood Road, Herne Hill, London SE24 9AF. E-mail: HermioneT@aol.com

A

A C Design 58
Acacia 68
ACG – Arts Centre Group Ltd 178, 184
Action Centres UK Ltd 182, 186
Adelaide's 182, 186
Agape 68
Aldous, Alex 156
Alexander, Paul 106
Alkazraji, Muthena Paul 124
Allen, Mary 117
Ally! 163
Ampleforth Youth Net-Work (AYNW) 184, 189
Anderson, Dudley 152
Andrews, Colin 163
Andrews, Nicola Ellis 60
Angel Studios 190
Anno Domini Designs 120
Ansell, Evelyn W P 134
Antcliff, Chris 145
Ark Studio 197
ARM – Audio & Recording Ministries 178, 181, 199
Armigate, Lyn 134
Armstrong, Bernie 163
Arnold, Gillian 156
Arts in Mission 178
As If... 68
Ash, Rob 68
Ashburnham Christian Trust 182
Ashmore-Turner, David 60
Ashton, Gill 106
Asylum 68
Atkins, Anne 117
Attwood, Lindsey 122
Au, Andy 98
Aura 156
Austin's Photography 141
AWM Graphics 187
Ayers, Janet 122
Ayling, Keith 68

B

B & H Sound Services – Northern 200
B & H Sound Services 196, 199
Babbs, Liz 98
Bailey, Jim (Kingdom Creative) 163
Bailey, Robert 134
Baker, Simon P 141
Baldry, Cherith 117
Ball, Linda 149
Ballantine, Olwen 134
Baly's Cream Jazz 69
Barclay, Ian 117
Barker, Ella 98
Barnard, Adrian 152
Barton, Trevor 149
Bate, Darrell 106
Beal, Karen 106
Beal, Steve 122
Beale, Robert 124
Beard, Gill 163
Bebb, Erica 98
Beehive 69
Berrett, Alison 134
Berry, Peter J 58
Bessem, Theo 69
Beswick, Kate 69
Betts, Pat 134

Bevon, Christopher 130
Beyond Jordan 164
Beyond the Barricades 99
Bible Society 188
Bicknell, Julia 124
Big Boss 69
'Big Jack' Kelly 70
Big Picture, The 70
Bijou Theatre 106
Bird, Fru 99
Blackman, Rob 70
Blackman, Sharon 156
Blaithwaite Christian Centre 183
Blaylock, David 164
Bloomer, Paul 134
Bluestone 70
Boddington, Mary 130
Boddington, Ruth 130
Bogle Band, The 70
Bollen, Philip 99
Bomber, Heidi 99
Bonnett, Caroline 70
Bonser, Jeff 152
Boot Brothers, The 71
Boote, Julian 159
Boulter, Russell 159
Bourne, Karen 130
Bowen, Eleanor 134
Bowman, John T 71
Bragg, Dr James 71
Bramall, Richard 159
Bran, Henry 71
Brand, Christine 60
Brassington, Peter 145
Brewin, Rebecca 130
Bridge Communication & Design 187
Bristow, Elizabeth Anne 164
Brittain, Paul 71
Brooke, Mark 134
Brooke, Ursula 135
Brown Bear Music 164
Brown, Robert 159
Bunn, Davis 117
Burman, Susan 151
Burns, David 130
Burr, Fiona 135
Burton, Jane 99
Bye, Peter 60, 190

C

Caiels, Janette 152
Callister Communications Ltd 179, 187, 194
Campbell, Janel 58
Campsie Litho Ltd 187
Capitaan 71
Carberry 183
Carpenter, Max 106
Carter, Jason 72
Carter, Philip 60
Cartledge, Sophy 60
Catholic Communications Centre 190, 201
Catley, Marc 72
Cavallini, Karen 143
Cavallini, Marc 143
Centre Stage 107
Chalmers-Brown, Elaine 107
Chance, Andy 72
Childs, Dave 164
Chime 193

Christian Arts Promotion Ltd
Glastonbury 188
Christian Banners 156
Christian Copyright Licensing Ltd 179, 181, 190
Christian Dance Fellowship of Britain 185, 190, 193
Christian Music Ministries 193
Clarke, Andrea 100
Clarke, C P 145
Clearwater Communications 194
Clelland, Tom 164
Clements, Michael 72
Cliff College Conference Complex 183
Clifford, Ann 143
Clinton, Graham 124
Clouts, Dan 135
Clownin'g Glory 65
CN Productions 179, 193, 195, 197, 201
Coburn Television Productions 201
Cohen-Stone, Gerry 107
Colbear, Kevin 58
Collett-White, Thomas 130
Colling, Brian 65
Collins, Hazel 145
Collins, Mike 141
Communiqué Design Associates 120
Connections Personal Management Ltd 188
Constant, Audrey 117
Conway, Jennifer 131
Cook, Alexander 72
Cook, Susan M 131
Cooke, Dave 73
Cooke, Jenny 117
Coomes, Anne 149
Costello, Jenni 124
Cottingham, Christine 61
Cotton, Iain 154
Covenant Players 107
Cox, Robert William 135
Cox, Susan 135
Crampin, Martin 131
CRE 8 100
Creative Audio 179, 200
Credo 165
Crew, Shiloh 73
Critchley, Paul Ian 165
Croft, Maggie/Alison Holmes 73
Crofts, Adrian 159
Crossfire 73
CrossView Audio Visual 179, 195
Crow, Gillian 124
Crowley, Martin 165
Crowther, Susanna 107
Cruickshank, Carol 100
Cruickshank, Neil 165
Crystal Clear Audio 200
Crystal Sound Gospel Concerts 189, 190
Cudby, Alison Eve 100
Cullen, Andy 73
Cullum, Andrew 107
Curry, Nick 117
Cuttill, Anita 73
Cutting, Alastair 131, 190
Cutts, Jeff and Susanne 74
CVG Television 179, 181, 194, 201

index

D

d.votion 166
Dakin, Paul 124
Dale, Carol 100
Daltry, Stephen 159
Dance for Christ (DFC) 101
Daniel, Geoffrey 145
Davenport, Clive 166, 197, 200
Davenport, Clive 179, 193
Davies, Judy 131
Davies, Kathryn Sarah 101
Dawe, Barbara 135
Dawning, Tracey 135
Day, Sally 160
December Blue 74
Deeks, Dave 74
Deliverance Ablaze 74
Dell, Gary 160
Denning, Revd William C 190
Diakonos Physical Theatre 108
Dick, Rose 108
Digital Audio Co, The
180, 191, 195, 198, 202
DIO – Dominion International
Opera 189
Discovery 74
Distant Light 75
Dock, Ian 127
Dominion International Opera 61
Douglas, Paul (Band) 75
Douglass, Heather 118
Downey, Jocelyn S 145
Downey, Olivia 135
DRIFT 108
Ducker, Deirdre 131
Ducker, Ruth 136
Dunamis Dance Company 101
Dunkerley, Chris 125
Dyer, Hilary 125

E

East, John 75
Eastside Studio 198
Eastwell, Patricia 156
Eaton, Judith 156
Edenfield Communications 180, 200
Elastic Band 166
Elfick, Hilary 146
Elle M Theatre Company 108
Ellel Ministries 183, 186
Elliott, Colin 75
Ellis, Beth 109
Ellis, Penelope 143
Ellsmore, Stuart A 61
Emery Theatre, The 186
Emmaus Road 75
Emprint 191
Endgame 75
English, Peter 109
English, Steve 122
Envoy 76
Essential Theatre Company 109
Euphoria 76
Evans, Malcolm 76
Eve and the Garden 76
Excursion 166
Eynon, John 58

F

Face to Face 76
Falkirk Christian Centre 183

Farthing, Ian 109
Fellowship of Christian Writers 178
ffg 198
FGOT (Fine Gentlemen of Trout) 77
Field, Marion 149
First Conference Estate plc 183
Five Gables Charitable Trust, The
185
Flannagan Andrew & Peter Ryan 77
Flashman, Steve 77
Flow 77
Flowers, Dave 166
Footprints Theatre Trust 109
Forde, Ben 160
Foreman, Bridget 109
Forman, Yvonne Anne 156
Forty, Elyse L 136
Forward Vision Communications Ltd
180, 181, 195, 202
4th Dimension 77
Francis, Catherine 78
Francis, Zafar 125
Free Copyright Commission 191
Fresh Claim 78
Funktion Junktion 78
Funky Monk Music 197

G

Gabbatiss, Jane 136
Gage, Faith C 146
Garden Music Duet 61
Gascoigne Palmer, Julia 136
Genesis Arts Trust 191
Gethsemane Rose 78
Gibson, Elizabeth 118
Gill, Yvonne 157
Givans, Ray 146
Glenfall House Trust 183
Glover, Phil 78
Gof The Clown 65
Goldmime 127
Goodwin, Marion Irene 146
Gordon 'Honky Tonk' Smith 92
Gough, Mike 141
grace 167
Graham, Sandra 61
Green, Colin 78
Green, Kate 136
Green, Mark Andrew 79
Greenbelt Festivals 186, 191
Greenwood, Derek 110
Gregory, Steve 79
Grieve, Philip 136
Griffin, Patricia M 131
Grimstad, Iver 167
Grosch, Mal 101
Grossmith, Revd Frederick 125

H

Haastrup, A 160
Hadler-Mayor, Candida 102
Hadley, Susan 154
Hagues, Robin 61
Hale, Colin T 136
Halsall, Martyn 125
Hampton, Roger 146
Hands + Feet Trust 110
Hardwick, John Creative
Communication 65
Harlow Causeway Drama Group
'Living Stones' 110
Harmony Trust, The 194

Harrington, Susanna 102
Haswell, Diana 157
Hathaway, Mary 149
Hathorne, Revd Carol 118
Havilland, Jean 141
Hawkins, Sam – Boo Designs Ltd
122
Haworth, Bryn 79
Haynes, Gerda – van der Bijl 136
Hays, Ruth 167
Heley, Veronica 118
Heming, David 79
Heming, Julian 167
Henderson, Angus 132
Henley, Janice 137
Hepburn, Graham 62
Hewitt, Garth 80
Heyman, Paul 167
Hilton, Julie-Ann 110
Hoare, Brian 168
Hobbs, Paul 137
Hodges, Nick 80
Hodgson, Ken 102
Hodgson, Ruth 157
HOG 80
Holburt, Phil 80
Holland, Peter 168
Holmes, Alison 62
Holt, Revd Stuart 151
Hopper, Keith 160
Hopwood, Lynn 122
Hothorpe Hall 183
Hughes, Sylvia Mary 102
Hymus, Chris 80

I

I'ons, Stephanie 122
Ice House Christian Centre 184, 186
Inreverse 80
Inside Out 81
International Films 195
IONA 81

J

Jack, William J 81
Jackson, Ira 168
Jacobs, Sheila 118
Jakes Ladder Theatre Company 110
James, Cynthia 137
James, Steve 81
Jasper, Tony 111
Jayne, Helen 81
Jireh.co.uk 120
JNR MACK 81
Jo and Matt 81
Jolly Jack the Clown & Emilé
the Mime 127
Jones, Paul – Associates 120
Jones, Simon 198
Jong, John de 82
Jubilee 82
Juggling John 128

K

Kane, Carole 157
Kato 82
Kettle of Fish Theatre 111
King, Amanda 157
King, Joe 82
Kirk, Dale 128
Kirkham, Jayne 144

KiS 82
Knowles, David 83
Knox, Jay 152
KSM Recording Studios 198

L

Label of Love 83
Lacey, Rob 111
Laird, Graham (Fine Furniture) 58
Lamplight Productions 195, 202
Langton, Andy 168
Latty, Cid 168
Latty, Geraldine A 168
Lawson Johnston, Philip 168
Lawson, Steve 83
Legg, Steve 65
Leokadia 137
Leonard, Christine 149
Lewis, Paul John 137
Lewis, Peter 169
Lewthwaite, Phil 169
Life-givers Puppet Theatre 151
Lifestyle Designs 182, 187
Lighthouse Christian Rock Band 83
Lime Tree Studios 198
Little People Puppets 151
Living Horns 83
Livingstones Dance 102
Lloyd Griffith, David 137
London Magnificat Orchestra 62
Longview Training & Video Services 180, 182
Loose Goose 84
Lord, Julie 84
Loring, Keith (Kit) 111
LSS – Lighting & Sound Services 200
Ludo the Clown (These Foolish Things) 66
Luff, Bradley 169
Lulubelle the Clown 66
Lunt, Rose 111

M

Mabbs, Louise 157
MacDonald, Shona 169
Maclure, Alison 169
Mae, Linda 112
Malaika Ministries 84
Mallon, Mary 154
Man, Jeanny 132
Mangan, Paul 154
Marbleous 154
Maries, Andrew 170
Marriott, Audrey 102
Marriott, Ian 170
Mart, Terry 137
Masterpiece Theatre Company 128
Mather, Revd William B G 138
May, Iain 84
McArthur, David 62
McCabe, Felix 84
McCahon, Peter D 66
McCalla, Howard 152
McGovern, Phil Andrews 147
Meer, Carolyn A 132
Meilak, Marlene 147
Menist, Chris 84
Message Graphics 120
Mid Wales Christian Holiday & Conference Centre 184
Mike & Jon 170
Miller, Bill 103

Millward, Peter N 138
Mimeistry – Todd & Marilyn Farley 128
Mission through Music 85, 189
Mitchell, Andrea 147
Mitchell, Chris & Linda 194
Mitchell, David (Morning Star Music) 85
Montgomery, Marion 85
Moore, Gill 103
Moran, Peter 170
Morris, David Lyle 85
Morris, Stephen 62
Morrison, Giles D 85
Mosaic Theatre 112
Moss, Katrina 161
Mudheads Monkey 85
Munro, Jean S 125

N

Nave, The 178, 187
Neilands, Lynda 132
Nelson, Steve 86
NET School of Ministry 184, 185, 194
Netherbow, The 132, 178
Network 170
Network Crafts 154
Network Music 170
Never on a Monday 86
New Creations 112
New Directions Theatre Company Ltd 112, 144
New Forest Fire 171
New Horizons Choir 171
New Jerusalem Dancers 103
Newby Entertainments 66
Newid Record Label 197
Newnham, Tony 63
Nia 86
Nishimura, Kyoko 138
No Limits 86
Norman, Steve 126
Norris, Christopher 161
Northumbria Bible College 191
Now, The 171
Nuffsed 86
Nuprint 188

O

O'Conor, Richard 171
Oak Hall, Otford Manor 184
Oasis 171
Ocracy, The 171
Oehler, Rosemarie 138
Oldham, Tom 138
One Way Ministries 112
Organised Chaos 87
Other Phil & Jon, The 87
Owen, Graham 87
Owen, Stephen 141

P

Page, Nick 161
Pantry, John 172
Parfitt, James R 138
Parsons, Benedict 141
Parsons, Steve 87
Paterson, Evangeline 147
Paterson, Michael 191

Pathway Productions 180, 195, 198, 202
Payne, Jan 172
Payton, Mark 113
PC+ 161
Pegler, Heidi 63
Pegler, Joanna 103
Penny, Stuart 87
Perkins, Julian A 172
Perry, John 87
Persson, John 129
Persuasion 88
Phillips, Penny 132
Phillips, Penny 192
Phillips, Sandy 103
Phoenix Performing Arts Trust 113
Pierson, Lance 113
Pilgrim 88
Pinnacle Creative 188, 202
Pinnington, Angela 172
Plankton Records 197
Poetic Justice 88
Pollitt, Graham A 153
Positive Design 188
Postema, Cassandra 157
Poulton, Paul 88
Pray Naked 88
PRISM (Praise In St Mary's) 172
Pullinger, Mark 59
Pure Silk 88
Pusey, Laurence 138

Q

Quinta Conference Facilities 184, 187

R

Radiators, The 89
Radius 185
Raine, Andy 104
Randell, Janet 104
Rann, Sue 118
Ratcliffe, Nigel 173
Rawe, Timothy 58
Rayne, Julie 89
RDA 89
Re: creation Sound Ltd 200
Ready to Assemble 157
Reed, Alan 139
Reelife Recordings 180, 182, 199
Reid, Paul & Sharon 89
Resurrection Theatre Co 113
Retallick, Debi – Textile Artist 158
Retallick, Jono – Artist 154
Return to Eden 89
Revelation 89
Rhee, Nanette Heather 139
Richards, Noel 90
Riches, Colin 155
Ridgley, Sandie 126
Riding Lights Theatre Company 113
Right Way Up 196
Rinaldi, Sue 90
Riols, Noreen 119
River 90
Roberts, Geoff & Judith 173
Roberts, Ian (Photography) 142
Roberts, Nicola 139
Robinson, Sandra – Boo Designs Ltd 147
Rochelle, Lea 113
Rodd & Marco 90

index

Rodger – A division of ROLAND
(UK) Ltd 192
Rodger, Elizabeth 63
Rogers, Andrew 173
'Rokey' the Clown 66
Roly 67
Rootes, Shane 90
Roper, Matt 142
Roquefort Duo 63
Rose, Lynda 119
Rosemary 173
Ross, Guy 147
Round, Peter James D 91
RtH Publishing Ltd 193
Rugby Methodist Praise & Worship
Band 174
Rumble, Coral 147
Rumours are True, The 91
Russell, Joan 174

S
S'dANCE 174
Saffery, Michael (Act for Christ) 114
Sampson, Fay 119
Sanctuary 174
Sarner International Ltd
180, 196, 199, 200
Sawyer, Nancy 91
Schwob, Claire 142
Schwob, John 123
Scott, Danny 114
Scott, Ruth 63
Scowcroft, Joan 119
Scripture Union Sound & Vision
Unit 181, 199
Seal Christian Arts Resources 201
Secret Archives of the Vatican 91
Seeds 114
Seeds 185
Selecta Sound 182
Shalom 174
Sharma, Kiran 139
Shaw, William 153
Shepherd, Mary 148
Shepherd, Sue 192
Sherwen, Russell 144
Shorehill Arts 189
Signature 91
Silhouettes of Christ 174
Silver Fish Creative Marketing Ltd
120
Simeon & John 92
Simon Jones 181, 202
Simpson, Fiona The (Band) 92
Simpson, Rosemary Inglis 133
Skinner, Susan 119
Smith, Annette 158
Smith, Claire 92
Smith, David 92
Smith, Jean 93
Smith, Raymond & The Hillside
Singers 59
Smith, Rosie 133
Snell, Adrian 93
Snelling, Olave 161
Snowden, Kate 104
Snowden, David 175
Sokell, Brenda 93
Solar Sound 201
Son-Rise Theatre Company 114
Sound Supplement 181, 196
South Asian Concern 196, 197
Souza, Ava de 114

'Spider' Webb 161
Spice Theatre Co 115
Spivey, Christiane 104
Springs Dance Company 104
St Clair Fewins, Adrian 120
Stairs & Whispers Theatre Company
115
Stamp, Roger 153
STAMPS (St Andrews and
Methodist Players) 115
Stanier, Paul 142
Stephens, Shan 161
Steven, Kenneth C 148
Stevenson, Rachel 158
Steventon, Julie 175
Stockman, Steve 148
Stonehouse 93
Storytelling Project 133
Stovold, Graham 93
Strong, Andy 175
Stroud, Marion 126
Sumner, Barbara 144
Swarm 94

T
Tandem TV & Film Ltd 196
Target 94
Taylor, Elaine 94
Telling Pictures 196
TEN 94, 202
Theatre Roundabout Ltd 115
Theology Through the Arts 192
Thomas, Audrey 64
Thomas, Edgar 64
Thomas, Paul James 121
Thomas, Tina 94
Thompson, Jason A 94
Thompson, Neil 175
Thompson, William 175
Tilley, Angela 59
Timberlake, Charles 95
Tindall, Laurence 155
Tinnin, John (Mixed Visual Media)
133
Titanic Brothers, The 129
Tongues of Fire 175
Traynar, Ian 133, 192
Tsouris, Dimitrios G 139
Tsouris, Vivienne 105
Tubbs, Revd Gordon L 123
Tun, Sarah Ross 173
Turner, Paul 162
Turner, Rob 95
Two Across Physical Theatre
Company 115
Tyler, Sarah 95

U
UCCF Arts/Media Relay Worker
Project 185, 186, 192
Ulmer, Ellie 64
Unity 95
Urwin, Steve 95

V
Velvárt, Marianne 96
Viles, Carlyon 64
Vineyard Christian Fellowship 192
Vineyard School of Worship 194
Visual Ministries Concert Choir 96
Visual Ministries 189

W
Waite, Alison 139
Ward Ling, Sheilah 139
Watson, Lydia 176
Wayland, Clive 176
Weaver, Pam 126
Wedding Songs –
Catherine Francoise 64
Wells, Linda 105
What 4, Cutting Edge Band/
Drama group 116
Wheeldon, Isabel 155
Where's Harry? 96
White, Kathleen 150
White, Virginia 105
Whitehead, Wendy 126
Willes, Samantha 140
Williams, David W J 59
Willson, Gayle 155
Wilson, Ali & Karen 96
Winfield, Sharon 96
Wingfinger 188
Wiseman, Stella 126
Wood, Christine 150
Wood, Douglas C 150
Woodall, Captain David 67
Woodland Photographic 142
Woolgar, Chris 176
Woolgar, Jan 176
WorldWide Christian
Productions Ltd 201
Worner-Phillips, Nigel 97
Wray, Paula-Marie 140
Wright, Charlotte 140
Wright, W Margaret 140
Wrightson, Tessa 97
Wylie, Marlene 158

Y
Yemm, Bryn 176
Young, Jason 153

Z
Zundel, Veronica 150